Stargazing in Solitude

Suzanne Samples

Published in North America and Europe by Running Wild Press. Visit
Running Wild Press at www.runningwildpress.com Educators, librarians,
book clubs (as well as the eternally curious), go to www.runningwildpress.com.

ISBN (pbk) 978-1-947041-92-9
ISBN (ebook) 978-1-947041-93-6

for e.e. samples and w.w. thompson

Years ago, my heart was set to live, oh
And I've been trying hard against strong odds
It gets so hard in times like now to hold on
Well, I'll fall if I don't fight
　　　　—*Big Star*

I don't mind how quick the seasons change
You know to me they's every one the same
The sweetest sunshine drips the drain
Death's comin', I'm still runnin'
　　　　—*Two Gallants*

preface
Spoiler alert: I'm still fucking alive.

a summary of frontal matter: glue gone wild (also an overview of my life)

I was diagnosed with Glioblastoma Multiforme three days after I turned 36. GBM is cancer most often reserved for men over the age of 55. (See: John McCain and Beau Biden.) After a seizure in a coffee shop, I was transported from Boone, North Carolina, to Winston-Salem, North Carolina, where I had a craniotomy four days before Christmas. I resided in the hospital's rehabilitation center until the end of January. I had to relearn walking and using my right arm; unfortunately, some functions of my right side never returned to normal. Although I was convinced the brain tumor was just a quick distraction from playing roller derby and teaching college freshmen, surprise! It was the worst brain cancer of all, and I had a survival time of 11-13 months. The surgeon removed most of the tumor, I did 33 rounds of radiation, and I took chemo for nine months.

Quick update: While I was in the hospital and after I returned home, I wrote a book about the whole thing called *Frontal Matter: Glue Gone Wild*, and two years later, I'm still alive.[1]

I'm still here.

Maybe writing saved my life.

---

[1] I would like to address one major mistake in *Frontal Matter*. I originally wrote how Victoria, my neurologist's wife, was finishing her master's degree at Auburn University. I could not remember at the time exactly what was happening, but she was actually working on her Ph.D. and unable to completely finish because of…life. It was an unintentional mistake on my part but one I clearly wanted to address, especially because of today's political climate. Apologies, Victoria! I probably made other mistakes in the book, but this is one I recognized and wanted to correct.

part one: escape

boone, north carolina

I do not know where I am going. I get in my tiny purple Scion and head toward Asheville. It's a route I am familiar with; for three years, I commuted two hours to work at App State when I was living in Asheville and married to Kevin, who is now married to Tristan.

I wish them the best.

I really do.

I leave my phone and computer but take my wallet if I get pulled over. I do not know what, exactly, I am driving away from, but I have to *get the fuck out of here*. I need to leave my apartment, and I need to desert the cozy candles I light every night. Despite losing my sense of smell after the tumor, I still love candles. Right now, though, I can't stand to look at *Vanilla Boysenberry or Parisian Café* any longer. Still, out of my senses, I am glad smell is *the one that got away*.

I have read online it is *typical for brain tumor patients to lose their sense of smell.*

I am so typical.

I pick up speed before the crying starts. I have never had a panic attack before, so it takes me a minute to realize I'm not having a heart attack or a stroke. I am driving nowhere and heaving and crying and trying to get away from something, anything, everything. My emotions desperately have no place to escape except for the confines of my car. How many times have I heard *there's nothing we can do for you*? How many times have I heard *there's just no way we can fix this*? How many times have I heard *there are just some things that have no solution*?

And then comes the repetition in my head, the repetition I hear in my nightmares every night: The neurosurgeon saying *glioblastoma glioblastoma glioblastoma*. It is as if he is rehearsing for a play and trying to get the words just right. *Glioblastoma glioblastoma glioblastoma.*

If I could get away, get away from everything, then no one could deliver any further bad news. If I could hide from everyone and no one could find me, I could live forever. I could pull off the Blue Ridge Parkway at some point and exist between two trees, cover myself in leaves for warmth, and linger like a feral child with adult sensibilities. I would not have to go to MRIs, appointments, or hospitals.

Just me and nature, baby.

This thought allows me to stop crying and gasping and wheezing.

Fuck. The initial blow of *everything that happened* has finally worn off. Fuck.

I have shed the shock of terminal brain cancer like a snakeskin in Winston-Salem, where the ambulance shipped me *same day delivery* after the emergency room doctor in Boone declared that *there was a mass on my brain.*

I could go to Kyle and Kelly's.

Kyle, my first cousin, lives in Asheville; I love him and his wife like they are my siblings. I could burrow there, convince them I need to *stay for a few days* until my thoughts clear up like the mountain views and my brain settles down. I could persuade them to keep all of this mess a secret until I stop crying and clutching my chest. I could play with their dogs and get a good night's rest, or maybe a few.

Maybe I would stay there forever.

I could go to Chris's, but she is going to be *reallll mad at me* for leaving Boone and forgetting to tell anyone I was gone. This is what happens when you're diagnosed with terminal brain cancer: People want to know where you are all the damn time.

But I don't think about people looking for me; no one should need to. I'm not required to be at school today, and my animals have food and water. CK, my girlfriend, would be over later, but she would understand. She would know I just needed to get out for a minute. An hour. A few years.

If anyone is looking for me, I am easy to find. I've driven this road so many times, it feels like another circuit in my brain. I know every abandoned house and overlook associated with this route. Of course, this is where I would be.

Suddenly, I feel the need to hide. The panic attack has ended, but there is still something lurking in my brain that does not feel right. There is something that needs to come out, something I need to shake.

I pull onto the parkway and feel paranoid. *Paranoid on the Parkway: The Suzanne Samples Story.* I've been watching way too many Lifetime movies since being released from the hospital, and I fear too much television is starting to affect my mental state. I reach an overlook and pull up next to a huge SUV. I can't see them, but they must be elderly. The leaves have not turned pumpkin orange and apple red yet, so the parkway is not crowded with leaf lookers, just bored older people looking to share an easy afternoon with nature.

And me.

If I had my phone, which I was smart enough to leave at home, anyone could find me. They would just need to contact my mother, otherwise known as Jenifer-With-One-N. She gave me an ultimatum: Either download an app that continually shows her my location, driving speed, and battery percentage, or live at home.

I downloaded the app and cursed her for being a Baby Boomer proficient with technology.

The worst of both worlds.

I want these people to drive away so I can get out of my car and stretch. I think about jumping off into the mountains once these nature lovers leave. Knowing me, I would leap, end up breaking both legs, and suffer for days before rescue squads would eventually find me and scold me for being such a brat. *Don't you know the value of life? Don't you know you have survived way longer than you should have? Don't you know how lucky you are?*

I discover a trail looping around the overlook, and I ponder crouching in the damp grass to think. Or not think. I might calm down then, maybe. But when I try to squat, I realize I can't bend without falling. My coordination and strength are so weak, I can't simply sit and rise again. I would either collapse and petrify like a leaf in stone or keep standing and hope for the best.

I don't really want to die.

I really don't.

Please.

brooklyn, new york

A Delta Airlines attendant wheels me to baggage claim where I am supposed to meet my sister, Sarah.

I do not see her, so I stand, very slowly and achily; later, I transfer myself to an abandoned suitcase dolly and wait for her. Someone paid a quarter to use the cart but never returned it to its final resting place, probably because of the broken wheel screeching to provide a soundtrack that welcomes everyone to the grand city.

Like the dolly, Sarah's phone is dead, of course, and I don't know if she'll be able to find me. I sit on the broken piece of metal and wonder if someone will yell at me, but no one seems to care. *Welcome to New York*, I think to myself. Others might find this lonely, but I am comforted no one needs to know why I am sitting on an apparatus meant for a suitcase and not a short, disabled woman.

I test out the wheels and discover I can scooch myself into an abandoned corner of baggage claim. Although this might make it more difficult for Sarah to see me, I ensconce myself into a cobwebbed window crook.

I feel safer here.

I can watch the flurry of people grabbing their bags (or someone else's) and not worry I will lose my balance and fall over someone's Louis Vuitton luggage trio they earned selling overpriced lotion in a multi-level-marketing pyramid scheme.

I worry Sarah will not find me; I worry I will sit here forever, abandoned and alone like that guy in the Tom Hanks movie who lived in the airport, but because I can't walk, I'll have to wheel myself around on this forgotten, broken dolly to use the bathroom or find food.

I have this self-indulgent thought when I notice someone lean against the outside of the window. She is barely shorter than I am, wears a black long-sleeved hoodie (although it is June), has a pink skullet—a somehow stylish fusion of a mullet and shaved neon yellow sides—and can't get her cigarette to light.

As if I am observing a nefarious parrot in a concrete jungle, I watch her struggle for a few moments.

Flick. Flick. Flick.

In a classic older sister move, I wait until the cherry glows red before I bang on the window.

You gonna leave me here inside all day, bitch? I mouth.

She blows out the cigarette and puts it behind her ear for later. Sarah dances into the baggage claim area, places her tiny hands on the dolly's grip, and wheels me around. I nearly fall off, but I feel free.

"You made it! All by yourself!" she says.

"I like the pink and yellow," I tell her as she offers me her hands. I am always surprised by her strength; although Sarah barely weighs 100 pounds, I remember her lifting me off the dirty hospital floor with a quick pull under my armpits.

"Where's your cane?"

I point toward the wall where my aluminum pink and purple cane leans. There are navigation symbols on the instrument, and I keep hoping they will guide me somewhere new. I scoured Amazon for at least twenty minutes before I found the most flamboyant $12 mobility aid the world could offer.

"Is this the only bag you have?" Sarah asks as she lifts up the purple duffle bag her then-boyfriend helped me buy when I was in town last.

I always travel light.

We get into an Uber, and I feel the need to explain myself.

I always do.

I have some…mobility problems. It might take me a second to get in the car. I'm…I'm sorry.

"It's okay, it's okay," the Uber driver tells me as Sarah attempts to help.

Once we settle into the car, our drive into the city begins.

"Are either of you Jewish?" the driver asks.

"Um, no," Sarah answers.

"And you?"

"We are sisters," I say, "so no, I'm not Jewish either."

"You cannot be sisters. Full sisters? No way, no how."

"We have never looked alike," I say, as if this explains everything.

"But you are not Jewish?" he asks, and Sarah looks at me with confusion.

"No," Sarah says. "We are not Jewish."

"Good," the driver says. "Because Jewish people, they stink! They get into my car, and the smell lasts for days. Days! I never get the smell out! You can probably smell it now!"

I do not dare look at Sarah because I know I will laugh. I should not giggle at our anti-Semitic Uber driver, but I always do this in uncomfortable situations. It's a lousy defense mechanism, and I hate it.

Jewish people do not stink.

Our driver tells us he came to New York from Pakistan in the 1990s. I imagine he has endured racism at some point, so I am surprised how his hatred of Jewish people still festers like a hidden piece of food left behind by white girls in his car. Maybe my surprise shows my ultimate privilege, but I do not have time to consider this for very long.

"See that building over there?" the driver asks us as he points to a nondescript three-story open parking garage. "That man built it! He built that in three days! Can you believe it?"

That man? I mouth to Sarah. Perhaps *that man* is some sort of New York City code for the mayor, the president, or someone in the city with a lot of money. But instead of providing answers, Sarah shakes her head at me with confusion.

"That man built that over there, too," the driver says as he continues to point. "That man! He has so much money!"

"He sure does," I say, trying to sound confident.

"How do you make your money?" the driver asks.

"I do hair in Brooklyn," Sarah answers.

"And you are not Jewish?"

"No, we are not Jewish."

"My sister-in-law does hair in Florida. If you hate it here, maybe you could join her. She's in Ft. Lauderdale. Laudy-Daudy. The sun, it shines all the time. It's not like this dirty shithole. See that bridge? That man made the bridge. He has been very busy."

"Sounds like it," Sarah says. "That man makes so much stuff."

Sarah is, at her best, an actress. Although I have been around her for her entire life, sometimes she can convince me of anything that isn't true.

The Uber driver drops us off in the middle of a Brooklyn street, and I struggle to ascend from the car. All the traveling has worn me out, and I can barely walk at all. My right leg is simultaneously stiff and weak, like a piece of cardboard that might blow away at the first trigger of wind.

I wonder if *that man* could rebuild my body.

Probably not because he is *very busy*.

"I'm sorry," I say.

"Take your time," the Uber driver says. "I don't want to drive today. I'd rather be in Laudy-Daudy with my sister. Maybe she would let me do hair."

Sarah and I have to walk through a deli to get to her apartment. *It's just easier this way*, she says, and I am happy to visit for a few days and go home. The deli employees slap salami on some ciabatta and wave to Sarah as if they are best friends, and naturally, Sarah would know everyone in New York City by now.

Of course, she would.

boone-ish, north carolina

I lumber back into my tiny purple Scion. I can't live on the parkway, I decide. I can't cover myself with a blanket of leaves and eat berries until my brain tumor returns and begins feasting on me from the inside. I should just go back home and take a nap or go to bed and sleep through Tuesday.

No.

I want to go skating.

I haven't skated since December of two years ago, right before I received the diagnosis of a *mass on my brain.* I haven't skated since I had the seizure that completely paralyzed my right foot. I haven't skated since I lost all my balance and coordination because a *T2 signal flair* keeps showing up on my post-resection scans.

I have a tough time getting shoes and socks on my feet, so skates? Absolutely not. But I could try. I could drive back home, grab my skates, and head to The Greenway in Boone and roll for a few minutes. If I happened to fall, which I did continually without skates on my feet, someone would be able to help me back up.

It's what I need.

I don't know how much time I take to get home, but I feel like I've been gone for about twenty minutes. Not too terribly long. I spot two cops parked at the top of my driveway and praise them in my head for setting up such a clever speed trap.

And then one follows me down the hill toward my apartment, and the gravel from my driveway feels as if it is rising through my legs and into my stomach. I'm sure I was speeding; I always do. The faster I drive, the faster I can get away from the shitty stuff in my life.

I pretend I don't see the policeman and slowly lift myself from the car.

"Are you Suzanne Samples?" he asks.

Shit.

13

"Yes," I answer with too much confidence. "Am I in some sort of trouble?"

"We have been looking for you. Your friend called us and said you might want to hurt yourself?"

I mean, sure, I had considered burying myself in the parkway leaves forever, a living grave, but I didn't plan on actually hurting myself. Not really, anyway.

"I mean…I thought about it."

I can't make eye contact with the officer. He has ginger hair and looks about ten years younger than I am. He wears a wedding ring. Although my driveway is a mess, his black shoes look spit cleaned.

My dog barks.

"You have babies in there," he says. "You know I have babies too. They need us."

Well, well, well, Officer. You found my weakness: my pets.

"That's true," I say. "They certainly do need us."

"If you hurt yourself, your babies would be alone."

"I have terminal cancer."

I don't know why I decide to tell him. Maybe to explain my actions, although he hasn't asked me to. I stare at the woods behind my apartment. The river runs quietly behind my words.

I have terminal cancer.

"Oh, man," the officer says. "I don't know what to say. I'm really sorry."

I appreciate him. He seems genuine. He acts like he cares, perhaps more than a lot of my so-called friends.

"I'm fine," I say. "I promise I won't hurt myself. I swear."

The truth is, I'm still a little out of my mind. I don't know what I might do next, but I still want to go skating. I haven't skated for almost two years; I can barely put on a shoe. I don't know what makes me think skating is a good idea or will actually work, but it's something I need to do. A release of some sort.

"Here's my info," he says as he hands me a yellow business card. In all my 37 years, I didn't know cops had business cards. This is something I never learned from Dateline or Discovery ID. I shove the paper in my pocket and avoid his truth-seeking eyes.

"Thank you," I say.

"It's no problem. We are here for you."

The Watauga County police force is here for me.

I've lost so many friends. I've lost so many people who could not speak the word *cancer*. But the Watauga County police force is here for me. They are in my driveway, and they want to make sure I am okay.

The officer leaves. I keep standing in the gravel. I pull the business card out of my pocket and look at the name. There's a chance I could have had him in class. *Wilson Williams*. His cell phone number is below a picture of a badge.

You're a good one, Wilson Williams. My dog keeps barking, unaware it's just us again.

No one else is here.

No one.

As if it's a patient on a gurney, an entire fish flopped onto a steel serving plate stares up at Sarah's friend Kelley for dissection. The glossy eyes gaze up at her hip black bangs and dare Kelley to tear them out and consume them whole. Instead, Kelley picks around the globs surgically, as if she's a trained doctor.

I hallucinate the fish becoming buoyant again. Instead of Kelley masticating the glittery gills, the fish reanimates, floats from the table, and swims to me in a series of slow blubs. The slimy scales expand before the feisty fins reach around my neck. The radial cartilage chokes me until I am underwater completely.

Drown me, I dare the fish. *Splash me onto the plate when I am gone.*

I have not quit drinking since I entered the city limits.

"So, how is teaching going?" Kelley asks me.

Kelley is the only true friend Sarah has in New York. She cuts hair with my sister but is also in school for architecture. Kelley has dreams of designing buildings instead of shit on peoples' heads.

"Uh, you know, it's okay. I'm only back part-time, so I had three classes this semester. I'll go back to work full-time in the fall."

"What is the weirdest thing a student ever said to you?" Kelley asks.

Sarah orders another round of drinks. I'm sipping some red wine I could never afford on my own. I was lucky enough to take an entire semester off work after my surgery, during recovery, and most of my treatment. Because of the Family and Medical Leave Act, I still got paid. Now I am back part-time but getting paid full-time.

Was it enough to live on?

Kind of.

Was it enough to continue paying my medical bills?

Absolutely not.

"Definitely the time a student was trying to send me a paper but accidentally emailed me a picture of her dorm markerboard that said *it's dark i'm drunk i love you.* She was a good student, but she did not look at me for the remainder of the semester."

Kelley's mouth drops, and I wonder how her burgundy lipstick stays so perfect while she's consuming the fish head.

"It was a total accident but funny nonetheless."

Sarah is paying for all of these drinks and fancy food. I ordered mushroom truffle ravioli that no doubt, a very special pig named Guinevere snorted in some woods in upstate New York.

I try to leave my phone alone, but I want to know if Alex, my love interest from the closing of *Frontal Matter: Glue Gone Wild*, has texted or sent me a Snapchat.

Nothing from Alex but a text from Chris.

Don't drink tonight.

Oops.

Chris's brother passed away a few years ago when he decided to put a bunch of fentanyl patches on himself before he fell asleep forever. At the time, no one really knew how dangerous fentanyl was, and he just *wanted to have a good time.* The girl beside him in bed called Chris the next morning and asked if her brother *was a really heavy sleeper.* Chris knew something was terribly wrong and later had to identify his body at the local hospital to spare her parents the grief.

I can understand why she does not want me to drink. I'm on a heavy dosage of seizure medication, which could easily fuck me up. I also have suicidal ideations about a third of the time. It's a control thing—if my brain is going to be the one to kill me, I would, at least, like a say in the matter.

I cannot help myself.

I text Alex and say *Busy tonight?*

Alex and I text continually throughout the day; we send Snapchats about every ten minutes.

Yes, I am passive-aggressive. Yes, I should probably have fun with my sister and not worry about Alex. Yes, it's weird I have not heard from her all day.

Before dinner ends, I get a text back: *I think I want to fuck Brad.*

I do not respond. I met Brad, Alex's friend, when I went to visit Alex in Minnesota. I should not have been traveling alone, but I saw the trip as my *last chance at love.* Who else could understand me? Sure, having brain cancer and being trans were not exactly the same thing, but Alex and I had a lot of similar issues. No one understood what we were going through. Our bodies had changed and were changing. We lived on the fringe of the world where no one cared to find us.

During that trip, Alex and I slept in the same bed and clutched each other as if we might lose one another or ourselves in the middle of the night. We watched *Troll 2,* the best-worst movie of all time. I got to see Alex perform in one of her shows, and she told me later she *watched me the entire time just to see my reaction.*

I met Brad and his boyfriend, Mark.

Brad and Mark are friendly and funny. Brad and I sit on their couch and discuss the true-crime Jacob Wetterling case and how everyone was singing a song called "Jacob's Hope" while poor Jacob was not missing at all but dead. Brad remembers the song and sings it with full bravado. Brad's voice fills the apartment with 1980s hope while the rest of us eat pizza.

"Werrrrrrk," Mark says as Brad finishes the song. "Isn't he great?"

We all agree as we finish our slices. Brad and Mark are kind enough to order me a pizza without red sauce because I hate tomatoes almost as much as I hate brain cancer. Mark wears a Britney Spears t-shirt and works as a barista. A former barista myself, we discuss how awful it is when people talk about *expresso* and bitch about cold coffee after they have forgotten their cups on the bar for twenty minutes. I feel connected to Brad and Mark, and I see them as an adorable couple.

"What's wrong?" my sister asks.

"Nothing."

"Give me your phone."

I know this is not a fight I'm going to win, so I hand her the device. She reads through my texts.

"Christ," she says. "Let's pay up here and go to the bar."

"The Commodore?" I ask. Last time I visited, before *everything happened*, Sarah loved The Commodore.

"No, we're going someplace different."

Kelley's fish stares up at all of us, gutted and picked except for those slimy orbs. This is how I feel sometimes. Watching everyone go through life while I can do nothing but stare up from my own plate, too many parts of me missing to create any meaning.

boone, north carolina

    Call me. I'm out looking for you, the note says. *I'm not mad at you. Love, CK.*

brooklyn, new york

"Are we going to The Commodore?" I ask again.

"No," Sarah says.

"I thought that was your favorite bar? And it's close, so I won't have to walk far."

I have been walking a lot in New York, and I am tiring fast. I can only clumsily stride about fifty feet before the fatigue sets in. While Sarah has been slapping rainbows on customers' heads during the day, I sit at her apartment with her dogs and only leave the flat to get food from the taqueria across the street. Sarah and I ate lunch there on the first day, and the employees know I have trouble getting up the stairs and carrying my food to the table. They have all been friendly and willing to help, so I do not dare try another restaurant. I would rather starve or eat the canned cold green beans Sarah has in her minuscule kitchen cabinet.

"The Commodore is full of douchebags," Sarah says. "I hate that place now."

Kelley catches on before I do.

"You got kicked out of there, didn't you?"

I am surprised, though I am not sure why, that Sarah has already gotten booted from a Brooklyn bar. Unlike Asheville, where her picture is posted on nearly every bouncer's podium as a DO NOT LET IN offender, I figured Brooklyn would be too full of other problems to worry about a 98-pound stylist with a skullet.

Apparently not.

The Commodore is right in front of us, and I cannot walk any farther. Plus, they have really great piña coladas and a fun outdoor area with yard flamingos and plastic palm tree accouterments.

"Sarah, we can totally sneak you in," Kelley says. "Who kicked you out?"

"A bartender named William."

"Okay, well, I'll go in and check the bar to see if he's there. No one else is going to remember. They probably kick a bunch of people out every night."

"But do they kick out petite ladies with skullets?" I ask. This is Sarah's hubris: looking the coolest but being a tad too rambunctious.

Sarah and I stand outside The Commodore and wait for Kelley's recon mission.

"Full of douchebags, huh?" I ask. "Good one."

Kelley returns a few moments later with pertinent information.

"William is in the kitchen tonight, so you just have to scurry by the galley really quickly and get inside. I'll stay with Suzanne to make sure she doesn't fall. I'll order all the drinks."

Everyone needs a friend like Kelley.

There is no bouncer, so Sarah shimmies past the kitchen and bar area to get outside where freedom waits. Kelley and I stagger behind her. There are steps, and I really fucking hate steps. And curbs. And anything where my foot has to drop down from a ledge.

Kelley leaves me outside with Sarah, but I have to sit about fifty feet away from her because she is smoking. Sarah smokes and drinks more than a lonely trucker but does not have a damn thing wrong with her.

"Hi," I wave. My voice travels over the plastic flamingoes and small, rocky pond.

"Hi!" Sarah waves back with her cigarette. "How's it going over there?"

"Oh, just great. You know, when I moved down here, I didn't know if I could stand the heat in the summer, but it's been just fine. It's nice to be in a park where people have the same decorating style as I do. After Walter died, I didn't know if I would make it out there in the world, but this is the place for me."

It doesn't escape me that this might be the closest to retirement I will ever get.

"Well, if you ever need a smoke or a bit of peanut butter, you know where to find me."

Sarah finishes her cigarette before Kelley comes back with a round of piña coladas. I was never really into drinking and always tried to watch my calories, but since treatment began, I stopped caring. What could hurt me now? *Sugar causes cancer* is a complete myth. So is *sugar causes diabetes.* Lies, all lies. I was in the gym six days a week, barely drank, and never smoked, and all I got from it was terminal brain cancer.

I try to walk over toward Kelley and Sarah but nearly trip over a plastic frog.

Ribbet.

"We'll come to you," Kelley says, and she and Sarah walk toward my lime green plastic chair. I should go with this color scheme—pink and lime green—for my apartment. That way during the grueling Boone winters, I might feel a little warmer and cheerier.

Or maybe not.

"To the plastic flamingoes," I toast, and everyone takes a drink.

boone, north carolina

I totally understand why CK is worried when I took off on my little adventure.

My computer displays nothing but a folder with a question mark. I had no idea why it was doing that, so I just left it alone. However, to CK, it looks as if I deleted all of my computer files before I drove to my death. I also left my phone behind. I don't think I was ever planning to completely off myself, but this differed from *hurt*. Why did it matter if I hurt myself now? Wasn't my brain, the most important organ in my body, already eating me from the inside? What would a few bumps and scratches matter?

They matter because they give me control.

I have not felt any control since this whole mess started.

I have felt at the absolute mercy of every MRI, every round of chemo, and every imbalance that causes me to trip over air.

I've fallen, and I can't get up! has happened to me so many times I've lost count. Mostly, I can rise through a slow process of getting on my knees and pressing my palms into the ground. I can then push myself up using the floor for stability. However, sometimes the falls are so bad, I cannot get up on my own.

Then I just start crying and hope someone can hear me.

After I read the note, I call CK.

I'll be there in a minute, she says.

CK swears she's not mad at me, but she has to be. We have been dating, although I know this is a terrible idea. She has to be furious with me, even if she says she isn't. Who wouldn't be? I ran off to the Middle-of-Nowhere, North Carolina, and I didn't tell her where or why I left. I was expecting her at my apartment in a few minutes, but I didn't think I had been gone so long. Had I been gone a long time? I wasn't sure. I wasn't sure of anything except for that shitty CD I had to listen to because I left my phone at home. The CD was some indie girl group

24

that should have been good but wasn't; their songs were so blah that after listening to them for the whole trip, I didn't have a single one stuck in my head.

I'd almost forgotten about the skates.

Although autumn was here, I still had a few hours of daylight left. Plenty of time to toss on my old skates and take a swing around The Greenway past downtown. I go to the closet where my Antiks have burrowed in a backpack for two years. I am scared of how they might smell, but I'm pleasantly surprised. For one, I can't smell much of anything. For two, I love the smell of old derby gear and sweaty skates. My nostalgia for happier times goes into overdrive. If I could just get the fucking skate on my paralyzed foot, I would feel a bit better about life.

CK pushes the door open before I can finagle the skate on my foot.

"Jesus Christ," she says. "Did you know that there are four purple Scions in the Boone area? Four. I saw the cops pulling over one of them, and the lady was probably straight-up arguing she was not Suzanne Samples. Did the cops see you pull down here?"

"No," I lie, and I can tell she sees right through my skin, shirt, and straight into my tangled stomach. Has everything rotted down there? I wonder. Sure, my cancer cannot pass the blood-brain barrier, but what if my other vital organs aren't getting enough circulation? What if they aren't getting enough support? What if, like my right foot, they aren't getting any messages from my brain at all?

This is all entirely possible, I convince myself. Entirely.

"Okay, I hope you're lying because otherwise, they are still out there looking for you."

"Fine. I talked to one. But it was about my speeding."

CK grabs my arms gently. These grabs will become less gentle as her time with me progresses, and my time here dwindles. I'm still sitting on the futon and trying to tear through my skate bag. Nothing is working out the way I planned.

"You don't have to do this. Just stop."

I don't stop.

"Stop."

I realize then, she has no idea what I need.

CK takes the backpack away and tosses it into the closet.

"You're going to stop right now. Tell me what happened."

But I can't; instead, I cry. I have been doing a lot of that lately. All the times in the hospital when I couldn't cry are coming back to haunt me now. I cry at least once a day, and most days, twice. I cannot control my emotions.

And I broke up with my therapist.

It started to feel really exhausting to sit in her office for an hour and talk about nothing but my complicated relationship with my mother and my short story publication record. There were a lot of awkward silences and phrases such as *it seems like maybe you have boundary issues*, but oh no, there were no solving of those issues. Most of the time, I would just sit there and drink whatever coffee I brought with me and hope she would offer some sort of advice about dying young. But she had nothing to say about that, so I ended our relationship. There was also that time she emailed me when I was in the hospital after my craniotomy and requested I send her $300 because my insurance had been billed improperly.

Thanks, Babette.

I sent her a text in May that I was *taking a much-needed break* from therapy, and I never returned. I didn't respond to her follow-up text about her *wanting to help me* once school started. If we couldn't discuss dying, what was the point? I needed someone to help me navigate the end of my life, and she wasn't able to.

The problem was, I couldn't find anyone capable. Boone is a small town without a ton of options. I would need to drive to Asheville or Charlotte; neither of those seemed tenable at the moment.

Or affordable, especially with my speeding record.

"Look, it's okay," CK tells me. She is fourteen years younger than I am and has a lot of experience with mental health and self-care. While my parents thought therapy was *for crazy people*, CK's mom had her in a therapist's office when she was six, all because she was experiencing disassociation from her body. During the office visit, CK did nothing but draw hand turkeys. I once heard from a mutual friend a psychiatrist *diagnosed her with Borderline Personality Disorder, but CK didn't believe the diagnosis.* I didn't think much of it at the time. Still, she knew therapy could be helpful in any situation.

I feared I was too far past any situation.

"Where were you?" CK asks.

"I drove to Linville."

"Why the fuck did you drive to Linville?"

It's a fair question.

"I...needed to mail something."

"What the fuck did you need to mail?"

"A thing."

I am a terrible liar.

CK hugs me as I cry. I have no idea what I'm doing. I honestly thought I would be dead right now. I was not supposed to survive a year, and here I am almost two years post resection. Not many people[2], especially me, thought I would still be alive. Just like I was driving around Linville with no plan, I have no map for what to do next in my life. I navigated surgery, rehabilitation, chemo, and radiation more easily than most people, yet I have no idea how or why. Sure, my age helps. Sure, my dedication to health before surgery helps. Sure, the surgeon getting most of my tumor helps.

But damn.

I still have a paralyzed foot and fatigue that prevents me from

---

[2] Except my editor. Thank you, Barbara.

walking very short distances without needing to sit down. Sure, I smile all the time, but the cancer has spread from my brain to my emotions. I feel negative. Hopeless. Without a chance.

Glioblastomas always come back.

That's the refrain.

"Oh, honey," CK says. I don't like when anyone calls me honey, especially younger people. "Let's get you some tea and maybe a nap. We will talk to the doctor and see if we can get you something for anxiety next time we go."

brooklyn, new york

I'm two piña coladas in and drunk off my plastic lawn chair.

I decide it's time to Facebook message my mom.

You know I'm dying, right? You know god cannot heal terminal brain cancer?

I feel as if I have finally expressed my feelings to her. It's taken me a trip to Brooklyn and two piña coladas in a bar Sarah has been booted from once already, but here we are, among the plastic pink flamingos, drinking and pretending we are retired folks in Florida. Here I am finally telling my mom how I feel.

My mom, the only spectator in the room when my surgeon came to reveal my diagnosis, ended that night hugging me and telling me she *didn't cry*, so don't expect her to. I didn't expect her to cry, or want her to, but I thought it was a strange thing to say. *I don't cry, so don't expect me to.* Um, okay, well, that's fine.

I told her I wanted to be alone, so she left.

I appreciated that.

And then she went the full-fledged *god is going to heal you* route. I should have known it was coming, but I was too shocked by my diagnosis to even think about it at the time. She was the type of mom to post pictures of babies with cancer on Facebook and copy lengthy updates about how god's work was creating *small but steady progress.*

Of course, those kids all died.

I'm not saying it's not incredibly sad, but I am saying god did not heal them. My mom and her church have faith; no one can blame them for that.

I have another piña colada and a mean streak.

She has not messaged me back, so I decide to message ol' Jenifer again.

You know god isn't going to heal me, right? It's a deadly cancer. The deadliest.

I put down the phone and take a few sips of my drink. Sarah tries to steal my cherry, but I swat her away with my left hand. My left side is still strong, still quick, still agile.

My phone buzzes.

I don't think I'm going to be able to stand losing you.

The retirement yard freezes around me. This is the first time my mother has ever expressed *a feeling* toward me. Sure, she has said she loves me. Sure, she gave me everything and more I needed when I was growing up. Sure, she has prayed for me and made certain the church sent me money after my hospital stay, which I was more than thankful for. However, besides once telling me *she never imagined having a daughter as smart as I was*, my mother has never been open with me about how she feels, about our relationship, or about any issues we may have had. They were all hidden in cabinets with the Disney-themed glass cups my sister and I collected as kids.

"Who are you talking to?" my sister asks with that I-told-you-you-shouldn't-be-on-your-phone annoyance in her voice. I know she thinks I am talking to Alex, which I would be if she had not told me she wanted to *fuck Brad*. I had no idea how to respond to that.

Sarah, quick little Sarah, grabs my phone and starts reading through the Facebook message from our mom. Never in my wildest imagination did I think Sarah, the party girl and youngest in the family, would have to take responsibility for our mother and me, but here we are, with the plastic flamingoes, piña coladas, and lawn chairs, all sitting around trying to heal my relationship with Jenifer Childers Samples.

I start crying.

I cry all the time now.

Ed, Sarah and Kelley's boss at Hair Metal, their Brooklyn salon, shows up with a buddy and a skateboard. Ed, a leftover Gen X grungy dude with a small daughter and love of alternative hair styling and heavy metal, has no idea what to do. He gives me a hug, and we all try to act normal.

I stop crying when Ed performs his Jessica walk.

Jessica, a girl from the salon, has to eat gluten-free, vegan, and low sodium. Sarah calls her *Stressica* because she always worries about what might upset the balance of her body next. Stressica is nearly an Instagram influencer because she looks like Siouxsie Sioux and models herself after the singer in her clothing, hair, and makeup. As a follower of her Instagram myself, I'm surprised Stressica seems to have so many negative issues in her life. Her Instagram looks fun, carefree, and full of Brooklyn parties. Sarah told me that she ordered a small $40 pizza the other day because of her dietary restrictions. Then Stressica spent the rest of the day crying because she did not have any money. I just assumed all influencers, even near influencers, had money.

But back to the walk.

Ed struts like a runway model on one of the bar's sidewalks. Then he turns with his back facing us so he can whip his head to the front again and stare at us with an intensity unrivaled by a sphinx guarding the most precious treasures. Tyra Banks would call this a *smize*, and Ed could have been a top model. We all watch Stressica's Instagram video of the same walk, and it already has over 1,000 views. Ed does the strut again and again until we are all laughing so hard, I accidentally spill piña colada down my shirt.

Ed stays another twenty minutes and then zooms off on his skateboard.

"That's wild Ed came out," Kelley says. "He's been sober for years now, and it's hard for him to show up to bars."

"I think he likes you," Sarah says. "His brother lives with his mom because he has brain tumors. Ed probably understands you on some level. He had another sibling who died in a skydiving accident."

We finish our drinks, and Sarah leaves the bar from a back entrance. Kelley helps me with some steps, and we make it outside unscathed. *Poor Ed*, I think, but all I can see is Stressica whipping her head around to tell us how uncool we all are.

boone, north carolina

I have stopped going to my MRIs. You would not believe how easy it is to cancel them all and then say *I'll call back to reschedule.* I'm a much better liar on the phone than I am in person.

And then I don't call back. I don't call back to reschedule, and I don't call back to discuss with anyone why I don't want to have MRIs any longer. But since you're reading this, I'll tell you:

1. No one can ever find a vein good enough for an IV, which I need for the gadolinium contrast that will illuminate any tumors in my brain.
2. I don't plan on seeking any further treatment for my cancer; I am just going about my normal life while waiting to die.
3. The MRI paired with the two doctor's appointments I always have afterward total $900. My medical team wants me to do this once a month, and that amount of money is nearly double my rent and a little under half my paycheck.
4. My MRIs have been looking good. Dr. Stroupe explains yes, I still have cancer because, well, that is just how glioblastoma works. However, the MRIs show *tumors and not cancer*, so the best I can hope for is stability with my scans. They have been stable every single time, thankfully, so I really don't see the point in spending so much money to hear that everything is the same.
5. MRI days are like a full-time job. I already have one of those, and I have to pay for the MRIs instead of the other way around.

I enjoy a few months of living: going to work, getting annoyed by students, trying to write a mystery novel that never leaves my computer, and hanging out with CK.

You might remember CK. (CK has a different name in the last book because things get messy in this one.) She was my roller derby teammate who brought me underwear and sent me that long text about liking me from the minute she saw me, blah blah blah. I brushed it off at the time but commended her for sharing her feelings so openly. She sent me the text right after I finished radiation and was still taking chemo, so I could not deal with unrequited love at that time. I was into pursuing this thing with Alex, who had asked me to move in with her. *The Mayo Clinic is right down the street. It would be perfect.* I was trying to convince my boss to let me teach all of my courses online because I did not want to depend on Alex for financial assistance. I could sit at the apartment and grade papers all day while Alex prepared for her musical gigs and played video games. *I think we would be good roommates*, Alex said, but what I heard was *we will be lovers and in love and happy and hey, we also have to be roommates, so let's be mindful of that.*

And then that did not work out.

Alex did not want to be my lover. Alex wanted to be my roommate and friend, and I was just not in the mood to hear that.

But anyway.

One weekend when Sarah came to visit me in Boone, we went to CK's restaurant and drank a lot of wine. There was this plan to hook me up with one of the restaurant's regulars, a woman named Anna, and I was all for it. Why not? Everything with Alex was a quick flame put out by the Minnesota snow, and I had nothing.

I wanted to have a one-night stand.

This seemed perfectly reasonable to me. If love did not work out, then I would fuck someone and call it a day. I did not want to die without experiencing sex again. *I didn't think that would be important to you*, my friend JC told me, and that immediately made me wonder exactly why I did care about sex when I was dying.

Maybe because I knew it would be *an experience.*

At CK's restaurant. I get so drunk off red wine I decide to change my phone background to Sufjan Stevens and declare that if anyone did not know who he was, I could not be friends with them.

I am not always a likable person.

"Your musical taste is definitely *I grew up in West Virginia, but then I went to college and got super pretentious*," CK says as she slings beer and wipes her hands on her rolled-up jeans. I am delighted CK and I are friends. I did not know if we would get past the whole weird text thing, but then she acted completely normal the next time I saw her and knew our friendship would be okay. I really appreciated that about her; most people would have pouted or been angry with me, but she just went on as if nothing happened.

Sarah falls off a barstool.

The entire restaurant echoes from the wooden stool and the 98-pound yellow-pink head on the floor.

"I'm alive!" Sarah exclaims as she pulls herself up from the beer-stained tiles.

A few of the bar regulars cheer for her, including my empathetic friend Erin who knows me from Starbucks, and Sarah turns in a circle with her hands raised as if she just won a wrestling championship belt.

I motion for CK to cut Sarah off, but I know there is no stopping her.

The whole hooking up with Anna thing does not work out. The conversation goes nowhere, and I can't tell if the girl is gay, asexual, or completely fucking straight. Sarah tried to go out and smoke with her to gauge the situation, and she tells me she doesn't think it's going to happen.

I'm actually not upset, which surprises me a little.

In matters of romance, I take rejection hard. I spend a lot of time building someone up in my head and creating these individuals who end up being more holographic than anything else. But in my mind, these people and I would maintain a healthy relationship (while living in separate houses, of course, just like my aunt and uncle did before her death). This person, whoever they might be, would have similar interests. A perfect night would be drinking a bottle of wine, discussing Zadie Smith's latest essay, and then snuggling together in a big queen-sized bed before the other person went back to their own house. I would fall asleep happily sprawling all over that colossal bed with two cats at my head and my dog at my feet. We would listen to Sufjan Stevens on long road trips to see all the cheesy landmarks from Memphis to San Francisco. We would engage in lengthy discussions about existence and the possibility of poltergeists and telekinesis. (I have always had an interest in the paranormal and refuse to believe a dead person cannot communicate through a Ouija Board or automatic writing. Whatever.) We would spend a lot of time together walking my dog, Gatsby, with the other person taking the leash so that she would not pull and cause me to fall.

I keep forgetting things are different now.

I could still do all of those other activities except walking Gatsby, so I really needed to find someone who liked dogs but did not yet have one.

I also wanted to find someone nice.

After the dating Chole, which was more than a disaster, I decided kindness was what I needed. The person could be a little boring, sure, but they had to be nice. No alcoholics. No people who blacked out on bar floors and needed to be pulled by their Vans out of the bar and stuffed into my tiny Scion, all the while accusing me of stealing their wallet and calling me a *worthless piece of shit*.

Nope, I was moving on from that.

Nice people only.

They had to exist.

They had to be out there.

brooklyn, new york

When we return to Sarah's apartment, Kelley comes inside to play with Sarah's dogs. The dogs, Jared and Claire, weigh 13 pounds total. Definitely an example of pets matching their owner. Sarah sleeps in a loft, so I have to hand the little monkeys up to her once she gets settled.

But tonight, there is no settling.

I finally decide to text Alex back. *I don't get it*, I write. *You want to fuck Brad? I thought he was just your best friend. Plus, I thought we had something going here.*

I am usually not this bold. Typically, I wait for someone to pursue me; however, Alex had been pursuing me, I thought. We held hands. We snuggled in bed together. We talked all day long. I went up to Minnesota in the cold with my cane to spend time with her. She came to Boone to see me, and we spent a weekend in Asheville with my cousin Kyle and his wife Kelly. We held hands throughout breakfast, slept in the same bed, and cuddled with Kyle and Kelly's dog, Scout.

I don't kiss on the lips right now because I'm too afraid of fucking up my surgery. If I get any infection, then they won't do it.

That seemed legitimate to me. I did not want to mess up the most important event of Alex's life, so I only kissed her on the cheek. She rubbed my back, and everything seemed real.

Until it didn't.

She texts back immediately.

I have intimately emotional connections with a lot of people, not just you.

Oh, okay. Sure you do. I did not take my disabled ass to Minnesota so you could text me later and tell me I was one of many.

I take an Ambien.

So, what we had was nothing? I don't get it.

We are friends. I hold my sister's hand all the time. We sleep in the same bed. Just because I sleep in the same bed with you doesn't mean I want to fuck you.

I get it. You want to fuck Brad, who is in a happy relationship with his boyfriend. Cool.

My sister never liked Alex; Sarah said she *knew her type*. She was angry when I went to Minnesota to see Alex instead of heading straight to Brooklyn. Any kind of traveling is extremely taxing for me, so all of these visits mean a lot. After reading Alex's last text, I feel terrible for not running straight to Brooklyn and being with someone who actually cared about me.

I mean, I would never hold Sarah's hand or sleep in the same bed cuddled up to her; that was weird as hell. Then again, the Samples family has never been a *touchy bunch*, so maybe we are the weird ones.

I call Alex. I want her to understand that although it would have been nice to fuck her one day, once her surgery was over and she felt entirely mentally and physically comfortable doing so, this relationship with her was not about fucking. It was about emotional intimacy and being there. It was about love with a different set of rules. It was about attraction, sure, but it was more about showing up. Alex showed up all the time until she didn't.

No answer.

I call again.

No answer.

She texts me. *I'm not answering. I know you're drunk.*

And? I text back. *That's why I finally felt bold enough to share my true feelings with you.*

I never hear from Alex again.

I fall asleep (thank you, Ambien) until Sarah's ex-boyfriend Steve shows up. Sarah initially moved to Brooklyn because of Steve, but they broke up when Sarah adopted Claire. *It's the dog or me*, Steve said, and Claire was the obvious choice. But like she always does, Sarah became friends with Steve again, and now here he was, having a dance party with Sarah in her studio apartment.

"Suzanne!" Sarah shouts. "Steve is here!"

She starts playing dance music—is it Girl Talk?—from her television while she and Steve flail around without worry. I pick up my phone and hope that I have an apologetic message from Alex, a change of heart, but there is nothing.

Nobody.

I post the following on Facebook before I fall asleep again, the dance music pounding through my brain like another growing tumor:

It's funny how everyone is your friend until you get brain cancer.

boone, north carolina

Sarah and I leave the restaurant and head downtown to the most well-known undergraduate bar. I do not belong there, but I do not give a fuck right now. I'm drinking and having fun and declaring my love for Sufjan Stevens and his music. His mother died of cancer, and though she also had a lot of other problems, I feel quite connected to his album about her struggle and death. *How could something so terrible be so beautiful?* I always wonder as I listen.

I suppose life can be beautiful and terrible simultaneously.

Once we get to the bar, Sarah orders shots. I do not even know what they are, but she confesses she has befriended the bartender and told him I had cancer, so all of our drinks are on the house tonight.

Only Sarah could manage this.

I would never, ever use cancer to my advantage, not in a bar anyway.

As much as I don't really drink (despite my recent alcohol-fueled adventures), I can take shots like a college frat boy. I never need a chaser. The alcohol burns my throat like a chemical compound, and I think if I can handle this night, I can handle death by glioblastoma.

"Tell your friends to come out!" Sarah says.

I do not have that many friends, and the friends I do have are old like me and too tired to leave the house on a blustery winter night.

But I have an idea.

I text my friend Dollfin, the derby teammate who watched Gatsby while I was in the hospital. She's always down for a good time, and I have a weird suspicion she has a crush on Sarah. I mean, everyone has a crush on Sarah: guys, girls, trans folx, and dogs. The only person who does not like Sarah is my cat, Pru.

Dollfin arrives three minutes later, and CK is with her. I am confused. How did they get here so fast? Wasn't CK going to sleep with her coworker, Paige? That's the last I heard when we left the restaurant.

"Oh, and I forgot to tell you. I convinced my friend to give me

Adam Duritz's cell phone number," Sarah says.

"Um, what?"

I am not ashamed to admit my very first CD was *August and Everything After* by the Counting Crows. My cousin Emily and I were regular forum posters to annabegins.com, a message board for all things related to the band. I had been to quite a few of the band's concerts, the last one just a couple of years ago with my ex-girlfriend, Jamie.

When Sarah and I were kids in the late 90s, we finally got VH1 on a cable package in WV, and I'll never forget how excited I was to see Adam Duritz singing and jumping around in a fringed leather jacket as if the world *had to know* all the important, poetic verses he wrote in his journal three days before.

"I swear it's him. Let me see your phone."

I give Sarah my phone and let her put in his supposed number. After one shot, I am drunk enough to give this a try.

Hi, I text, *do you remember meeting me at a party a couple months ago?*

I see those three little blinking gray bubbles and think someone is immediately going to tell me I have the wrong number.

What's your name?

Suzanne.

I don't remember meeting anyone with that name.

It was at a party in NYC. We even made out. I can't believe you don't remember me!

Send a picture of your face. You have one minute to prove I actually know you, and if I don't, I'm going to block your number.

I send him a picture of a miniature donkey.

Whatever forever.

Sarah orders another round of shots for everyone. I suppose these shots are all on my non-existent tab. I am done drinking, but Sarah is having none of it.

"Just act like you're drinking it and then toss it under the table," CK tells me as she ties her blonde, slick hair into a high bun. "I've been in a lot of situations where everyone around me is super drunk, but I don't want to be. I've learned some tricks."

CK is my ally, I think. I'm ready to go home, but she is the only one listening to me. Everyone else is drinking and dancing and having a good time, but I was never this person anyway. I was never the person drinking and dancing and having a good time. I was the person at home, reading a book and drinking tea without sugar.

That was me.

I look up and see that Sarah has saddled up on our booth and is riding it like a bull. This causes her to give the guy in the seat next to us a strange sort of lap dance, and he is embarrassed but likes it.

Dollfin becomes the documentarian and takes pictures of it all.

I move closer to CK. I need to feel understood and like I belong. *This is a weird thing to say, but the top of your head smells good*, she says as she pulls me closer to her. She cups my chin in her hand and kisses me.

This was not supposed to happen.

This feels strange.

I feel like I don't belong.

Dollfin at least saw some of it, if not everything. Dollfin is CK's ex, and although they remain good friends, I have no idea if Dollfin still has feelings for CK. Simultaneously, I feel loved and like a terrible person. Who makes out with their friend's ex right in front of them? Sure, I feel as if cancer gives me a free pass to many things, but certainly not that.

I am freaking out.

"I'll be back," CK says.

She returns with a black t-shirt for Sarah that has the name of the bar emblazoned across the front. Sarah hops off the booth bull to put on the t-shirt.

"This is fucking awesome!" she yells. "More shots for everyone!"

"She's going to wake up in the morning and wonder where the hell she got that shirt," CK says. "Don't worry. I'll make sure you get home safely."

Instead of buying more shots with my Brain Cancer Credit Card, Sarah talks to the guy running the sound for some awful band I've never heard of and will never hear of again. Sarah has a thing for sound guys. One of her more serious boyfriends works as a professional sound guy now, and the addiction stuck. This sound guy is cute, and totally Sarah's type: dark hair, beard, skinny enough to wear her jeans if he needed to.

He also looks exactly like every other guy in Boone.

I am hopeful she has forgotten about the shots.

I hold CK's hand. What the fuck am I doing? I knew she had a crush on me, past tense, but I never thought I would indulge it. Christ, she's fourteen years younger than I am. I'm like one of those old ladies featured on television for dating younger men. *A cougar.* I mean, sure, I look younger than I am (thanks, Mom), but fourteen years is a decent age gap. I was learning to drive and tasting alcohol for the first time (at the one, singular party I was invited to during high school) when she was still toddling around in diapers with her super cute blonde hair. I was a sophomore in college when the 9/11 tragedy happened, and where was she?

Maybe in kindergarten.

I was never good at math, but since my surgery, simple math had become more challenging than ever. What's 5+9? I needed my fingers. 10x13? I had no idea. I could pass through life without these skills, though. Adding tips to receipts at least let me see the numbers on paper, and that was really all I needed to know how to do.

What. Am. I. Doing?

Dollfin had definitely seen.

I do not know if she saw us kiss, but she had seen something. She had seen how close we are sitting.

I'm a terrible person.

I'm also kinda like *fuck it*.

After I got home from Brooklyn, where Alex unceremoniously dumped me over text messages (did she dump me? We were never officially together, but still. There needs to be a word for this, the dumping of an *almost relationship*), I started blowing up Tinder and OKCupid. I was looking for a one-night stand. I'd never had one, and I felt like this might be an experience I needed before I died.

I never made it past messaging and meeting one person, a polyamorous woman named Jesse, whose bed I slept in while she made seedy pumpkin soup we spit out on little paper towels purchased by her main partner, who turned out to be *kinda like Ted Bundy*. I never got the full explanation on that one, but I did spill some type of diet soda sweetened with Stevia all over her bedroom floor, and my sister, who dropped me off at Jesse's house, had to wipe up the mess because I could not bend down safely while holding a handful of paper towels.

Sarah needs to move my car off King Street in Boone because I cannot drive us home, and neither can she. I'm not sure she should even be moving the car, but she already has my keys, and no one can stop a drunk Sarah Shambles. CK and I sit in her Kia Sorento and make awkward small talk about roller derby and the upcoming season.

"It's going to be weird not skating," I say.

"Yeah, I'm sure."

"Where is Sarah taking my car?"

"To a school parking lot. You have your faculty pass, so the car will be fine there."

"And you're okay to drive us home?"

"Yes, absolutely," she says.

I had forgotten, for a moment, that CK was only 23 and probably accustomed to drinking a lot more in one night than I had in my entire life, although she was super thin and as willowy as the branches on the King Street trees.

Sarah hops into the back of CK's Kia Sorento, and we start the drive back to Foscoe, the community near Boone where I live. The locals call it *No Snow Foscoe*, and it's mostly true. The entirety of Boone could have a foot of snow while the sun shines in my part of town.

"Uh, I got pulled over," Sarah says.

"You what?" Even when I'm drunk and ready to start another round of chemo for brain cancer, I am forever the responsible older sister.

"Yeah, I saw the lights start spinning and the siren going, so I pulled over. When he came up to the car, I rolled down the window and asked if I could have a hamburger with fries."

"You didn't," I say.

"I did. He actually laughed and said he'd never heard that one before."

"How the hell did you get out of a DUI?" Despite her penchant for partying and snorting coke off that guy's dick while I was in the hospital, Sarah has never been arrested. I do not know how. Once in New York, she pulled down her pants, yelled at a bunch of security guards, and asked them if her *butthole looked bleached enough* because her boyfriend broke up with her for not doing that very thing. When she lived in Wilmington, North Carolina, Sarah kicked a police officer in the shins when he yelled at her for being disorderly in the streets.

Every single one of them laughed it off.

I guess that's what happens when you're barely five-feet tall, 98 pounds, and have colorful hair.

"Well, I got lucky," Sarah says. "As soon as I asked for the hamburger and fries, this college student started driving down King Street the wrong way. The cop told me good luck finding some food and sent me on my way."

"Oh my god," I say.

"Hey," Sarah says as CK laughs. "Where did I get this shirt?"

brooklyn, new york

"Suzzzzanne?" a weak voice calls from the loft in Sarah's studio. I look up and see two little dog noses poking out over the rail.

I guess Steve danced his way out of the studio.

"Yes?"

"Um, have you been on Facebook yet?"

"No, I'm still asleep. Well, I was."

"I just wanted to warn you. It's bad."

Shit. I'm a little thirsty but not that hungover. What did I post? Along with the drinking, my short-term memory is still abhorrent *since everything happened.* I couldn't even fathom the phrases *since I had brain surgery and was diagnosed with the most malignant form of brain cancer out there.* I had to think and say *before everything happened.* That word, *everything,* meant so much and nothing at the same time.

I pull out my phone and open Facebook.

Fuck.

There are over 60 comments on my *It's funny how everyone is your friend until you get brain cancer* post. I have started an argument. I have started a discussion.

I have started a revolution.

I got drunk, felt sorry for myself, and now everything has gone to shit. In person, I'm pretty quiet. I don't say much unless the situation calls for it. However, I have found that as a writer, social media gives me a place for self-expression.

Sometimes, I just don't realize how far that self-expression reaches.

Let me make one thing clear: I have handled the whole brain tumor, brain cancer, and learning to walk again gracefully and forcefully. I never once quit doing physical therapy, writing, and trying to return to the life I once knew. Sure, that came at a price. I did not have the time or energy to keep up with my friends' social lives or upcoming destination weddings. I did not have the time or energy to hop in my

45

car and drive a couple hours to someone's house and have an entire night full of gossiping and drinking. I did not have the time or energy to talk to someone, anyone on the phone for two hours about their feelings regarding my diagnosis.

The first comment is from my new friend Adam (not Duritz), who, like me, was diagnosed with GBM in young adulthood. The disease affected his left side, so together, we make a whole person.

It's funny how everyone is your friend until you get brain cancer.

Adam: *Ain't that the truth.*

Okay, good. Some support.

And then the entire thread devolves.

Martin Christopher Goodman: *I gave you a goddamn futon and didn't even get a thank you.*

Martin Christopher Goodman, or Marty, did give me a futon with his partner Lori. Lori, whom I did not think checked Facebook often, got a handwritten thank you note from me. Although I could barely write and had to have my sister drive me to the post office so I could mail the note, I was proud of myself for being thoughtful. My mom was big on thank you notes, and she told me that even if my writing looked childlike and it was hard for me to hold the pen, people deserved their thank you notes. I did not disagree with her; at the beginning of *everything happening*, people had been kind and generous, and I did want to thank them. Of course, for my mom, it was more than a gesture; it was an image thing. Her daughter would write thank you notes, goddammit, even if it killed her.

So, I did.

I sent Lori and Marty a lovely thank you note, and I assumed I was absolved.

I wasn't.

Heather W.: *You know, you should never put the burden on the sick person. If you do something for someone who is struggling and then expect them to do something in return (especially when they are so ill), why do it at all?*

Heather W. coming through! I did not know Heather W. well, but I knew she suffered from migraines and had a good friend with terminal cancer whom she helped and dearly loved. If anyone knew how to deal with someone like Martin Christopher Goodman, it was Heather.

I am thankful for people like Heather W.

From there, people discussed who had the burden of care[3] for the sick person, and the sick person's responsibility (or not) to respond to that care. I did not know at the time, but this would become a pervasive theme in my life.

I expected to die much sooner.

But here I am in Brooklyn, looking at a phone screen and trying to discern just who, exactly, is going to remain my friend. I have always had a difficult time letting people in to see the true me. Maybe it's my INFJ Myers-Briggs personality type or my 4w5 Enneagram, but I've found the self I show the world is not precisely the self I feel.

I'm sure most people can identify with this, no matter their personality acronym or number combination.

I cry for a minute, but I grieve silently, so Sarah doesn't know I'm sad. She has fallen back asleep. Jared the Yorkie hears me, though, and sticks his little face out of the loft so he can show me he cares.

This makes me sob harder.

Animals are so much better than people.

I thought I was doing the right thing. I thought sending a thank you note was the right move, the thing to do. (This is beside the point, but the futon was an absolute lumpy piece of shit, and I felt bad for anyone sleeping on it. But it was what was given to me, and I accepted it gratefully.) I thought I was being good.

---

[3] Isn't this a terrible way to put it, though? It's a colloquialism, but a bad one at that.

I feel betrayed. I have terminal brain cancer, and sure, I'm not dead yet (like I thought I would be), but I do not feel safe. I feel scared every second that something is coming back or that I will pass away in my sleep somewhere strange and without my pets beside me.

Like Brooklyn.

As I cry, I think about how different my life is now than it was a year ago. I've lost so much: my ability to walk, my short-term memory, my right foot—well, I have it, but it doesn't move—and my energy. Sure, I can say I have also overcome so much: I learned to walk again, I learned to type on the computer again, I learned little tricks to help my short-term memory (repetition is key), and I was going back to work full-time. Most people with GBM never get to return to work at all, but I needed a sense of purpose. I *had* to have a sense of purpose. I did not have human children, which I think helps some people regain their emotional strength, but I had *kids*. I had 93 students who would need me to help them adjust to college life and make it out of Expository Writing without hating school, their teachers, and their lives. I had to, I needed to prove to myself I could get back to who I was, even if that meant falling into my bed at 4 p.m. after a school day and staying in that bed until 8 a.m. when I got up to do it all again.

Fuck you, Martin Christopher Goodman.

I decide I'm not going to let him ruin my day. Sarah and I have plans to go to Times Square, find a Sbarro, and pretend to be Michael Scott from *The Office* so I can *get me a New York slice!* It's one of my favorite moments from the show, and I would seriously regret not taking the picture while I was in the city.

But seriously, fuck you, Martin Christopher Goodman.

Sure, Marty has problems. He can barely string a sentence together because of all the drugs he did in his younger years, but he had always been kind to me. He had given me rides to work when my car was not running, and he and Lori had lent me money when I was in need. I had paid it all back, but the gesture meant so much to me. Even that ugly futon meant so much to me, and I thought I had done the right thing.

I could hear my mother's voice in my head: *These people deserve a thank you note. It's the right thing to do.*

Sarah is awake.

"Help me get these little dogs down, and we will go get breakfast."

It is way past breakfast time for ordinary people, but we are abnormal today and maybe always.

We are abnormal, awake, and alive.

Somehow.

She hands me Claire first, who immediately grabs one of my socks from last night and runs around the studio showing off her new find. When Sarah passes me Jared, he licks my nose.

He knows how sad I must feel.

As CK drives us back to my apartment, we listen to 90s pop music. I have no idea how someone 14 years younger than I am knows all the words to Third Eye Blind's "Semi-Charmed Life," but here we are. I feel safe with CK's driving; I feel much better with her at the wheel than I would if Sarah or I tried to drive.

I'm having a good time, which does not happen very often. I'm still taking chemo one week per month. I typically have so much fatigue, I turn down the rare invitation when it comes. I'm not trying to isolate myself, but this is how everything has turned out, and yes, I'm secluded, but what am I supposed to do about it? Since I can't skate any longer, I don't see friends that often. Since Alex broke off communication, I don't have a Daily Person. I still talk to my ex, Chris, but she is busy with her job and doesn't always have time to deal with her *ex who has brain cancer.*

But this feels fun, lighthearted.

Sarah somersaults into the front seat and puts CK's car into neutral. Jesus, save us all.

Sarah is small enough to sit on the console and spread her legs without messing anything up, but because she is drunk, she miscalculates, and we almost die. CK is a quick thinker, though, and gets the car back into drive without any trouble. I suppose she is accustomed to dealing with the drunken antics of young people. Sarah, who isn't quite young anymore, never let go of the drunken antics part.

But hey. We got free drinks. Gotta use that Brain Cancer Credit Card more often.

My dad told me a story once about seeing my sister behind the hospital glass after she was born in 1984. *Your baby?* the guy beside him said as he lit a Marlboro. *Yep*, my dad said. *Born this morning.* The guy puffed his cigarette, and messy ashes dropped to his shirt like he was burning the photograph of a scorned lover. *I know*, the guy said. *I delivered her this morning.*

50

Explains everything.

Although I should feel carefree, and to a certain point I do, there is this nagging twinge in my brain about what comes next. Monthly MRIs with IVs filled with gadolinium. More chemo. Starting teaching again in a couple of weeks while I'm still taking chemo.

I panic.

With 90s pop music as my backdrop, I panic.

How will I be able to do any of this? All of this? I squeeze my eyes shut and repeat the following mantra: *I have brain cancer I have brain cancer I have brain cancer.* I think by doing this, I might ease some of the shock.

Of course, this never works.

Mantras are supposed to be positive, or some shit like that, but I'm hoping the *I have brain cancer I have brain cancer I have brain cancer* repetition will finally convince me this is *real shit* happening, whether I want it to or not.

I should be dead by now.

"Hey," I tell CK once Sarah gets settled in the backseat again. "You can stay at my house. You can sleep in my bed, but we can't have sex."

My messages are more mixed than a 90s pop music CD.

"Are you sure? The last thing I want is for you to feel uncomfortable."

"I'm sure. It's just two people sleeping in a bed, right? We don't have to make this weird."

I am still nervous but also into it. My main concern is hurting Dollfin. How would I feel if one of my close friends slept with Chris? I would probably rage and, at the very least, post some passive-aggressive comment under any picture they might post together on social media. I am not as kind as Dollfin, which makes what I'm about to do even more nefarious.

Once CK and I are in my bed, I press my ass against her. I can only sleep on my left side; I haven't slept on my right side for over a year now. Although I can use my right side, it remains painful. My shoulder never quite recovered, and my leg aches constantly.

She touches my bare leg.

"Are you sure this is okay?" she asks.

It is okay. Maybe? It is okay except I don't want to become embroiled into a full-on Millennial Scandal. Sure, CK is not a student, but I am closer in age to her mom than I am to her. Hey, this can be my one-night stand. CK is cool enough to deal with it, and we can still be friends. I can explain this away to Dollfin, and she will understand. She is interested in a woman named Becky, so I don't think she will be furious.

But she would have the right to be.

"Are you sure this is okay?"

"Yes," I say, and I have no idea what I'm getting myself into.

I am nervous.

I've never had a one-night stand before, and my sister is asleep (maybe?) in the next room. The person I'm about to have the one-night stand with is 14 years younger than I am and still plays on my old derby team.

If this goes wrong, it is going to go horribly wrong.

Fuck it.

She touches me, but I do not touch her. I feel like this is the way it is supposed to be. Lesbian sex can basically be anything you want, free from the patriarchal *let me put my penis in you and call it a day.*

It is great.

I cry afterward, but I don't know why. I can't stop crying, and I feel like I'm ruining the whole night. CK handles it well; she holds me, but something feels off. I feel like I've made a mistake.

I cannot have a one-night stand.

This isn't me.

I feel like I am betraying myself. I push myself off the bed and go into the bathroom to finish crying.

While I finish crying, I hear CK finish herself off.

I am going to vomit.

I am definitely sick from the liquor. I start doubting everything; am I even allowed to be drinking while I am on chemo? I mean, I am not taking chemo this very night, but I will be again soon, and the chemicals remain in my body. Will I screw something up? Should I even be around other people? Was I going to help another tumor form in my brain?

My sister sleeps in the living room on that fucking futon, an unlit cigarette hanging from her mouth like a lost cause.

brooklyn, new york

"We're just going to forget about social media today," Sarah says as we slowly walk to a coffee shop where we can get croissants and iced caffeine. When we sit down, she takes a picture of me smiling, the croissant and iced drink in front of me like I'm in a Parisian café. I do not have any makeup on, and I have a bandanascarf on my head. I call it that because it has the print of a bandana but serves as a head scarf.

Sarah sent me a red, black, and blue one once my hair started falling out.

They are me.

I tried other scarfs, but they looked too fanciful and not my style. I am a bit more casual and did not need a long, flowing headscarf to let the world know that *yes, I definitely have cancer*. I did not even consider wigs; I knew they would itch and look unnatural on my head. Although Sarah shaved my head when my hair started falling out, brown spikes had begun to grow back. Unfortunately, the radiation caused the new, baby hair to fall out all over again, leaving a strange circle of brown sprouts like a ring of wilted flowers around my scalp. There was one spot missing in the wilted flower ring and also a chunk of my eyebrow.

Thank goodness for makeup.

Although I am uncomfortable with her taking my picture, I actually look cute.

"Okay, post it to Facebook," she says. Obviously, we aren't all the way done with social media today. "And then give me your phone."

I like this strategy. This happy picture of me can show the people ragging on me that hey, I'm strong enough to make it past your hateful comments. I'm good enough to move on with my life without people.

I am still alive. I am still smiling. I am still fucking here, bitches.

boone, north carolina

CK drives me back to my car the next morning.

Gavin DeGraw plays on her radio, and for some reason, the 90s and early 2000s music of last night do not sound as sweet and fun the next morning. I situate myself in her Kia Sorento so my knees point toward the mountains surrounding us. I cross my arms over my chest and make myself very clear.

"What happened is fine that it happened, but it can never happen again."

I am nervous, I guess. That is why I use a form of *happen* three times.

"That's okay," she says. "But if you change your mind, let me know."

I close my eyes and feel like I might vomit—not because of what I did with CK the night before, but because I drank too much. Even the few drinks on the Brain Cancer Credit Card was a lot for me.

Although I am still alive, I live in constant fear I am *fucking something up*. I am beating the odds, but I do not necessarily want to be beating the odds. Sometimes I do. Sometimes I am happy to sit outside and do nothing but watch the river run beneath my apartment. Sometimes I am happy to sit and read for hours (something I have had to reteach myself to do—not because of the letters and words but because of the cognitive ability I have lost to remember anything short-term). Sometimes I am happy to watch *Jeopardy!* reruns and concentrate on nothing but Alex Trebek's mustache.[4]

Then there are the other times.

I have this lingering thought that I wish I had died during surgery. If I had, then I would not have had to face chemo or radiation or any of the friends I lost along the way. If I had, then I would have avoided facing the constant rebuilding of a life lost on December 18. If I had, then I would have just been gone, and that would be enough.

But hi, here I am.

---

[4] Goddammit, cancer. What is: You are the fucking worst?

Having one-night stands and acting awkwardly the next day. Sitting in CK's Kia Sorento with my knees pointed as far away from her as they can possibly be. Folding my arms like a moody teenager.

Just like I was in the 90s.

I wonder about people who have one-night stands all the time. Does the person eventually give up on feeling awkward? I know myself well enough to understand that although I am pleased I tried the whole one-night stand thing, the morning after is not for me. I can't even look at CK, who is being very sweet and keeps asking *are you okay?*

I repetitively say *I am okay*, but I'm actually extremely apprehensive I fucked up the relationship between us; I'm even more concerned I fucked up the friendship between myself and Dollfin, who had been nothing but there for me throughout this whole ordeal.

CK drops me off at my car, which hasn't been towed. Although everyone promised me no one would move the tiny Scion, I didn't believe them.

I didn't believe anything anyone told me anymore.

"I'll see you later," I say as I attempt to get out of the Kia Sorento. But like one-night stands, Kia Sorentos are not for me. CK has to come to the passenger side and help me out, so I don't bust my ass on the concrete.

"Thanks," I say as I refuse to look at her face. Shit. I have really screwed all of this up. "Maybe we could talk later?"

"Sure, yeah, of course."

Say what you want about Millennials, but they are awfully mature about this whole one-night stand thing.

I drive home and suddenly remember: Inspectors will be at my apartment today because the owner of my building is selling the property. Sarah, if I had to guess, is still asleep on the troubled futon with that damn unlit cigarette hanging out of her mouth.

The ride home takes forever, no matter how many Sufjan songs I listen to. What on earth was I thinking? I knew CK, at some point, had a crush on me. I was supposed to be the responsible one in this situation. I was supposed to be accountable for me, for CK, and for Dollfin.

I had no right to do what I had done.

When I get home, the cigarette has moved from Sarah's mouth to her forehead.

"Hey, you have to get up right now," I say as I gently shake her. I don't want her to puke before the inspector arrives.

"Whhhhhhy?" she asks as the cigarette falls to the floor. I suddenly wish the cigarette was lit, and this building would just burn down with the two of us inside of it, together with all of our pets.

"The inspector is coming, just like I told you yesterday."

"Ah, yesterday was yesterday. Inspector Gadget! Why am I wearing this shirt?"

She is still drunk.

Someone knocks at the door.

The inspector and the realtor, Scott, come through without a second knock or invitation. At least I know they aren't vampires.

The inspector wears quite an interesting outfit: a tan jumpsuit and a wide-brimmed brown fedora.

"He needs to take a look in all the corners," Scott tells us as he glances sideways at my sister, her pink hair all askance.

"I'm her sister. I'm drunk."

The inspector does just as Scott says: He takes a small flashlight and looks into every corner of the apartment, including the cobwebbed crannies of the laundry room no one ever visits.

And that's it.

After they leave, Sarah looks at me and says, "Why was Indiana Jones just in your apartment? I thought you said it was going to be Inspector Gadget."

I don't know what to tell her, so I say, "I think he was looking for the Temple of Doom."

I know the truth.

The Temple of Doom is nowhere in my apartment, not even in the laundry room.

The Temple of Doom is in my head, ready to explode at any given moment.

brooklyn, new york

Sarah and I are in Times Square, and there is a naked guy playing country songs on a guitar. Since brain surgery, I have had difficulties hearing more than one sound at the same time. I immediately go into sensory overload and feel the world around me start to spin.

I don't know why I thought it would be a good idea to come to Times Square.

Sarah takes a picture of me in front of the hubbub, in front of all the signs, people, and excitement. I am a regular Cancer Tourist with my cane, bandanascarf, and gray fanny pack. (To be fair, though, fanny packs did come back into style.) When I see this image later, I look happy but terrified. What if someone accidentally knocked me over? What if the sounds and bright lights made me have a seizure? What the hell was I actually doing here?

But as a Cancer Tourist, I want to experience everything. Last time I was in New York City and I was healthy, I got mad at my sister after we had a fistfight and left halfway through the trip.

Things are certainly different now.

I try to avoid fighting with her, and as far as I can tell, she does the same for me.

Until we start looking for the Sbarro.

Sarah has this habit I can't handle; she stops in the middle of moving crowds to look at her phone. If we were in Boone, this might be fine, but we are in the busiest place in one of the busiest cities. I'm trying to walk with my cane and end up losing her at least three times. When I stop with her, people keep running into me, and I am afraid I will fall and be unable to get up.

I am not the only one annoyed.

People curse as she suddenly halts, and finally, I tell her *we need to stand under an awning* to avoid running into everyone.

We seem to be walking a lot to find this Sbarro. If Michael Scott can do it, then we certainly can.

But we can't.

We turn corner after corner and end up in this decrepit alleyway, where a rat jogs across the road. I swear the rat has his own briefcase.

Sarah, Jesus, this cannot be right.

And then across the street, we see the Sbarro. We have been circling the restaurant the whole time, completely unaware of where we were.

This is what happens when you're short.

You never look up.

Stacked atop one another, Sarah and I are barely as tall as the rat running toward Wall Street.

"I'll stand across the street and take the picture," Sarah says.

I pose with my cane in front of the Sbarro. When I first moved to Auburn, where I studied for my Ph.D., I did not have cable or internet. I also did not have any friends. I did nothing except write, study, and watch *The Office* DVDs. I felt as if Michael Scott had become my quirky best friend; I knew everything he was going to say before he said it. I felt as if he spoke directly to me. Eventually, I realized how unhealthy it was to be best friends with a television character, so I joined a gym and made an effort to get to know the people in my program.

"Smile!" Sarah says. "You gonna get yourself a New York slice."

I do as she says and don't think about anything else for a moment.

I live for these times.

boone, north carolina

I check my phone and have a text from CK.

How are you feeling?

Fine! It really can't happen again, though.

Indiana Jones is gone, and I have a hungover Sarah on my futon. The cigarette has made its way to a different place on the floor, and I feel like I'm living in a weird, alternate universe where I'm dying but still need to be responsible for the feelings of everyone around me.

Sarah has to leave today, but I do not want her to. If she could stay just a little bit longer, perhaps she could help me clean up this mess. I sure could not do it on my own. Plus, Sarah had messes like this all the time, and they always turn out okay.

*

Sarah left, and now there is a foot of snow outside my apartment.

So much for No Snow Foscoe.

I do not remember how she got back to the airport. Did that one dude who lived in Boone she dated while she was in Wilmington take her? He must have. I know she did not drive herself because she didn't have a car. Plus, my tiny Scion would have never made it to the airport in this.

Dollfin calls me.

I am scared. I am convinced she hates me. I answer the phone anyway.

"Hey," she says. "I'm going to come over and shovel your snow so you can walk up your driveway and get to your car."

Fuck. Dollfin is the nicest person I know. For real.

I always leave my car at the top of my apartment building when there is a threat of snow. I live right beside a highway but on the bottom level. If my car is at the top, then I can easily make it to the road, if I can walk up the steep gravel hill to get there.

I wish I remembered the conversation about CK that Dollfin and I had. I think it went something like this:

You and CK were really close the other night.

Yeah, dude, I don't know what to say. I'm so sorry. I feel awful. I don't know what I was thinking.

We go outside. Dollfin shovels while I keep talking.

I would be so mad at me right now.

I mean, CK slept with someone else I know before she slept with you. That hurt worse. I was still in love with CK at the time. Now I'm not.

I know people like to shit on the Millennial generation (or *Millenniums*, as my mom calls them), but as a whole, they seem more mature and helpful to me than any other. Dollfin keeps shoveling as we make jokes about lesbians sleeping together. The pool here in Boone is small—I'm talking your ex-girlfriend is now dating your current girlfriend's ex-girlfriend—

so we all know how this works.

I still feel terrible.

The Brain Cancer Credit Card (who is going to pay this off?) may have gotten us drinks at the bar, but I did not want to use the excuse to hurt one of my closest friends.

There is so much snow, at least a foot. When I moved to the mountains, I did not expect I would be diagnosed with terminal brain cancer, and I would lose mobility on my entire right side. I did not think about how difficult it would be to maneuver around the snow and ice with a walker or a cane. I did not think about how I would open the door and immediately feel my right side lock up whenever the wind blew.

I should have moved somewhere warmer, but here I am.

I don't remember what else Dollfin and I talk about, but when she leaves, I know I ruminate about *everything being okay*. I should have apologized more. If one of my friends slept with my ex, I would, at the very least, send a scathing email. I'm not terrible enough to physically hurt someone, but I would use my words as a rusty nail and fantasize about the person getting tetanus from my efforts. (Well, I would do that if they slept with Chris. If they slept with Chole, I would put them in my tiny Scion and drive them away from her as soon as possible).

I text CK.

I have no idea what I'm doing.

I'm a Xennial, so I have all the ennui of Generation X and the need for recognition of a Millennial. As I often feel, I am stuck between everything, even generations.

Some serious character flaws.

CK braves the snow and comes to my apartment. I tell her she can get in bed with me, but I have to face the left side because of my body. This means I am talking to a wall while she listens behind me.

I do not remember exactly what was said, but it was a lot of *we will always be friends,* and *nothing needs to change,* and *we have great physical chemistry, but I'm fourteen years older than you, so this is not a good idea.*

When she leaves, I feel good. Everything will be okay. Everything will be fine. Everything will work out just the way it is supposed to.

brooklyn, new york

Before I leave Sarah's, we play our favorite game. I do not know how this game originated or why we are such sick fucks that we play it, but we have been doing it for years. Now, the game simultaneously seems funnier and even stranger.

"Sarah," I say dramatically while making direct eye contact. "I have something to tell you."

She doesn't say anything.

"I'm dying."

I then look into the corner of the room.

The first person to laugh loses the game.

boone, north carolina

After my one-night stand with CK and resolution with Dollfin (but did she secretly hate me? I didn't think so, but one could never be sure about people and feelings), we all decide to go to Basil's, where CK works, and where I tried to convince everyone Sufjan Stevens was a god. CK has other friends who are going to be there, and I'm interested to see how this turns out. It was only two days ago when CK and I fucked, and besides Dollfin, I don't think anyone else knows about my Millennial escapades.

Dollfin and our mutual friend Beast will also be there, so even if CK's friends are jerks, I will not be alone.

We show up and order some drinks. I need to quit drinking. Drinking has got to be bad for someone still taking chemotherapy. But fuck it. I'm going to die anyway. Why not have some fun beforehand?

Dollfin brings Becky, her new love interest.

Dollfin has Becky. We are okay. Becky has Dollfin.

I still loathe myself for what I have done.

We sit in the corner of the restaurant where they keep the games. As I watch CK and her friend Megan flirt with one another across from me, I can't help but think the only games being played tonight will involve people and emotions.

Megan takes CK's glasses from her and puts them on her face. CK slaps Megan's arm playfully. They giggle, and I am immediately disgusted. What the hell is happening to me? Am I jealous? Am I mad?

Am I losing my mind?

There is a legitimate hole in my brain. I have seen the black cavern on the MRIs. Healthy brain tissue never grew back where the tumor once resided. Now there is a black hole in my frontal lobe that could contain multitudes of gravitational acceleration with the potential to pull my whole damn brain into the vast unknown.

The noise of Basil's starts to sound like I am actually in outer space and unable to come home. I am trying to rectify all the noise I hear with what those sounds mean. Everyone seems like they are talking at once, yet I hear nothing but symbols of words and no correct pronunciations.

Unfortunately, I am not one of those people who have brain surgery and can now fluently speak French or Arabic. I can't see into the future or make Jackson Pollock paintings with my foot. The best I've got is sounds that all morph together like badly spliced audio or galaxies crashing together, and I can't separate them from one another.

I stand to go to the bathroom, to get away from it all. I have trouble getting up and wobble a bit, but this thankfully goes unnoticed. Once I shut the bathroom door, the silence gives me time to breathe. There are no sounds in the stall to fuck with my brain. I wash my hands and text Beast.

This is kinda awkward, but I slept with CK the other night. I didn't think I had feelings, but maybe I do. I don't like how much she is flirting with Megan.

I know Beast is a safe person to text. She won't say anything. I need to tell someone, and Beast is someone good at keeping secrets.

When I return to the crowd, something has happened. I don't know what, but thankfully, it has nothing to do with me. I start to feel very nervous, like I need to get out of there before something, whatever it is, escalates. I've always been intuitive, but perhaps brain surgery and the loss of half of my left frontal lobe has given me something: even more discernment.

"I need to pay and get out of here," I tell CK. She will go and get the iPad and close me out, no issues, no problem.

As she closes my tab, CK asks, "Hey, can I come with you?"

I am surprised.

I thought she would end up taking Megan home with her and not give me a second thought. I will find out later the night after CK and I slept together, Megan slept in CK's bed, naked. There is nothing I could say about this, but it does upset me.

"Yeah," I say. "Let's get out of here."

I am sober enough to drive home, so CK follows me.

Once we get back to my apartment, CK tells me what happened.

"Megan hit Becky," she says. "Dollfin is pissed."

"Like she hit her across the face?"

"No, she hit her arm. Megan gets drunk and starts wailing on people sometimes."

"That's not the best excuse I've ever heard. I would be pissed too."

"It left a mark," CK says as she throws her clothes on the floor and crawls into my bed without asking. I guess this is a thing now. "Megan just gets drunk and doesn't know what she is doing."

Oh, the mid-20s and the drama. I had forgotten about those days, like when I dumped a beer on a guy who was into me until his friend told him I was *a slut*, and then he ignored me. I later snubbed out a cigarette on his carpet and left it all behind as I drove to graduate school at Auburn with nothing in my car but my cat Pru and a few clothes.

However, I never hit anyone. No one hit me.

I do not know Becky well, but I do know Dollfin. Although she is a very forgiving person, Dollfin also knows how to draw boundaries around the people she loves. I imagine Dollfin wanted to slap Megan across the face for hitting Becky, but Dollfin is not a violent person.

As CK and I cuddle closely in my bed, the familiar feeling of guilt strangles my heart. What right did I have to invite someone so young into my very complicated life? I didn't. I had no right.

I knew CK had kindled a weird *cancer crush* on me for a while now, and here I was, throwing gasoline on the dream.

Except I knew, although she didn't, this dream was a fantasy destined to eventually flame out.

I could never give her a normal life, and if this turned into something serious, my death would fuck her up forever. I knew even if I lived a few more years, she would have to take care of me. She might even have to wipe my ass if the timing was right.

Those few wispy flames could still burn someone.

I should not do this. I should not do this. I should not do this.

But I do it anyway.

boone, north carolina

I get home from Brooklyn and start my next round of chemo. Choking down those pills and waiting for the vomiting and nausea to stop is the loneliest thing I have ever experienced. There is no one to talk to and nothing to do but wait until the puking begins.

Since my initial chemo I took each day I did radiation, the medicine has gotten more potent, but I only take the pills for a week once a month. I dread that week more than anything. I will do this for nine months, and then we—my medical team and myself—will *watch and wait* to see what happens next.

I have already decided: I do not want anything to happen next.

My first surgery was so shocking and traumatic, I knew I never wanted another craniotomy, even if a further resection would give me a few more months. I do not want any more chemo, even if sticking a port in my chest would give me a few more days. I do not want to spend any further time in a hospital, even if it would give me a few more hours.

The unfortunate part of my tumor is that the damn thing never knocked me out. Except for the eight-hour surgery, I remember everything. I remember the seizures in my right arm and leg, I remember the three IVs, and I remember waking up in ICU and begging for iced tea they would not give me. I remember the long hours of listening to my mom call my dad and discuss what color to paint my deceased Nana's house (seriously, how long could they consider such a thing? Hours, apparently. Days.). I remember all of the ways my physical therapist Brad tried to get my right leg to move. Some ways worked, and some didn't. I remember the surgeon[5] and my mom leaving me that night with the devastating diagnosis and me begging a nurse for *something to knock me out, please.*

I remember waking up the next morning and the world being the same for most people outside of the hospital's doors.

---

[5] I wonder how Van Gogh is doing these days? I hope he is well.

I do not want any other memories like those.

I do not want to be sexually harassed by all the old men at breakfast. I do not want to call two nurses into the room whenever I need to piss. I do not want to be told I am not allowed to stand up from a wheelchair because everyone fears I will fall.

Plus, I want to die at home, wherever that might be. My parents have put increasing pressure on me to move home, to *their* home, and I'm not sure how I feel about it yet. They planned me. They gave birth to me. Therefore, I feel like I am their responsibility.

I think they also feel that they need to take care of me, which is lovely.

However, my hometown is a wilder place than my cancerous brain.

Harrisville, West Virginia, has a little under 2000 people, and the town has one stoplight that my mom is always sure to tell people *we don't really need.* There is only one restaurant, The Pizza House, that I trust. The Pizza House was my first job, and goddamn, if they don't make the best pepperoni rolls in all of West Virginia. The town and surrounding areas really rallied behind me after my diagnosis and surgery. They graciously gave up money, gifts, and even had a potato buffet and gave me the profit. They are amazing people with giving hearts.

I'm just not sure I belong there.

My shaved head is gone now, but people know things about me. Being in the hospital for a month and having some random surgeon pulling back my dura mater to gaze at everything inside my skull reveals certain secrets I never planned on telling anyone.

I stare at the chemo pills in my hand. I had to pick them up at the UPS station because I was not there when the driver tried to drop them off. They needed a signature. Of course, they did.

Unless you are one of my cancer buddies, I bet you did not know chemotherapy can arrive in the mail.

Well, it can, and when I stare at those two gargantuan pills in my hand, I wonder just where I went wrong in my life. Sure, I've heard it all—*you didn't do anything wrong, it's only a weird gene mutation, this has nothing to do with your diabetes*—but there had to be something I did to deserve this. Did I treat people like shit in a past life? Did I steal horses? (I would not put it past a Samples to do such a thing.) Did I try to convince people windmills were giants?

I have no answers, but I sure thought about all of this a lot.

Red pill or blue pill? I think as I stare down at the temozolomide.

These are both.

I have no choices to make.

I wash the medicine down with iced coffee. Sure, it's 7 p.m., but I will be knocked out anyway.

Except I need to know things.

As someone with a Ph.D. in Victorian literature, I have $94,000 in research skills, and boy, do I plan to use them. I stay up every night reading articles about glioblastoma. You know by now GBM usually occurs in men over the age of 55; however, they can happen to females and younger people. No one knows exactly why GBM pops up in certain people's brains (except for a small percentage who have very uncommon risk factors for a cancer that's uncommon enough), and few researchers have enough interest to study the tumors or find out why they happen.

There's no funding.

There's no money.

Nobody fucking cares.

Well, people care, but you have to find them.

I see different statistics for lifespans: Eleven-13 months. Thirteen to 15 months. There is one lady named Cheryl who has had GBM for over 18 years, and she is a heroine in our community, except for that one time she talked about hunting deer for her dinner, and people freaked out on her because out of everyone, she *should understand the value of life.*

Cheryl explained to people she was actually a wildlife conservationist and knew precisely what she was doing. She and her husband used all parts of the deer and blessed the land upon which the animal walked.

Stay you, Cheryl, I think before I fall asleep.

Stay you.

I've done everything I can to stay me.

part two: swimming

boone, north carolina

My mom buys a cruise.

Instead of dealing with the feelings I am dying, she purchases a seven-day adventure to the Western Caribbean. Sarah is also going and will room with my mom. My mom wants me to take a friend to make the trip more fun, so I invite Rolli.

Rolli has been there through it all: The initial ER visit in Boone, the transfer to Wake Forest Baptist, the physical therapy, and the aftermath of a cancer diagnosis. *I'm devastated for you,* she said once I was back in my own apartment.

I still don't think I completely understood what was happening to me. I heard the words the doctors said, and I pretended to understand them. I heard Rolli say *I'm devastated for you,* but I could not genuinely grasp why my friend would be so upset. I did what the doctors said and heard their precautions, even if I didn't listen. I went to my appointments—which were still furiously frequent—and took my chemo once a month.

This month, my doctor graciously scheduled my chemo so it is not during the same week as the cruise. I ingest the drugs a week before so I can enjoy myself.

The last round was perhaps more brutal than my time in the hospital.

As advised, I tried to eat regularly and avoided starving myself. I took the anti-nausea medicine three hours before I gagged on the pills, and then I ate dinner before going to bed around seven. At eight, I woke up and knew I could not make my way to the bathroom. The side of the bed I sleep on is nearest to the kitchen, so I stumbled into the kitchen and grabbed a trash bag. The goal was to make my way back to the bedroom and then use the bag if I needed it.

I never made it back to the bedroom.

I fell onto the living room floor with the bag in my hands. I puked up the frozen rice I ate for dinner and then rested my head on the floor.

Everything ached as if I had avoided training but run a marathon anyway. My muscles hurt, my bones hurt, my *skin* hurt.

I vomited again into the bag.

This was absolute bullshit.

This was fucking bullshit.

I was alone on my living room floor, puking into a trash bag, and there was no one here to help. Where were the visitors now? Where were the people who signed up for a meal train? Where were the people who promised to take me to appointments?

Where the fuck was everyone?

I sleep on the floor next to the bag, my closest ally, and puke the night away.

In the morning, I text JC, who drops off Gatorade.

We have had some issues but are still friends.

One Sunday morning, we were supposed to meet and attend this Unitarian church JC knew about. I waited in the parking lot of a diner for a text telling me where to go; that text never came. Later, when JC did contact me, I passive-aggressively responded and in that moment, did not care if I ever heard from JC again. When Alex visited, I was insistent she stay with me instead of JC. I wanted Alex's attention, and I was still mad at JC about the church visit.[6] Even if Alex and JC had been friends long before I came along, I wanted things to go my way.

So many things had not gone my way lately.

During the visit, things did go my way.

Alex and JC spent some time together without me. I wanted them to see one another, but I desired for Alex to stay with me, sleep beside me, love me. I thought if they were able to spend time together without me, then I would not be pouty around JC, and they would have more

---

[6] At a later time, JC and I did end up attending a church service where there was a weird baptism event. The pastor baptized the entire church by tossing water all over everyone. JC got the worst of it.

fun without my sorry cancerous brain around. After the whole church debacle, I had been incredibly petty with JC and felt I was doing everyone a favor by letting them spend time together without me burning everyone's friendships to the ground.

They did, and everything was fine.

Afterward, Alex slept in my bed every night, and everything was fine.

Everything was fine until it wasn't.

But anyway, Rolli and I need to drive to Asheville so we can get on a plane that will take us to Florida, where we will meet up with my mom and sister before boarding the ship.

Before that, Rolli has to get her coochie waxed.

"Are you okay with waiting in the car?" she asks.

"Of course. I mean, some things need done before boarding a cruise ship."

Rolli and I are accustomed to being in the car with one another. We commuted together when I was living in Asheville but teaching in Boone, and she was living in Boone but playing roller derby in Asheville. She always drove, and I sat in the passenger seat, sometimes grading papers but still making conversation. Mostly, we talked shit about roller derby rosters and why we weren't on them, or we listened to murder podcasts or music from her Sirius radio stations. We had our special songs ("Thunder Clatter" by Wild Cub!) we always turned up, and we tried to make the arduous two-hour (really an hour-and-a-half when Rolli was driving) as fun as possible.

This created a special bond not even the temozolomide could destroy.

As we drive on the curvy roads from Boone to Asheville (there is no direct route), Rolli gives me some insight on why everyone is *so fucking mad at me.*

"You know why Lori and Marty are actually angry with you, right?"

"No, I'm really unsure. I sent them a handwritten thank you note for the futon. I don't really know what else they expected from me."

"They were mad because you made a Facebook post about Nodya and David, but you did not mention them in the post."

"You're fucking kidding me. That's what they are mad about? I thought I was doing the right thing. I didn't think Lori or Marty really gave a shit about a Facebook shout out, but apparently, I was wrong. Plus, David worked like he was on salary to make my apartment safe for me. And Nodya cleaned every corner of that apartment."

David made me a sidewalk from my gravel parking lot to my door in January, when I first came home from the hospital. The work was challenging and took hours. Nodya and I could hear the brunt of the shovel hitting frozen mud as he made a place for each brick.

And now Marty and Lori were pissed I did not give them a Facebook shout out.

What. In. The. Fuck.

I did not realize a post about a futon on Facebook would be the demise of a years-long friendship, but I had started to notice people behaving suspiciously around me. Like they did not know what to say. Like they did not know what to do. Like they just didn't have time to deal with this all.

But Rolli is the opposite, and that is why she gets a cruise, and no one else does.

Like the sea waters soon to surround us, my friends have been impossible to navigate. Of course, some have been supportive. Some have come over to help me fold laundry, an impossible task since I cannot really lift my right arm. My colleagues all still love me, especially Mel and Kate. Although I'm not playing roller derby and never will again, I have been helping out with the team. This gives me a sense of purpose, a sense of belonging. Jenna brings me Starbucks, and, of course, Dollfin and CK keep me entertained. Nodya pays for Angie, a cleaning lady, to come to my apartment every two weeks to do what I cannot: the simplest tasks of dusting and vacuuming and wiping down the stove.

Others, not so much.

boone, north carolina

Feeney, the friend who saved me from my initial seizure signaling I *had a cancerous brain tumor*, steals my birthday.

To be fair, I had the initial seizure on Feeney's birthday last year, so maybe I stole her birthday a year ago. It wasn't my fault, though. I could not help what was happening to me.

But this year is different. Birthdays mean something special now. I do not know how many more I will have.

After letting people take advantage of my kindness for most of my adult life, I wanted my final years to be all about me, baby. Didn't I deserve that? Didn't everyone?

I did, though, feel a bit uneasy about going out for my birthday. Maybe I should just stay home, I thought. Maybe I should just pretend I didn't already outlive my initial survival time. Maybe I should just thank Jesus, Gaia, or Buddha I made it this long at all.

In the end, I conjure up friends of my past lives like spirits from a Ouija Board. Dollfin, CK, and another former teammate and friend, Bang, all agree to go to The Cardinal, my favorite Boone restaurant. I need this. I want this, maybe. I want some semblance of my life *before everything happened*, and this would be a fresh start.

December: the close of another year. A year I did not think I would live to see. A year full of seizures, pills, gadolinium contrast, and the type of specified anxiety correlated with receiving a terminal diagnosis.

As soon as I walk into The Cardinal, I see them.

A massive table in the middle of the restaurant.

Some people I don't know and worse than that, a handful of people I do know.

I try to reason with myself. I attempt to wish my birthday away. It doesn't matter. I shouldn't even care. I should sit with the three people I invited, cheers to myself, and then go home.

But there's a beautiful blue birthday cake with sparkling candles, no

79

doubt made by Feeney's pastry-chef sister. I watch the table in the middle sing a slightly off-key happy birthday to Feeney. They are all cheerful after a farm-to-table meal, which seems to be the never-ending hipster, college-town trend. Dirty napkins and cocktails and local beers litter the table in a sign that *friendship exists here*. Love. The celebration of Feeney being alive and healthy and able to do whatever she wants for another year.

She did not invite me.

This hurts way more than her stealing my birthday.

CK and I stand there and secretly hold hands. I'm thankful that someone cares, that someone has taken the time to recognize me, that someone wants me to have a good time.

Dollfin and Bang are on their way, which also gives me some hope.

But how could Feeney do this to me? Why didn't she invite me? I thought Feeney was supposed to be one of my best friends. She did not quite save my life, but when the first seizure happened, she got me to the ER without the use of an ambulance, and I was so thankful for her. I was so thankful she came to visit me on Christmas of last year, right after my surgery. I was so incredibly thankful for her friendship.

Which I apparently was not a part of anymore.

It takes a few seconds for the crowd at the table to notice me and CK standing against the wood-paneled wall of The Cardinal. As a popular, small restaurant, space is always crowded, so we can't pretend we don't notice one another.

Shit, CK whispers, and I know she understands the sheer uncomfortable awkwardness that will transpire in about ten seconds. Sure enough, my friends at the table wave to me after Feeney blows out her glittering candles. Candles meant for a healthy person. Candles meant for someone who is the poster woman for strength and vitality.

Candles not meant for someone like me.

My friends at the table give me a quick *hi*, and right then, I know I am not welcome. Not welcome in the restaurant or the derby team, which I once so much loved. Sure, a lot of them came to see me in the hospital, which gave me so much hope and so much desire to live.

So much so much so much.

But once the diagnosis hit, the *glioblastoma multiforme*, a tumor no one knew anything about or could even pronounce, people started to slip away from me and the dark, cavernous hole that now took up unwanted space in my brain.

It is scary, and I get that. It is frightening, and I understand. It is almost impossible to comprehend that me, Suzanne Samples, a healthy (except for the damn type one diabetes which has been destroying my islet cells since 1986), non-tenure track college freshman instructor (with a Ph.D. in Victorian Literature), and a gym rat (unless there was derby practice) could suffer such a cruel fate.

Read: a normal person with overachieving tendencies.

Happy birthday to me! Happy birthday to me! Most of my friends have abannndoned me!

Against her better judgment or maybe because she feels terribly guilty, Feeney approaches me as we wait for our own small booth on the outskirts of the main dining room, far away from the better, cooler people at the big table. Partly, I get it. I waited until the very last minute to plan my birthday celebration. Most people did not have time to return my texts. But clearly, Feeney had planned her party far in advance with plenty of time to invite me.

And she didn't.

Happy birthday, she says.

Thanks, I say.

She returns to her birthday table, and we never speak again.

Well, I did send her a text that said *Hey, thanks for stealing my birthday and being a cunt after I discovered I had cancer.*

And then I *INFJ Door Slammed* (a perk of my Myers-Briggs

personality type) Feeney and blocked her number.

Yes, it was mean, and yes, I have a way of being a total bitch when I am upset. I have discovered that since the removal of my tumor, my good qualities have increased, and my terrible qualities have gotten so much worse. I assume this is my new method of survival, my new way to fight.

I mean, I have to do something.

I have read all about people disappearing when you find out you have cancer. These blog posts are full of anecdotes and excuses about how friends drop away after diagnosis. *You may notice your friends disappearing after you find out you have cancer. This is completely normal. They are often afraid of their own mortality or just don't know what to say.* Yet there is one thing they always forget: These people who drop away have zero compassion and are terrible friends.

Maybe this is just part of everyone's life and has very little to do with cancer. People become more of who they are the older they get, and they continually become more disappointing with age.

My three remaining friends and I sit at our table in the corner. Don't get me wrong: I am thankful CK, Dollfin, and Bang have remained in my life. But before *everything happened*, I would not have guessed these three would still be around. They are all younger than I am and have lives full of things to do. Despite my surprise, they are here, and I am grateful.

Our derby coach comes to our table before Feeney's birthday party leaves.

Happy birthday, Hammer, my coach says.

It was stolen, I say, *but thanks.*

The next day, I go with CK and Dollfin to a brewery so we can hang out with Beast. Feeney has been Lifetime-movie-style preoccupied with Beast the second Beast hurt her ankle on the derby track. Feeney and Beast had a lot in common, like playing derby, loving dogs, and being strong swimmers. While Feeney played the ever-faithful EMT and helped Beast wrap her pain, Feeney fell in love.

One problem: Beast did not return these feelings.

Another problem: Beast is so nice, and Feeney mistakes these feelings of kindness for romantic love.

I've had to hear about this unrequited love from Feeney for the past two years.

I didn't mind.

I discussed my own unreturned love interests. However, Feeney turns a crush into a full-blown obsessive endeavor by coincidentally showing up everywhere Beast is, even if it's the Walmart parking lot. Feeney chased Beast down there one Sunday afternoon to give her a love letter. Beast has a shadow, a ghost who won't leave her alone.

Another problem: The whole time this is happening, Beast is dating someone else.

There we sit drinking our beers when Feeney pops up behind our table. She only makes eye contact with Beast and pretends as if the rest of the table does not exist.

Hey, she says to Beast, her blue eyes attempting to elicit feelings of love from her in what Feeney perceives as a weak moment. This has been going on for way too long. Most crushes begin with fiery comets in the sky and end with nothing more than a matchstick flicker. But oh, not Feeney. She still burns brightly for Beast and has no plans of dimming the flames. *I have your dog's water bowl. Do you think we could meet up sometime so I can give it back to you?*

She traps Beast in the kiddie pool, where it doesn't matter if you're a strong swimmer or not. We all knew she would.

Um, sure, Beast replies. *I'll…I'll get in touch with you.*

Later, our teammate Jenna expresses concern over Feeney. *I just worry her mental health is okay.*

When Jenna says this, I realize no one has checked in with me about my mental health since my diagnosis. It's all about the physical matters.

What about me? Why is no one checking to make sure I'm okay?

the atlantic ocean

Let me get one thing straight: I do not morally agree with how cruise ships destroy the environment or how they treat their employees.

But damn, it feels great to be floating in the middle of nowhere with people I love.

My mom has been keeping a secret about the room she got for Rolli and me.

OH MY GOD THERE IS A BALCONY! Rolli cheers.

Our room also has a mini-suite with a couch, desk, extra storage, and a chair. Rolli's excitement feeds the quiet Samples' family concealed feelings. It's hard to avoid smiling as Rolli and I explore the room and balcony.

However, I have one other thought. My mom knows I might never get to experience another vacation like this, so she went all out. No matter how much she denies I have terminal brain cancer, she knows. I know she knows. She knows I know she knows.

We just don't talk about it.

Instead, she buys cruises for me, my sister, and one of my closest friends.

I worried about Rolli and Sarah being too much alike to get along. They are both extroverts who enjoy almost never-ending social events and fun. They thrive being at the center of the dance floor. They both drink, but one is more responsible than the other. (If you read my previous book, I'm sure you can figure out which one I'm referring to. If you did not read my previous book, here is the more responsible one: Rolli.)

Near the end of the cruise, I ask Sarah how she and Rolli got along so well. I am more accustomed to hanging out with extroverts to balance me out. I can't imagine what might happen if I were sequestered on a cruise ship and had to hang out with another introvert the whole time. Well, actually, I can. We would spend some time together but then go our separate ways in the evening to find a cruise window nook and read books we will talk about in hushed voices later. *It's easy!* Sarah says. *She entertains for a while, and then we switch. It gives us both time to reenergize.*

Rolli and Sarah become well-known on the ship. Whereas I barely squeak a hello to anyone who makes direct eye contact with me, Rolli and Sarah make actual friends in the Skywalker Lounge: Wynstón, a cruiser celebrating the completion of his bachelor's degree, and a spritely group of gal pals from the northeast.

Although Wynstón is super nice and has amazing light-up shoes, making friends on a cruise ship seems like a nightmare to me. Why would you want to make friends on a cruise ship? That means you have to talk to them whenever you see them. They can corner you behind the lion mural in the Explorers Lounge (and no, there is no apostrophe). There is zero place to escape unless you want to take a dive off the boat into the vast, deadly ocean.

No matter how nice they all are, I will remain solo, thank you.

Here is the problem: My current issues make *being solo* impossible. I need help with every. Single. Thing. I didn't think about how a ship is in constant motion and how I have zero coordination and fall all the time. I didn't think about how I would need to use the ship elevators for everything, and many people who have no disability or issues always want to use the elevator because it's easier than walking up four flights of stairs. I didn't think about how although I am between chemo cycles, I'm still *on it* and still managing the fatigue and seizures and dead foot that never returned to life after the initial This is The Worst Day of My Life Because This Random ER Doctor Just Told Me There is a Mass on My Brain.

But being on this ship and exploring some new islands in the Caribbean is exactly what I needed after the shit I've been through. My neuro-oncologist can't believe I feel well enough to be on a cruise ship, but here I am. Most of my doctors, but not all of them, confided in me (after my craniotomy and after my rebirth as a new person who had to relearn everything) that they did not think I would ever walk again.

I knew, though, I knew I would.

Sure, my right foot is still dead, but it's incredible how the body can compensate for deficiencies. Of course, I know that my story is not everyone else's narrative, and it's not anyone's fault if, after a brain tumor, they never walk or talk again. I was able to, thankfully, but I don't forget about those people I have met and those I have encountered online whose bodies just decided not to compensate for those deficiencies.

I am one of the lucky ones, if I can call the whole brain tumor and incurable cancer such a thing.

I am still alive. I am still upright. I am still moving, even if the boat is rocky.

boone, north carolina

When I was still in the hospital, I started writing about my experience. I didn't plan on sharing this with anyone, but I knew I needed to record everything that happened and was happening to me. *This is so fucking weird*, I thought about 165 times a day. *Who does this happen to?*

There was another reason I started writing everything. My short-term memory was shit now, and no matter how much longer I lived, I didn't want to forget this bizarre experience.

After the initial seizure and my craniotomy, I still could not use my right, dominant hand. A part of me thought that after surgery, I would wake up and be able to walk and use my arm again. Oh, how naïve and hopeful I was. I had no idea the work and hell I was about to go through. I soon realized, with a significant amount of frustration, surgery was the easy part.

During recovery, I had a lot of free time. Because I'm the type of person who never gets bored, being in a bed all day seemed more insurmountable to me than learning to walk again. Thank goodness, I purchased the iPhone X a few weeks before my life went to shit. This phone had a fantastic battery life and plenty of fun things to explore.

Although this was something I had never done before, I started recording my thoughts and experiences through an app. Nurses always asked me who *I was talking to on the phone*, and I would always answer *a friend!* so they would not mistake my words and thoughts as a hallucination (or something worse) and put me on any other medications. I had enough, thank you. I recorded sentences in stream-of-consciousness fashion and hoped I could make sense of it all later.

I wasn't sure I could.

But I wanted to try.

Before The Worst Day of My Life, my creative writing was finally starting to take off. I even signed (with my left hand) the publication rights for a short story twenty minutes before they transported me to that weird gymnasium-like room for eight-hour brain surgery. (There was also a prayer and some visitors I do not remember, all wishing me well and hoping I didn't die.) I was publishing smaller works I hoped would lead to book projects. I wasn't yet thinking of agents, book publications, or literary success, however one defines that, but I wanted to lead myself in that direction.

And then, I survived brain surgery.

To be completely honest, looking back, a part of me wishes I would have died.

Then there was the cost of the surgery, not counting the hospital stay: $185,000.

But anyway.

As I started recovery, I got bored. Sure, I had physical, occupational, and speech therapy, but there were hours when I was glued to that hospital bed with nothing to do. I was not allowed to leave the bed, and those damn beeps would alert the nurses if I was on my way to a bathroom escape, or god forbid, the window.

Writing kept me alive.

Also, I wanted to test myself. I had already lost so much; I needed to prove myself...to myself. Although I had played roller derby and been a faithful member of my local gym, athleticism did not come naturally to be. But my mind, oh my mind, had always been active (maybe perhaps too intense), present, and full of ideas I wanted to share with the world.

So, I began.

At first, I just voice recorded tiny notes.

the old man who lost his mind and wheeled himself into my room
the bacon that resembled a dog treat
the same old man who lost his shoe at breakfast
the dirty underwear Ang and I found in the laundry room
learning to walk again, or trying to at least, is like being reborn

Finally, Jenna brought me my computer, which was probably the best occupational and speech therapy I could have. I challenged myself. I wrote every. Single. Day. My right hand kind of worked, enough to type again, anyway, and my left hand performed perfunctory tasks perfectly. When I returned home, I wrote while my sister drove me to radiation. By that point, I knew my awful cancer fate (*most people with glioblastoma live 11-13 months*) and worried I would not finish anything substantial, so I increased my word count and pushed myself until I had no ideas left. I continued writing as I spent weeks in a hotel with my two cats when my sister had to return to New York. I got ideas from waiting on that radiation table with my freaky serial killer mask. I got ideas from my Uber drivers. I got ideas from sitting in that hotel room alone, late at night.

Yes, writing kept me alive.

My right hand remained weak, but my memory was slowly returning. Still, the fear of forgetting all the shit that happened kept me going. Kept me typing. Kept me from going really fucking moody.

When I finished the first draft, I panicked. What could I do with this? Where would this writing go? I couldn't think of a title. *Gray Matter* and *Grey Matter* were, of course, taken already. Hundreds of times. I thought I had heard somewhere that titles do not retain copyright, but I also thought it would be shitty and lazy of me to steal someone else's title. *Front Matter: Suzanne's Fight with a Brain Tumor.* No. *Front Matter: A Woman's Experience with a Brain Tumor, Brain Cancer, and Writing.* The potential titles got more ludicrous and longer the harder I tried. I settled on *Front Matter: Suzanne's Experience with a Brain Tumor, Brain Surgery, Brain Cancer, and Writing.*

It was terrible, I know, but at the time, critical opprobrium didn't enter my thoughts.

At the time, I felt as if I needed to get every single part of the fucked-up experience into that title. I self-published two copies of the draft and chose an atrocious font for the front cover: all of the T's looked like crutches. Oh well, I thought. The crutches at least gave the cover the ambiance of the medical milieu.

I kept one copy for myself and mailed one copy to Alex. Alex and I were still copacetic at the time. We sent each other about 20 Snapchats a day. (Fun fact about me: I only use Snapchat when I'm in relationships with people not suited for me.) *I have no idea why I'm Alex in the book!* she said after I mailed the book to Minnesota.

I should have known then.

One day while sitting outside in my nightgown—what my mom calls *a duster*—I looked out to the river from my concrete porch. *I want to be remembered*, I thought. *When I'm gone, I want people to remember me and know what I went through so suddenly and so tragically. I want to be remembered.*

At the time, sending one book to Alex and keeping the other book for myself seemed like the right thing to do. Alex would keep her copy safe, and someone would eventually find my copy amongst the literary journals I couldn't remember the names of now and other things I had self-published. (Were those books and stories good? Maybe, maybe not, but I wrote them. Only a few people read them, but here we are.) I wouldn't mind if no one read *Front Matter: Suzanne's Experience with a Brain Tumor, Brain Surgery, Brain Cancer, Writing, Cats, and The Failed Loves of her Life*; I took satisfaction in knowing I remained capable of doing something.

Sure, I was still having trouble walking. I fell all the time and only took a shower once every four days. Sure, I couldn't drive yet, and I stayed inside all day except for sitting outside in my duster. (To clarify, a duster, I learned, is a cross between a nightgown and a dress. Dusters aren't scandalous, but dusters are something to be worn at home and not in public. Jenifer would be horrified if she knew I wore my duster on the porch.) Sure, I isolated myself and kept forgetting to return texts because my short-term memory still sucked, but I was writing.

I was doing something besides sitting outside in my duster.

I did the self-publishing thing and tried to move on with whatever life I had left.

But I kept thinking about the advice my college writing teacher gave the class: Why does this story need to be told? If you could describe your work in one word, what would you say? (He had this theory that 99% percent of writers would choose the word *loss*, and now that I'm older and have more experience, I have to agree.) If you were in an elevator and needed to pitch a book to an agent or publisher, would you believe in your story enough to look that agent or publisher in the eyes and hook them?

The short answer was: I did.

Here is a slightly longer answer: The major percentage of young women burdened with glioblastoma were a) not writers b) dead or c) not feeling well enough to write their story down. (I once did the math, and I seriously had a .0000001 chance of getting GBM. I have also found scholarly research proving how higher blood sugars give people a better chance at avoiding glioblastoma. Ha! What a joke! What a lie! Who were these supposed scholars?) As I continued with the horror of having GBM, I actually found people who were writers and had published work about having the most malignant brain cancer out there, but that took some digging and late-night internet searches.

Even though my book still had an awful, terrible, cringe-worthy title, I sent the manuscript to one agent who seemed like she might have an interest in the story. After a couple days, she returned a very kind email to me expressing her sadness for my situation. She also said she *couldn't imagine the market* for my book, and I understood.

Writing is a business.

She was kind yet honest, and I appreciated her detailed response. She also gave me some advice to try small, independent publishers.

This idea appealed to me very much. Since college, I had loved discovering indie musicians through various searches online and in record stores. (And no, I do not have a record player, but I do have a typewriter. It's a family heirloom, and I do not take the typewriter to coffee shops or outdoor music festivals.) In college and during my first years of graduate school, I loved Bright Eyes, The Faint, Cat Power, Beirut, Tegan and Sara (special thanks to my very straight boyfriend at the time who introduced me to Tegan and Sara), and Sufjan Stevens. I particularly enjoyed even lesser-known indie bands like Two Gallants, Azure Ray, and Tokyo Police Club. (If you haven't guessed already, I really, really loved the Saddle Creek label.) I was perplexed at myself for not trying the indie book market yet.

With a new mission and purpose, I logged into Submittable and started searching for anyone who might take an interest. Before *everything happened*, I had great success on Submittable with short and flash fiction, so I was disappointed in myself for not thinking of this idea earlier. I chose about five places to send my shit-titled book. I uploaded the docs, made sure my cover letter was shining (but not too lengthy), and waited.

This could change my life.

the cayman islands

In a dirty white van with a trailing muffler, we go to Hell.

Hell, in the Cayman Islands, is definitely a tourist trap and definitely a place I want to visit.

Hell has these weird, menacing black rocks that stand up from a swamp like overused diabetic insulin needles from the 1940s. (This is especially relevant because our tour guide also has diabetes. We explain to him the reason I use a cane is *not because of diabetes*. He looks relieved.) The rock formations are limestone, I learn, and a unique mix of algae and bacteria cause the sharpness and holes in the rocks.

Will I end up in a place like this? I have not been attending church regularly. I was *saved* when I was 11, but I use the word *fuck* way more than any human should, and I called someone a *cunt* in a text message. I do not consider myself religious, but I believe in *something*. Anything. Nothing.

Naturally, there are pictures and paintings of the devil throughout the limestone landscape. Naturally, we have to take pictures. Naturally, we buy plenty of postcards from the gift shop. I imagine my own face plastered on one of these postcards, my *million-dollar smile* freakishly morphing into the blackish gray limestone stakes.

The tour guide does not want to take us to The Conch Shell House in Grand Cayman, but our bus insists that he go. *It was on the excursion brochure!* Carol from the back says, and this time, I agree with a Carol. *I would really like to see this*, I say. We can all tell the tour guide has seen this silly shell house far too many times. He tells us he drives past The Conch Shell House each day driving to-and-from work. It's kind of like how we Appalachian Americans frequently pass Dollar Generals or cow pastures.

Despite feeling disgruntled, our dreadlocked guide buses us to the landmark.

I am immediately enamored by the cottage-style house with the perfectly matching pink and tan conch shells baked into the concrete of the home. I can't imagine how long this must have taken. Like a lot of children, I was fascinated with shells and how they washed up from the ocean and the river where my dad grew up. I would spend hours looking for the tiniest shells and then put them into cool, vintage bottles I saved for that very reason.

I could create safe little worlds in those bottles.

Unfortunately, I am too weak to get out and swan about The Conch Shell House, but I enjoy staring at the building from the bus. How long did it take to create this gaudy monstrosity? The guide, who is also not surprisingly still in the van, tells me *The Conch Shell House was once a bed-and-breakfast, but the owners did not want to update the crumbling appliances inside.* Therefore, the inside was now closed to the public. *I guess it's kind of neat*, he says as he shrugs his shoulders up to his dreads.

My mom gets out of the van to take pictures of The Conch Shell House for me. Although she refuses to admit I have incurable cancer, she definitely recognizes my physical disabilities. She sees my weird leg seizures and knows I have terrible difficulty walking and getting up and down stairs. She somewhat understands my fatigue (after all, she has high blood pressure!) and allows me to rest on the cruise, even if everyone else is still exploring the ship.

So, what exactly happened to you? the guide asks.

Thankfully, everyone starts piling back into the bus before I have the chance to answer the guide and the shells trapped in that house.

I know my mom can't wait to get back to her Pentecostal Christian church and tell them all about how she escaped the fiery demons of hell.

boone, north carolina

I contemplate a saying my dad once told me. This saying, he explains, has been passed down through the Samples' family for generations.

There are two things you won't find in a graveyard: Samples and donkeys.

For the most part, this is true. My Grandma Samples lived until she was 99. My dad's oldest brother, Lincoln, is now 93. My dad and Uncle Mac are both in their 70s. My beloved Uncle Roger died of lung cancer, but despite that, he lived a long time. Not long enough, but still. Countless great aunts and uncles lived well into their 100s.

When my dad told me this quote, I assumed it would also apply to me. However, I know now the legend is absolutely false.

Untrue.

Very, very suspicious.

Sure, I have survived for two years now (exactly to the day I am writing this) but beating the odds cannot last forever. I wasn't supposed to live past a year, but my age, gender, and the amount of the tumor my surgeon was able to remove have given me more time.

And don't we all want more time?

I would never wish anyone any illness, but I am so jealous of Sarah. She stays out late, outdrinks 200-pound bouncers, and smokes who knows how many cigarettes each day.

She is perfectly healthy.

Sarah is a donkey.

Once, one of her boyfriends sent me a text telling me Sarah was okay after a long night out. *I just worry about her*, I say.

Well, she worries about you.

I don't respond because I am furious, not with her and her boyfriend, but with the way life works. I don't like how he equates my medical situation with the choices my sister makes. I don't want anyone to die. I don't like any of this.

It all seems very unfair.

I never was a big drinker or smoker. (I've smoked fewer than 20 cigarettes in my entire life. Remember the Newports, Emily? Remember the cloves?). Except for type one diabetes and being slightly overweight (I have big boobs, okay?), I was in perfect health. I maintained a strict exercise regimen and tried my best to keep my blood sugars in check. I got plenty of sunshine. I thrived on being busy with teaching, writing, and roller derby.

I had zero problems with anxiety.

Now, that's all I have.

I spend the hours before daylight obsessively studying glioblastoma. I was never a numbers person, but now I have a particular need. I need to know about percentages. I need to know other people's stories. I need the good and the terrible. When I tell my neuro-oncologist about this, he looks at me and says *Didn't you write a book about glioblastoma? You're an expert now, so stop that.* He read my book, and surely, he knows the memoir was strictly a creative piece and not scientific. Don't get me wrong: He is a fabulous doctor. He gives me so much support, and I could not believe he wanted to read *Frontal Matter: Glue Gone Wild.* Still, there is this other part of me that knows I need to find out more. I need data. Information. Logos. Statistics.

When I ask my doctor about my current lifespan, he looks at me and says *Hey, don't worry. We have a guy coming in here who has had GBM for 12 years. It's rare, but it happens.*

My words to my doctor—*You're saying I might have to do this for 12 more years?*

We all laugh because at this point, we have to.

We are not all donkeys.

the atlantic ocean

We get back on the cruise ship—I can't remember the exact name of the vessel, but it's something reminiscent of a gem in a ring: Sapphire, Emerald, or Ruby. Maybe Diamond. It's hard to say at this point. My mom, Rolli, Sarah, and I prepare for dinner. As we leave our room, an errant child comes bounding down the hallway as if he is running away from daycare workers and toward a mountain of candy. He almost knocks me over, but my cane and the railings save me.

Hey, SLOW DOWN, Rolli yells.

I love this about Rolli. She gives zero fucks about screaming at rowdy children (for the good of the greater community, of course). Rolli ensures I always get a spot on the elevator. I am a bit timid, but she is showing me I need to, I must ask for what I want.

After dinner, my mom and I go to our separate rooms while Rolli and Sarah roam the ship. I take my seizure medication, an antidepressant, an anti-nausea pill (just in case), four generic sleeping pills, and a prescription sleeping pill, also just in case. I've always taken that many generic sleeping pills, if you were wondering.

I simply can't sleep without them.

Writers and insomnia have always been in love.

Still, after downing half of my personal apothecary, I cannot rest, and Rolli and Sarah are probably singing karaoke or taking secretive shots with the ship's crew members. Despite Rolli and Sarah being up most of the night, Rolli always watches the ship's morning show when we wake up.

And boy, has she found a doozy.

People around the ship are encouraged to put birthday wishes or shoutouts to the staff or other cruisers into a box. Every morning, the cruise director reads out those wishes on the cruise network.

Rolli records the following interaction on her phone:

And a special happy birthday to Phil Latio! We hope you have a happy birthday. Good on ya, mate.

Rolli, Sarah, and I cannot quit laughing. We also can't believe someone else thought about this before we did. Before anyone can stop us, we are all blasting social media with this hilarity. Cruise internet is expensive, but we all bought it anyway.

Now we have a worthy cause.

When my mom comes into our room, Sarah attempts to explain this to her. I am horribly uncomfortable.

Phil Latio. Like fellatio. It's oral sex, Mom.

I want to sink into my cozy cruise bed forever. Maybe jump over the balcony. Perhaps go on a shore excursion by myself and never come back.

I know what it is, Sarah.

This conversation is so representative of the females in my family. I'm supposed to please my mom, and Sarah is supposed to shock her. I am the *good one*, and Sarah is not the bad one, but the one meant to be full of surprises. If I drank and smoked all the time and tried to tell her the definition of *fellatio*, my mom would have every elder in the church praying and *laying hands* on me. When Sarah says it, though, Mom laughs and is excited to be part of this inside joke. She *feels cool*.

Later, Rolli comes back to my room, and my sister returns to the cabin she shares with our mom. There is a full-wall mirror behind the duo of twin beds. As she opens the door to their room, Sarah sees a reflection of *Fifty Shades of Gray* playing on their television. But when my mom hears the door squeak, she quickly switches the station to something more innocuous.

Busted.

I know my mom will never mention this, but Sarah finds the experience hilarious and tells me all about it the next morning. My mom will get over it and not care Sarah let me in on the big secret.

Maybe my mom sees more of herself in Sarah, thus explaining why she accommodates her dominant personality. My mom always thought it was weird I did not care if I had a date to dances, and I did not put much effort into physical appearances. But Sarah, oh, she knows how to look good, and I think Mom appreciates that.

I am not a subject for others to gaze upon, for others to become inspired by my alternative good looks, for others to compare me to characters like Tank Girl. (*Do people ever tell you that you look like Tank Girl? Oh really? I thought I was the first!*) I am not someone to be taken at face value. I do not let people in quite so easily.

This is the part my sister will read and tell me *you're making me look bad*. I'm not, I will assure her. I'm just trying to portray you the way I know you, the way I see you.

It's not a negative thing Sarah resembles Tank Girl, my mom thinks she's way cooler than I am, or Sarah expresses herself through constantly changing hairstyles; it's just that we are two totally, completely different people who happen to come from the same nuclear family.

I am complicated, introverted, and the type of person who got unreasonably upset when someone made fun of a Sylvia Plath quote[7] I wore on a badge out to a bar (a place I wanted to leave even before anyone made fun of me, all because I announced my literary preferences on a button). I would prefer to stay home and play mindless games on my phone rather than take shots of Fireball with people I just met who wanted to call me friends.

If I survived a plane crash, I would be like the character Henry Bemis in "Time Enough at Last" from *The Twilight Zone*—as long as I could see to read and had enough books on hand, I would survive. If Sarah was in that same crashing plane, she would be more like Janet Tyler in "Eye of the Beholder" from the same series—someone whose physical beauty needed to be appreciated by someone around her.

Despite our differences, we can agree on a) the genius of *The*

---

[7] "I am, I am, I am." Someone later really fucked this quote up for me, but I'm saving that story for book three, universe willing.

Twilight Zone and b) we are both terrible at romantic relationships. How could this happen? we often think. Our parents have been married for 43 years and actually seem...happy. Sarah and I had a relatively stable childhood full of people who loved us and wanted the best for us. Besides my diagnosis of type one diabetes, we were normal, well-adjusted kids who liked spending our summers dancing to videos on VH1 and cruising around the West Virginia backroads once I was awarded a driver's license after a couple failed test attempts. There was no identifiable reason why neither of us was able to sustain functional romantic endeavors.

Although we share this toxic trait, of course, we approach the matter differently. Sarah flies through relationships at the speed of Chuck Yeager (the pilot who was the first to fly faster than the speed of sound and also a West Virginia native), and I end up pulling people behind me wagon-style, hanging on way too long before I let them go. Sarah cuts and flies, but I drag mine all through the mud before I leave them to wash off any damage I might have caused.

Both of these methods do not yield the best results; yes, we are both flawed. Imperfect. Real.

Before we left for the cruise, I wrote extensively about the vast differences between my sister and me. She read the book from my computer while I was sleeping (which is my number three pet peeve, the first ketchup and the second hearing people brush their teeth) and thought I did not portray her in the best light. I even encouraged her to add her own page at the end of the memoir as a chance to assuage her displeasure and let her speak her mind about the horror we both endured.

After all, she had a different perspective as the caretaker.

Here is something only writers will understand: Some people have better exposure on the page. When you move through the world as a writer, you become a photographer of unspoken words, and you simply cannot drop that filter. You begin to view everyone through their black-and-white typeface potential. There are the sweet, kind people who are absolutely wonderful but would leave no impression on readers through a few descriptive sentences and expository attempts.

Then there are the *people you write about*, and these folks could be a number of different personalities. They might be terrible shit talkers, excruciatingly bland, or have so much personality that they bubble up from the page and splash the reader right in the face, leaving a stain a squid would admire. These are the people you want to become main characters, even if you are writing a memoir.

Even memoirs need characters.

People want to read about Sarah.

I will not disappoint them.

After she surreptitiously read the first book, Sarah told me *I just don't want people to think I don't care about you.* This confounded me. I thought it was obvious she cared about me. After all, she left a remunerative job as a stylist in The Big Apple to help out her dying (maybe?) older sister. Who would ever think badly of her? I know I portrayed her as cartoonish, but that's what makes her enjoyable.

She is the fun part of cancer.

If she did not know that then, I hope she understands now.

boone, north carolina

I cannot wait to return to the classroom, but I understand everything *will be different.* At first, I return part-time, which means I will teach three classes instead of four. Whenever I tell outsiders that all of us non-tenure track (NTT) faculty teach four classes, they do not believe me. *Four classes?* they ask. *That's a lot!* But for our crew, this is just the norm. We signed our contracts knowing we would be teaching four classes, but we were not expected to do outside academic research or serve on *super essential* committees. Sure, we still have a service requirement, but it is far less intense than our tenure-track friends. NTTs get accustomed to the teaching grind, and we know what we must do.

Oh, also, we do not make any money.

Once I calculate my yearly salary after taxes, I am shocked to learn I make less than a public high school teacher. But how could I give this up? We largely determine our own schedules, and I *love* college freshmen. Most people think I am weird when I say that, but I'm absolutely truthful. They are young, hopeful, and fun. They do cute things like raise their hands if they need to use the restroom. They see me as not only their instructor but also as someone they feel comfortable enough to ask for help. I do not take my role in their lives lightly, especially after a suicide wave hit our campus a few years back. I understand they may come to me with *hard things*, and although I cannot counsel them, I can help them find the people who can.

Quite often, though, they need someone to listen.

Quite often, I have needed someone to listen to me.

I decide to theme my classes *Death, Dying, and Darkness: Expository Writing.* Why the hell not? Might as well get them thinking about the shitty stuff when they are young, so they are not shocked by it once they are older. To be honest, I also pick the theme because I'm hoping to learn from the readings myself.

I hope to understand just what the hell, exactly, I did to deserve this bullshit.

Before I even start teaching, getting to my classrooms takes more effort than my physical rehabilitation prepared me for. I am still on chemo that first week, and the medicine makes my legs feel heavy and fatigued like they might fall off as the top of my body moves forward.

This is not an exaggeration.

Although I have a handicapped parking pass, Boone laughs at me. The mountains open their jaws and rumble until rocks land at my unsteady and unsuspecting feet. I am simultaneously the punchline and tripping over the punchline to my death.

When I walk into the classroom on my first day back, I decide I will immediately tell my students what the hell is up with me. I do not want them to sit there and wonder why I have a cane, why I might seem tired, or why I have difficulty moving around in the classroom.

Just break them in now.

I certainly know this is not required of me, but I have the choice to tell them if I want. They're technically adults. They can handle this. They should know upfront, so they don't sit there and wonder about my physical state; I want them to focus on their first-day writing assignment.

Welcome to RC 1000! I'm Dr. Samples, and I will be your instructor. I was recently diagnosed with a cancer called glioblastoma. It caused paralysis on my right side and is a terminal disease. Although a lot of my paralysis was temporary, my right leg is still…messed up. Please have patience with me this semester as I adjust to new circumstances.

And magically, they do.

I am not surprised. Appalachian State students, I have learned, are much more laidback and understanding than typical college students. A few semesters ago, I had my students write a personal narrative. For the first time, I was trying "group conferences," which was a mixture of the peer review process and a face-to-face meeting with me. At random, I put the students in groups and instructed them to email their papers to the other group members and me before we met.

When I opened the first paper to review, my body wilted into my desk chair. The student wrote beautifully and lyrically about her experience as a transgender teenager in North Carolina. I loved the essay and was so impressed with the student's ability to be so honest and write so eloquently about the complicated issues she consistently endured.

Her essay was not what scared me.

What scared me was that every other student in the group was a cisgender male.

What scared me was that all of these students received the essay the same moment I did.

What scared me was that I might have directly put this student in harm's way.

What if her group members berated her? What if they teased her? What if they made fun of her and caused her to leave the conference in tears? What if they pretended she simply did not exist?

I thought I really fucked up.

Of course, I wanted my students to express themselves and be themselves, but I did not want them to suffer any cruel consequences from others.

We all met in Crossroads, the coffee shop on campus. We sat. I waited. I pretended my shoestrings were horse reins.

Her story happened to be first.

Brian, a kid with a backward hat and camping gear in his backpack, began. *This story is so brave, and I'm really glad you shared your experience. It's so courageous to write about things that are so personal. Plus, the writing was super specific and metaphorical.* A circle of hats shook their heads *yes*, and I could not believe this.

In a world of cisgender, straight white males hating everyone but hot cisgender girls and other straight, white males, this fraction of freshmen at Appalachian State University in Boone, North Carolina, has figured shit out. They have understood. They have looked past the brims of their trucker hats and seen a different perspective.

She exhaled. *Do you all think I should change anything about the writing?* she asked.

This is every teacher's dream: a class that teaches itself.

THANK GOD THANK GAIA THANK BUDDHA I chanted inside my head. I had expected this to be so much worse. I expected to step in and give the group members a lecture about *being good fucking people*, but all of this happened without me.

And that's the day when I learned students at Appalachian State are different.

Of course, I cannot generalize and declare the entire campus a safe space for all types of genders, sexualities, and racial backgrounds, but these students. These students! They got it! Even if they did not fully understand anything else, they realized this! If I did this type of conference at the other schools where I taught, and my brave student had submitted the same paper, I would have had to call Student Counseling Services to moderate the group.

I digress, but those types of moments with undergraduates throughout my seven years on App's campus have allowed me to be a bit more open with students. They have compassion, but they also just want to move on with the usual shit.

I continue to go on with my classes and my new circumstances.

The students are never the problem; the problem is I do not realize how difficult the classrooms in Sanford Hall (a building which I have frequently blamed my brain tumor on...wasn't there an email about asbestos when I first started teaching here?) are to navigate now that I have lost all control of what my right side can and cannot do. I do not realize how the handicapped parking on campus means I still have to walk up a large hill to reach Sanford. I do not realize that when I try to use the marker boards, the combination of lifting my arm and attempting to use my fine motor skills to write would cause my handwriting to resemble that of an angry ghost's scrawl. *Give me my life back. Get out of my way. Don't come back here until you know better.*

I wonder if I will ever know better.

roatan, honduras We get off the boat (it takes me way more time than the others), take a cab to a beach, set up some umbrellas, and look at the sparkling ocean; some guy shows off on this surf/hover board hybrid thingy by doing air flips in front of the crowd, and Sarah thinks he is *so hot* as she sips her flowery drink and wonders if she should slip into the ocean underneath him so he has no choice but to see her, and none of *Stargazing in Solitude* was intended to be a travelogue, but that's just what we decided to do after my shitty diagnosis; after the hoversurfboard show, we go to this shady area to eat some terrible tortilla chips and Coke, which I drink instead of water, and post-Stale Chip Lunch, I meet an iguana named Terry and get my picture taken with him as Capuchin monkeys steal pennies and pieces of candy from Sarah's mustard yellow Fjällräven Kånken backpack—eventually, we end up in this fancy private pool area, where after my mom assists me into the water, we relax in donut floats (well, I try, and it doesn't really work for me, so I just stand in the pool, which is actually quite refreshing), and this lady from our ship swims into my personal space to tell me she had *Stage Two breast cancer*[8] and *now she is just fine!* and because of this, I should take comfort *everything is going to work out*, and why wasn't I *having more fun and staying out later and jumping into the ocean with everyone else?* After all, I was *on a cruise and should be enjoying myself!* just as The Breast Cancer Lady has done! I WOULD TOTALLY BE FINE SO I SHOULD BE HAPPIER AND MORE POSITIVE GODDAMMIT, and she will not let me explain to her I can barely walk and have quit drinking at all because of the seizure medication I am on, and I *am* having a lot of fun, but fun for me is not getting plastered and singing Bruno Mars on the ship's karaoke machine at one in the morning, and then she tells me how she wrote a book about her Stage Two Breast Cancer (from which she is totally in remission now,

---

[8] I am not suggesting that any cancer is good, but all cancer is different. One should never compare their cancer to another person's cancer.

thank god!), and the book is about how her *positive attitude and wine nights with the girls really got her through her treatments and kept her going* and *did I plan on marketing my book as a self-help guide for others in my situation?* and she moves closer and closer to me, and I feel like my tumor trapped in my brain before my neurosurgeon performed the rescue mission, and *uh, no*, I say, *I do not even know if my book will get published, it was just something that kept me going when I had nothing else, and it was mostly written for me, but I guess if other people want to read it, then, that would be cool* and then she asks me what I like to read, and when I tell her I'm really into the mysteries of Tana French, who is the most literary of all the mysteries, something I said has offended the lady and she says *well, good for you, reading something like that*, and then she finally leaves me alone, and I am free except that I cannot get out of the pool without my mother's help, and I am so, so, so tired but also so, so, so happy I got to see the beach and watch the Capuchin monkeys rob my sister and float in a fancy pool, and I think maybe I should check my blood sugar (because yes, even though I have brain cancer, I did not swap brain cancer with diabetes), and when I see the numbers 29, I grab my mom's wrist and cannot talk but show her the numbers, and she alerts Rolli so someone can get me more Coke and a snack, but of course, I always have snacks with me, so I dig into my purse for some Welch's Fruit Snacks and sit on the bench and wait for the Coke, and the world around me feels so hot and so demanding and so unforgiving until I get that Coke and let the fizzy bubbles slide down my throat and bring me back to life.

boone, north carolina I am unapologetically, platonically in love with my friend Travis.

Part of me wonders if, in a past life, Travis and I might have been the same person.

Travis came to visit me in the hospital at least once (maybe twice?), and this is distinguishable because he came all the way from West Virginia. If the hospital were a Methodist church, Travis would have won the award for Person Who Traveled the Furthest to Visit Suzanne in Her Time of Need. He also stayed in a hotel room in Winston-Salem so he could visit me again the next morning.

Who would do that?

Travis would do that.

He gifts me a teddy bear with a tag that says TINA IS EATING HER BABIES. At first, I do not realize he has written anything on the label; it's not until I get home that I see the note, and immediately. I laugh. Travis and I have many inside jokes, and most of them reference strange documentaries or really terrible movies or unremarkable shit most people would have forgotten a decade ago. When I see the note that TINA IS EATING HER BABIES, I immediately know Travis is alluding to the documentary *Grizzly Man*, where Timothy Treadwell lives amongst bears until they actually devour him whole.

Travis and I both have these slightly sick fascinations for morbid endings and what-might-have-beens.

Travis and I met in a Creative Nonfiction class, and after he turned in his first story, I could not decide if I was jealous of him or in love.

We rather quickly became part of one another's Myspace Top 8 and fervently traded mixed CDs full of Bright Eyes, moody female vocalists, and the most indie songs we could find in the dregs of the internet. At the time, I believe he had a beautiful blonde girlfriend (or maybe they had just broken up?), and I was enamored with Kris Clifford, the blue-eyed, pierced eye-browed sexy nerd that every other person (male or female) in the English Department also had a crush on.

The difference was Kris also liked me, and one night after a party, I sat on his lap upstairs in his bedroom and made out with him while everyone else played Clue below us and tried to figure out where Kris was. (No one suspected Suzanne, in the Bedroom, with the Armchair.)

What I did not know was that an NTT instructor in the English department named Christy had a Joe-from-*YOU*-type crush on Kris and would do anything in her power to destroy me. She told Kris I had a boyfriend (not true) and steadily drove us apart until I ended up on a date with an actual guy named Joe, whom she had paid to distract me and take me to a dinner at the mall, where Joe bought shoes with money Christy gave him and later brought me back to his apartment so he could make me wait on his couch while he called Christy from his bedroom and let her know that *I was surely distracted now.* Anyway, the entire plan did not work because when Kris and I drifted apart, he immediately started dating this girl who had half of my name and looked so much like me (and his older sister) that I found the whole thing creepy and wanted absolutely no part of it.

But anyway, back to Travis.

After my terrifying brush with popularity and mean girls (why was Christy looking at grad students as her playground? Now that I have the same job she did, I am embarrassed for her that she would take that route), I got mono and did not leave my apartment except to go to class. The rest of my time was spent on a mattress I moved from my bedroom to the living room, where I could gargle salt-water and watch *The Price is Right* as if I were a kid again. I fell so ill that my grandmother had to live with me for two weeks; unfortunately, the night before my diagnosis, I hosted a party in my small one-bedroom apartment.

Travis came, and we each smoked a cigarette in my kitchen, like we were Beat poets ready to drop some free verse on an unsuspecting academic crowd.

There is a picture of this, the two of us holding our cigarette in the same hand and staring off into the distance. If I had to guess, I probably handed that cigarette to someone else after the picture and went back to drinking. I did not get drunk that night—after all, I was the host, and I needed to stay alert—but I purchased way too much beer for the number of people at my house. There might have been five of us, at most. I was probably trying to feel better about myself after the whole Kris debacle (Was he engaged now? Already married? Did he still believe the lies people told him about me?), and I wanted to have some fun.

There was also that weekend at some literary conference where I made out with Kris' best friend in an elevator. Our teeth clicked, and it was terrible. We were both wholly embarrassed.

But only safe people, like Lisa and my friends Jesse and Betsy, were at my apartment for the party, and Travis was included. Everyone had fun, we all felt a little depressed, and then everyone went home.

And then there I was, putting bottles of Rolling Rock into socks from my closet, and then stuffing those socks in a huge duffel bag so my dear Nana would not see those green bottles full of booze and feel ultimately disappointed in my choice of after-school activities.

Besides my friends Lisa, Jesse, and Betsy, Travis was the only person I talked to during mono and all the bad decisions I had made in my first two years of graduate school. In our Creative Nonfiction course, I turned in a poem about the abhorrence of popular music and how more people should listen to Bright Eyes, and my lifelong relationship with Travis became sealed forever, like twelve perfect indie songs on repeat, all contained in the most perfect mixed CD either one of us had ever made.

We would last infinitely longer than Suzanne and Kris, or Suzanne and Anyone Else I thought I should be around.

Once I felt better, I invited Travis to attend an Appalachian Writers and Studies Workshop with me on a warm May weekend. I was not sure what to expect, but Travis showed up, and we sat beside one another. Although I do not remember exactly what the first presentation was about, the lady speaking suddenly burst into a lonesome Appalachian ballad about a husband killing his potential wife on the banks of the Oh-hi-oh. Although the lady was not necessarily a terrible singer, the whole thing was just *so fucking funny*. There we were, sitting in a classroom at Marshall University, hoping to learn something about how to write poetry, and this lady explodes into an Appalachian show tune about death and destruction by the hands of a trusted loved one.

I do not even need to look at Travis; I can *feel* him laughing.

And I knew then, we would always be friends, even after I did a really shitty thing when I developed a major crush on his best friend, Josh, and almost-but-not-quite had sex with Josh in my apartment after we had to climb through my window after a drunken night at the V-Club, where Josh knew people, and sometimes worked the door. I knew I should not do anything with Josh, but I could not stop myself. Josh was, and still is, the opposite of myself and Travis; everyone knows who he is, he has no problem hugging strangers, and he can unflinchingly have a good time without thinking about what might happen weeks later or analyzing every little word while it is exchanged. Josh and I had a *very brief thing*, and eventually, I left town to get my Ph.D.

Somehow, Travis and I never let Josh get in the way of our friendship.

I went to Auburn to get my Ph.D., blah blah blah, and then there I was in the hospital, unable to walk, wearing a t-shirt with the state of West Virginia in the middle and the words HOME cradled inside of the two panhandles.

Travis walks into the room, and my mom is in love.

Suzanne, he is so cute, oh my goodness, I cannot believe you never dated, you would be the PERFECT couple, and I could really see this working out, and I JUST CAN'T BELIEVE YOU NEVER DATED HIM WHAT WERE YOU THINKING OH MY GOD.

To give my mom credit, I'm not sure why Travis and I never dated, except that I was in a very uncertain point in my life when I met him, and perhaps I knew better than to bring someone certain into uncertain circumstances.

As Travis and I talk, there is so much I want to tell him but cannot. Mostly, this is because my mom sits there and listens to every word. She wants to hear phrases like *marriage*, and *let's date*, and *why don't we go ahead and move in together*, but instead, she hears *remember when the dad in Troll 2 takes off his belt?* and *Remember when that girl named Angel in our Creative Nonfiction class wrote a story about an AXE MURDERER and half the story was in all caps?* and *Wow, I actually feel so much like Sylvia Plath in here, the tulips are too excitable, it is winter here!*

Soon enough, my mom gets bored, stops listening, and goes to get a tea for herself. Maybe she's hoping we will talk about more private matters when she's gone, and we do.

I don't want to be here anymore, I tell Travis. *I'm really scared. This is not good, not good at all. My family is just completely shrouded in denial about what is actually happening to me. I want to go home to Boone so badly. I don't want to be here, please help me.* Travis does not leave me. He comes back the next day.

Here's what my mom will never understand: Travis always has beautiful women desiring to know him better and love him. Through the years, I have become friends with most of his girlfriends, and they are always sweet and genuine.

I always have a mess in front of or behind me.

Whether it's a man or woman or person or someone who hasn't gotten it all figured out yet, I love people who have no idea what the fuck they are doing. I'm always drawn to unknowns, and unfortunately, I haven't yet realized that my romantic partners should not be unreleased episodes of *Unsolved Mysteries.*

Travis deserves more than that, and I had stopped believing in *the one* and *soulmates* a while ago. Why put him through that? I could not imagine myself getting married again or genuinely settling down, especially now. I wanted to have sex, sure, but why would I put anyone else through my tortured, cancerous life?

Travis gives me a hug before he leaves and says, *xoxo bdi*[9] *don't worry it will be your night to howl soon.*

No one else knows what this means, but I do.

It means *I will never leave you, not even if you want me to.*

---

[9] Hint: JonBenét Ramsey.

cozumel, mexico

Once the ship reaches Cozumel, I decide to stay on the jewel-named boat.

I've visited Cozumel a couple of times, and since my mom goes to the tourist city once a year with her *Cozumel Girls*, a group of her female friends (mostly from church) who tear up the city every October, she does not mind remaining with me on the boat. I could stay alone, but she is too frightened I will fall and have no one to help me get back up.

I cannot say I blame her.

We sit by the empty pool and drink Red Bull. Sarah and Rolli text me to see if I need any Xanax, Klonopin, or antibiotics they plan on buying in a Mexican pharmacy. I do not need any of that stuff, not yet, but I ask them to bring me a present.

When I start to get a little bored with the book I am reading, I use a few minutes from my internet package to check my email.

I have a notification from Submittable, where I uploaded five or so submissions of my terribly titled memoir about my shit show of a life.

Congratulations! the subject line reads.

Wait.

This all happened too fast. There was no way that within a couple weeks of submitting the memoir, someone at a small publishing house read the book and decided other people might want to read it too. I had visions of the book published posthumously or not at all, hence those two self-published copies that gathered dust on my bookshelf and Alex's wherever.

I squint at my phone a little more carefully to make sure I'm actually aligning the correct sender with the right subject line. Maybe I had confused the Submittable sender with spam about a Nigerian lottery.

Nope.

There it was.

Congratulations!

I open the email, but it won't load.

Fucking cruise ship internet.

I turn off the Wi-Fi and hope I can get a signal. I go straight to my Submittable account, and there is the same message: *Congratulations!*

My mom asks me if I am okay.

I am squirming like a little tequila worm accidentally released on a pool chair.

Yes, yes, I tell her and ask her to get me more Red Bull.

Whatthefuck whatthefuck whatthefuck.

Congratulations!? On a whole book? On my terribly titled memoir about dying of brain cancer? Sure, I had a lot of interest in my short and flash fiction, but whenever I had attempted to publish longer works, everything had failed miserably.

But *Congratulations!?*

This was wild.

This was *glue gone wild,* just like that part in my memoir where I discussed how glioblastoma pretty much translates to *glue gone wild* because *glio* is a prefix meaning glue, and my prefixes had gone bonkers in my head to make sure my 30s were as fucked up as they could possibly be.

This was Running Wild, who was the press that wanted to publish my book.

Before my mom returns, I press the green *Accept* button on my Submittable account, and then I panic. Wait. Did I do research on this press before I submitted the memoir? Was it legitimate? Was I already too excited? Were they going to ask me to pay them something in advance, which would mean they were absolutely *not* a legitimate small press? I put an ice cube down my suit to calm myself. I look out onto where Mexico meets the shoreline.

Yes, I researched the few places where I submitted. Although my memory sucks, I can recall looking into Running Wild Press and deciding if I were ever so lucky, I would love for them to publish *Front*

Matter: The Most Terribly Titled Memoir about Brain Cancer, Learning to Walk Again, and Writing About the Whole Thing by Using the Word Fuck a Whole Lot at the Young Age of 36.

Do you really like this title? my friend Shaina, who did an initial edit before I submitted the manuscript anywhere, asked. No, I hated the title, I told her, but what was I to do?

I would think about it.

A few minutes later, I receive an email from Lisa at Running Wild Press. I can't remember exactly what the email said, but it was something along the lines of, *Great! I'll send over a contract and further info in a few minutes.*

Well, fuck.

This is actually happening.

My mom returns with more Red Bull, but I do not say anything.

I have a secret.

I want to keep this a secret.

After a year of everyone learning every single thing about me through social media, family, and friends, I need to keep this one. What started as an attempt to keep *everyone informed* quickly became a social media kudzu that grew outside of my control.

Before I knew it, random people who graduated from my high school seven years after I did somehow managed to obtain my address and knew everything happening inside my head.

Even if you're a sociable open book, you can see how this might become a problem.

Before *everything happened* to me, I would post about roller derby on social media and occasionally, some links to stories I had published.

A lot of pet pictures.

But I did not post deeply personal matters.

Now, that's all I posted.

People needed to know about my latest MRI, and I did not have the energy to message everyone personally. People needed to know *how I was doing*; providing a mass update proved much easier than responding to thirty text messages every night. Of course, I was and am thankful people care about me, but it's just so strange to share my private hell so publicly.

Well, don't do it, you might say.

But then people would bug my mom, my dad, and my sister. My friends would start to hate me (obviously, most of them already do). People might begin to think I already died, and we could not have that happening.

Yet, for now, I am happy because I have a secret. I am (technically) in Mexico, drinking Red Bull on a perfectly sunny day, and I do not have to share this with anyone.

The secret is mine and mine alone.

No one even knew I had submitted my terribly titled book to anyone.

No one even knew I spent hours tightening the writing and editing and picking out the perfect small publishers to send my deeply personal story to.

No one knew I had a secret.

boone, north carolina

When the surgeon first came into my room at the Stitch Center to tell me I had *glioblastoma multiforme*, I had no idea what the fuck he was talking about.

If you remember, I had convinced myself wholeheartedly I had a benign tumor, and once the surgeon resected Alecia, I would recover and be back to my healthy life. I would learn to walk again, return to derby, get back to work, and everything would roughly be the same.

I had these false memories of the surgeon telling me directly after the craniotomy that *the tumor did not look cancerous.*

Now, I know a surgeon would never say anything of the sort, especially to a brain tumor patient. I had created these memories to trick myself, to make myself feel better about the horror soon to vivisect my life.

There I was on the table, not unlike J. Alfred Prufrock at his parties, being dissected and studied. Everyone had seen me. Everyone knew the dead tissue, the blood vessels, and the replicated cells that formed the tumor in my brain. Everyone knew exactly what I was made of. They had all seen me on that table, all discussed what needed to be done, and all realized what unknown horrors had to be surgically removed.

I really feel as if my body does not belong to me.

I belong to everyone else now.

What's left of me? The black hole of my frontal lobe and the remaining cancer cells waiting to become celestial bodies.

I did not remember every single thing the surgeon said to my mother and me that evening—I recall him writing down the exact name of the tumor for us, I remember my mom staying very calm and saying she didn't cry, and I remember I could not stop shaking shaking shaking because I realized then my body was no longer mine, and I was now at the mercy of medicine and science for the rest of my life.

There would be no leaving the hospital and never coming back, there would be no busting out of there and throwing firecrackers behind me with a big declaration of *I'm outta here, suckers!*, and there would be no chance for me to reflect on this experience with a *thank god, it was nothing worse* mentality. It was something worse, the worst of the worst, and all I could do now was take a Valium and think about what my dear nightly nurse said to me: *How's your faith?*

This question still haunts me every single day, and I'm no closer to an answer now than I was when this first happened.

After my surgeon and my mom left for the evening, I asked my mom to send me a picture of the words the surgeon had written down.

Glioblastoma multiforme.

I remembered all the words he said, I remembered all the things like *lifespan, chemo, radiation, okay, you look overwhelmed, I'll come back tomorrow*, and I remember one other important piece of advice he gave me: *Don't Google it.*

Of course, in the minutes after I washed down my Valium—the first time I had ever taken something of the sort— I got out my shiny iPhone X and went to work. But first, I had to deal with all the people I had already texted about *having cancer*.

That was the first time I realized having cancer had absolutely nothing to do with me and everything to do with everyone else. I was squatting in the middle of that burning ship while everyone else was saving themselves. It was now my job to dump buckets of water on everyone else to make sure that no one felt as scared as I did.

And this was complete bullshit.

I heard several ruminations from friends and family. Some were kind, while others were foolish and inappropriate. *Everyone has cancer cells.* Well, yes, we all have cells, or we would not be alive, but in some people, those cells replicate way too quickly and start to form masses that should not be there. *At least you made it through surgery.* Well, yes, I did make it through surgery, but now something completely different will require my time and energy. *Are they sure?* I mean, a renowned neurosurgeon made a special trip to the rehab center to tell me all about it, but nah, he's probably wrong.

Of course, others were sensible and compassionate. However, those sensible and compassionate responses do not make for an interesting book. Still, they existed, and I am thankful for them.

One of my friends actually told me I was wrong, and actually, I kind of was. I couldn't have stage four cancer because that meant it would be all over my entire body. This is where the power of Google came in handy. Sure, my doctor instructed me *not to Google it*, but I needed to sort some of this shit out. I needed to become an overnight expert so I could talk about this to other people. I needed to know exactly what the fuck was going on inside my body.

And here is what I learned: Brain cancer is vastly different than any other fucking cancer that exists.

Brain tumors are graded and not staged; they follow a similar numerical progress of other cancers, but because of the blood-brain barrier, brain tumors, if they begin as such, cannot go anywhere but the brain. Very occasionally, some brain cancers can be found in the spine, but otherwise, they sit right there in the skull. Other cancers can metastasize to the brain, but brain tumors remain the stars of their original universe.

This is great, right? Well, it is great until you think about what happens in the brain.

Everything.

The brain. Controls. Everything.

So, no, I do not like it when people act as if everything is okay just because my cancer can't grab a passport and travel to my kidneys or pancreas.

But anyway, a glioblastoma is actually a grade four astrocytoma. Astrocytes are a particular type of glial cells, which, if you read *Frontal Matter: Glue Gone Wild*, you will remember that in glioblastoma, the glial cells in the brain start doing their own shit and not listening to anything else going on around them. I could give you a further scientific report, but basically, glioblastoma, a grade four astrocytoma, means that before I was diagnosed, glial cells shaped like stars began their own little space showcase in my head. Then, those cells all gathered together to form a meteor intent on taking down my own body of dinosaurs and wildlife I had worked to grow and cultivate for 36 years. Because glioblastomas cannot be removed entirely or cured, those remaining cancer cells have formed shooting stars that are currently performing a beautiful cosmic mutation showcase in my brain. Should one of those shooting stars further morph into a meteorite and crash in one of my lobes, then I will need a surgeon to remove that meteorite and leave yet another black hole in my brain, similar to the one currently ailing my left frontal lobe. Those black holes interest me more than the meteorites and shooting stars; after all, no one really knows how people survive with vast chunks of healthy brain atmosphere removed with each meteorite, with each crash.

And after treatment, after surgery, and after rehabilitation, all I can do is wait.

Glioblastoma always *comes back*.

All I can do is sit stargazing in solitude as my black hole widens, and the majestic comets continue to flash across my brain in a space show meant for no one else to see.

Glioblastoma is very difficult to understand, but I feel as if it is now my job to explain to the world how those fucking dinosaurs died. I read so many comments on the internet and hear so many people say things like *my partner is so mean to me now that he has glioblastoma*, or *my wife just ignores me and won't do anything I ask her to. This isn't like her at all. Should I leave?*

No, motherfucker, you need to sit down and realize that brain cancer is a terminal disease and not a personality trait.

You think your life is hard now that you have to care for someone?

Did you ever think about what they might be going through? Did you ever stop to consider that they did not want this to happen to them? That they are no longer able to control their emotions? That, more than anything, your loved one wants to *feel normal* and *for everything to be okay* even though they know this is no longer possible.

Throughout most of my research, this is the most relevant thing I learn: Once you get the bad news, you're never going to be lonely again.

Brain cancer will be with you forever.

Sarah brings me a traditional Mexican handcrafted purple and red stuffed cat toy from Cozumel and nearly sneaks a real chihuahua onto the ship. Rolli snaps a picture of the dog, who lovingly gazes at Sarah as she holds him, and Sarah cries at the thought of leaving the little guy behind.

Let's get one thing straight: Sarah can sometimes be annoying.

But in her heart, she loves dogs, especially tiny dogs, more than anything. If she had her way, she would open a no-kill, free-for-all shelter for dogs under nine pounds. There would be hundreds of them, and they would be running all over, jumping on her, and licking her face. She would probably never adopt any of them out because she would love them too much.

I still haven't told anyone my secret.

Something else is bothering me.

I had plenty of time today to sit on the ship and think. Along with the lucky disbelief that my biggest dream in life was coming true, I also thought about my friends. I thought about how awful some of them had been. I thought about how some of them completely fell out of my cancer sky and dropped straight onto another earth that no longer included me in the population.

I thought about how this was absolute bullshit. Specifically, I think about Lori and Ariel, or Pint and Madness from my old derby team. At first, they had been by my side throughout the initial month-long hospital visit. They drove long hours to visit me, and Lori even shaved my legs. I was not allowed to touch a razor because of the medication I was on, but as a nurse, I trusted Lori with this task.

But then, when I returned home, everything shifted. I struggled to get through radiation and relied on my sister for everything. After my treatments, Sarah would bring me back home and make me eat lunch before I slept from about 1 p.m. to 7 p.m. At 7 p.m., we would eat again and watch *Wheel of Fortune* and *Jeopardy!* before I fell asleep and got ready to do it the next day. Once Sarah left and I continued radiation while staying at the Hawthorne Hotel in Winston-Salem, hardly anyone contacted me or seemed to care how I was doing.

And guess what?

I wasn't doing well.

A couple of friends stayed in touch (thank you, Nodya and David and Jenna and Rolli and Feeney, who still deserves this credit), but the majority of the people who were so vigilant and present in my hospital room (where looking back, *everyone could see them*), were now lurking but invisible, just like those little glioblastoma tentacles that haunted me every minute. Lori and Ariel had moved on and started planning Ariel's mega wedding reception, which was going to take place in Columbia, South Carolina, sometime soon. Although while in the hospital I told Ariel I would attend the party, that was before I received my devastating diagnosis and had to endure chemo and radiation.

Attending a mega wedding bash could not happen for me now, no matter how badly I wanted it to.

Still, this made both Ariel and Lori mad. How dare I say I was going to do something and then change my mind after being ravaged by brain cancer treatments? I was obviously unfair to them. They were there for me in my time of desperate need, and now I was supposed to be better. Be fixed. Be okay.

I was supposed to be partying, apparently.

I do not think most people realized how terrible my life became after leaving the hospital. Although it sounds strange to say now, the surgery and rehabilitation was the easy part. I had support. I had people cheering me on. I had people who cared.

A month later, I was alone in a hotel room with my cats, watching the Super Bowl and eating groceries delivered by Whole Foods. I hate football, but I needed some sort of rope to the real world. I needed something that made me feel normal. I needed something that made me feel connected.

I do not remember who won.

I did not care.

I still do not care.

I can't get something out of my head Rolli told me when she picked me up for the airport before the cruise: *I'm glad I can still be friends with both you and Lori, even though you aren't getting along because you didn't publicly thank her for the futon.* I reacted oddly because I did not realize Lori and I *weren't getting along.* Sure, I had that Facebook spat with her boyfriend, but Marty was known for talking a lot and never making sense. I think even Lori would agree with that statement; that's how difficult it was to deny. However, Lori had mentioned nothing to me about being mad or frustrated or even annoyed.

And then I remembered.

I sent Lori and Ariel a text updating them about my health, which they all said they wanted. They had begun bitching at me about not *sharing enough updates*, and I started to feel as if I was sharing plenty of updates but not sent to them personally and every single day. I even gave Lori access to MyWakeHealth, thinking that if she could see everything there, she would feel special.

And yes, Lori and Ariel were two of my best friends, but I could not handle the responsibility of texting or calling them all the time to reiterate what I had already put on Facebook or did not feel comfortable telling anyone. But oh no, they needed to feel important all of the time, and if I was not making them feel prominent or visible, then I needed to feel shitty and guilty and all of the bad things someone with cancer shouldn't have to handle.

This was total bullshit.

When I did text them, it took them both forever to reply. I did not care about this; I knew people were different and worked and had things going on, so I did not expect a text back right away about my latest fall and how I had torn my rotator cuff.

When they did respond, it was at the same time. Very cold. Very short.

I may have lost a lot of my executive functions, but I knew that when they weren't texting me, they were talking to one another.

You didn't tell us about that.

Thanks.

You're really shutting both of us out.

Well, okay, I thought. Time to cut some loose strings. Obviously, Lori and Ariel needed super personalized updates about my daily life, and I simply could not give that to them. With Sarah back in the city, I was alone all the time and having significant difficulties performing functions such as brushing my teeth, taking a shower every three days, and taking care of my pets, who did not ask for any of this bullshit. I did not have the energy to cater to Lori and Ariel's controlling need to know when I took a shit or what flavor chip I ate for lunch.

I changed the password to MyWakeHealth.

In a sudden realization, I understood I did not owe anyone anything. They chose to visit me in the hospital. They chose to help me when they could. They chose to shave my legs or examine the staples in my head or whatever else they did. I had terminal brain cancer and did not owe anyone, no matter how close they were to me and the details of my health. If I had to set them free from my close friend circle and make them casual friends, then I would deal with that.

Lori should have known how hard it was for me to write the thank you card. After all, my handwriting resembled that of a 90-year-old woman who had minutes to live. My grip strength was god awful, and my fine motor skills were worse.

I wonder how Lori and Ariel would feel if they woke up one day and lost their fine motor skills? It's not something people ever think about, not really.

After sitting on this information about Lori needing to be *publicly thanked,* I wished I could *publicly embarrass* her for being a dick, but I opt for the private route instead.

Before dinner on the boat, I send her and Ariel and Marty (because why not?) a shared social media message about this new information I have learned.

And yes, I did have to throw Rolli under the cruise ship momentarily, but I knew Rolli could swim.

I felt tempted to somehow make this a public open letter, since everyone seeing them was so important, but I was not that petty. Oh, I was petty, but not quite that petty.

Lori, Ariel, and Marty,

On the way down to Florida for our cruise, Rolli made the comment, "I'm glad I can still be friends with you and Lori although you two aren't getting along." What the fuck? After hearing her say that, seeing Marty's incredibly rude Facebook comments while I was in Brooklyn, and getting a text from Ariel saying I was shutting you two out, *I'm fucking pissed. No one has said anything to me directly about being mad or frustrated with me. You all have passive-aggressively jabbed at me numerous times now, and I'm tired of it.*

Lori and Marty, I sent you a goddamn handwritten thank you note. I could barely hold a fucking pen when I wrote it, and I begged a friend to take me to the post office so I could mail it. And Ariel, I sent you a super nice necklace because I could not make it to your wedding reception. (I did. I was actually at my mom and dad's house at the time of the reception, puking.) *But I'm the one shutting you two out?*

Listen, I have terminal brain cancer and last time I checked, no amount of positive thinking or Facebook shout-outs are going to cure it. (Rolli told me that's why you and Dave are really mad. Really? You're willing to lose a friend over a Facebook shout-out? Wow. Mature.)

I lost any hope I had at a future within a 30-second seizure. I've fought hard. I've tried hard…but I am a different person. My memory is so bad now that sometimes I cannot even tell my cats apart. I'm lucky to be returning to work at all. Sure, you might see a picture of me smiling on Facebook, but that's about a tenth of the story. Most days are filled with me vomiting all over myself during chemo treatments and struggling to step up the small ledge of my apartment door. I still get through my days and find happiness where I can. What else am I supposed to do? I don't have a bad attitude; I'm just realistic.

So have a great future, all of you.

We still had to eat dinner.

I don't think about Chole, my ex, much. Occasionally, though, I will remember how terrible she was and how obsessed she was with being famous. Charming and a decent storyteller, Chole had so many narcissistic stories tucked in her hoodie pocket, right next to her Camel Blues.

The most ridiculous tales were the ones that took place while she was living in Los Angeles.

Oh, sure, she lived in L.A., but she never *made it*. Oh, sure, there was an excuse for that.

I was blacklisted because I got hired to do this children's show called Rugrat Rock, do you remember it? I certainly didn't remember it, but I was smart enough to tell it was a fusion of *Rugrats* and *Fraggle Rock*. Her friends were not savvy enough to catch on, and they sat with rapt attention on her porch as everyone smoked and chugged shots of whiskey.

Not my thing.

It was before the other Rugrats, of course, but it blew the fuck up for a while. It was going to be me and this red, fuzzy puppet. (Elmo? I couldn't help but think. Now we have created a link to a third popular kid's show.) *I screen-tested for it, was hired, and was ready to do the first episode when I realized that I just couldn't do a show for kids. I would forever be known as a kids' show star, like the Blues Clues guy. Who would want to be that guy?*

We all sat and waited for what she would say next. As she spoke, I was already on my phone, looking her up on the Internet Movie Database. Nothing. I should have known then.

So, anyway, I decided to avoid the show, and I actually got blacklisted. No one in Hollywood would work with me after that. But I did meet Jennifer Aniston on my way to an audition. I was holding my headshots, and we totally bumped into each other. My headshots went everywhere, but she was like, Oh, sweetie, let me help you! She was sooooo nice. And she was

130

actually just as pretty in person as she is on screen. I also lived next to the drummer from The Strokes. We're friends on Facebook.

Her actual friends, very impressed with this info, gathered around her to see her Facebook connection with some semi-famous musician no one really cared about. But her friends, oh, they cared. They thought Chole was the coolest person they had ever met, probably because they were sheltered and caught up in her narcissistic web of sticky stories and brushes with fame. Of course, I did not realize this until later, but she would ditch them, emotionally manipulate them, lie to them, and then either buy them flowers to pull them back to her or discard them entirely with a single word. I watched them all go at one point or another, and then they would sheepishly return as if they had actually done something wrong; her *best friend* Katie once told me, *Oh, that's just Chole. She'll get tired of you and not speak to you and hate you for six months and then suddenly show up again and want to be your friend.*

And you let that happen? I asked.

It's the only way to keep her around.

I didn't like the way Chole treated her friends, but she would always charm me back into the fold, just like she did with them. Nothing added up with her; she told me she had made out with her roommate once, and later I heard her roommate casually mention before Chole and I got together, they made out at least a few times a week. People always *stole her drugs*, but no one would ever be in or around the house when they were supposedly taken.

But when you're the *most famous person in West Asheville* because you once lived in L.A. and almost became a kid-friendly superstar but were such a badass you got blacklisted, I guess people always want to be your friend.

I do not miss her, not at all.

the atlantic ocean

I am nervous during dinner.

Our servers bring the bread, the salads, the fish, more bread, and a dessert that sounds like a bathroom occurrence. Sarah starts calling the butter *butter corn* because well, the round butter has little indentations that make each pat look like a miniature corncob. We share the butter corn and laugh, but I still feel like my nerves might fray like the neurons in my brain that have already met an untimely end. I knew Lori would respond to my message; Marty might throw in something that made absolutely no sense, but Ariel would just agree with whatever Lori said.

Sarah orders an Aperol Spritz, which makes me even more uptight. Before the cruise, she asked my mom if it *would be weird* if she drank. My mom gave her a judgmental gaze and then said, *Well, you're 21, aren't you?*

And, oh, this would have never been a conversation I had with my mom, and I envy Sarah for that.

After dinner, I know what will happen.

Sure enough, my predictions are correct.

Still, it's Rolli's birthday, and we want to have fun. My mom has informed our devoted servers *this one has a birthday today*, and she also tells the servers that a special cake is fine but *no singing*. Years of working in the service industry have taught Rolli that nope, no one loves to sing that fucking song, and yep, although you might only hear it once a year, those servers have to sing *happy birthday to insert name here* night after night after night.

When they bring her the cake, Rolli bursts into tears.

In the eight or so years since I've known her, the only other time I can remember hearing Rolli cry was when her dog Caleb got cancer and had to be put to sleep.

I know why she is crying.

She excuses herself, and my mom and Sarah panic. *What's wrong? Did she want the song after all? Is she sick?*

I tell them her stomach may be upset from dinner,[10] but I know she is sad about me. *I just don't want this to be the last birthday you are with me,* she says when she returns, and I understand. *Hey,* I say, *no one thought I would make it this far, and now I'm in the middle of the ocean!* We all laugh, and we try to get back to normal.

We try.

I want Rolli to have a happy birthday, with or without me.

No matter how much happened at dinner, I know more drama awaits me once I open my social media. I waste more of my cruise internet to read my former friends' responses to my message. As predicted, Lori takes up the most airtime. I do not remember the exact wording of her response, but the gist is I have shown them they are *not important in my life,* and because of that, Lori will *be unfriending me and blocking me on all social media sites.*

Not before I block you, bitch, I say to myself as I press a few buttons and effectively remove her from my life. This was coming, I tell myself. I should have known. Everyone says friends will desert you during cancer, but for some reason, I thought this did not apply to me.

Oh, it did.

I wrongly assumed if people stayed with me throughout the brain surgery and hospital prison time, people would remain just as supportive once I was set free. Maybe even more supportive, since I was now going through chemo and radiation and mostly living on my own.

But they weren't.

They weren't at all.

Here I was, taking a cruise after radiation and in the middle of my

---

[10] After all, when you have something on the menu called a Chocolate Journey, what do you expect?

chemo treatments, and friends were dropping from my boat and paddling away from me as fast as they possibly could.

After months of reflection, I finally have an answer: They are fucking cowards.

And now, what you've all been waiting for:

The Top Ten Reasons You Decide to Abandon Your Friend with Cancer, and What it Means About You

1. **Because you are afraid of your own mortality.** Everyone is. Get over it and be there for your friend.

2. **Because your friend *is different now*.** No shit. They have been through so many surgeries, needle sticks, tubes, IVs, pills, nights with the toilet, scans, and changes in their body. You are a moron if you think they still want to hear you drone on about your unrequited love or the girl at the gym who keeps stealing your locker. I don't mean, though, that your friend never wants to hear about that stuff or that it's not important. There *is* a time for that type of conversation, and your friend still cares about your daily life. Just give them the space to direct the communication instead of jumping in immediately about how your *life sucks because Lindsay didn't text you back.*

3. **Because you just don't have time for them.** Everyone gets busy, but no one gets busier than a cancer patient. Your friend might be going through treatment while still trying to work and make rent, utilities, and car payments. They likely don't have time for you but will be willing to carve out that space because you mean something to them. If you can't do that in return? Then you're shitty.

4. **Because it's just too hard to be around their medical equipment.** You're afraid of needles. You don't like hospitals. You don't like being in the presence of someone who might

throw up at any moment. Again, get over it. What if it were you? There is an absolute guarantee it will be someday.

5. **Because you want to sit on your ass and make your friend come to you.** This is a complete deal-breaker. I was stupefied by the people who asked me as soon as I was released from the hospital, *When are you going to come see me?* I was not even cleared to drive yet and wasn't sure I ever would be. I could not even get myself to the Dollar General, which is less than half a mile from my apartment. I'm not coming to see you, but you can always come and see me. And unless you're the type of friend who helps with cleaning and is okay with sleeping on a futon, you need to stay at a hotel.

6. **Because you don't understand why you aren't a priority.** Once the word cancer becomes a part of a person's lexicon, the tectonic plates of priorities shift. Some continents break completely apart while new land masses form. Although you may have had coffee once a week with your friend and discussed your terrible boss and your husband's inability to untangle your necklaces every morning, just the way you like it, now your friend may need to spend more time with family. More time with their parents. More time with their siblings and cousins. After all, even if those relationships seemed fractured before, your friend probably has the desire to reconnect with the people who have been with them since birth. This does not mean they don't love you; things are just different now.

7. **Because you offered to help with something and don't understand why they quit talking to you when you backed out.** Sure, life happens. We—The Cancer Patient Collective— get that more than anyone. But offering to take someone to treatment and then backing out the day before? No. Offering to bring someone dinner they are counting on and then forgetting? No. Planning to help someone fold their laundry and never

showing up? Absolutely not. That laundry keeps piling up, and the pets aren't going to help with that.

8. **Because you aren't getting credit.** No one is required to hold up to a frequent check about how many times they have thanked you or what ways they have thanked you. If you don't want to do something or require *credit* for doing something, Don't. Do. It. At. All.

9. **Because they are making you mad.** Many cancer patients struggle with memory loss or the loss of limbs or severe fatigue. Yes, they may snap at you. Yes, they may *seem different.* Yes, they may have forgotten to thank you or not thanked you in a way you prefer. They are not intentionally trying to make you angry or inflame you in any way. They have so much going on with their bodies that sometimes the outside world seems completely untenable.

10. **Because this is all just too much for you.** It is too much for anyone, especially the person going through it. Especially if the cancer is not related to a lapse in lifestyle (and even if it is), it is challenging to understand (for the person and for you) why they are going through this. It scares them so much more than it scares you. And no, the chance you might get hit by a bus on your way to work is not the same thing as a terminal cancer diagnosis.

Even if you do not get cancer, this will be you someday. You will have *something.* You will sit sickly on a floor somewhere and wonder where all those people have gone, wonder where all those people have been.

boone, north carolina

I am the enemy of old people everywhere.

This can be traced back to one thing—I have a handicapped parking pass, and I am in my mid-30s. They don't know how old I am, and I probably look even younger to them (thank you, Mom). They do not understand why someone so young should join the elite group of those who *earned* those spots. They spent months and years and decades accruing points to get that little blue tag, so how on earth was I just entitled to one?

The glares are not enough.

They have stuff to say, and boy, do they say it.

What's wrong with you?

How the hell did you get one of those?

You know this is a handicapped space, right?

Yes, I do know, and I have the placard hanging in the proper place on my mirror. No, I am not using my elderly grandparents' pass while they hang out at home; they are all dead. No, I did not steal this from someone who left their car unlocked. No, I am not lazy.

No no no.

But I can tell they still do not believe me.

What they fail to see is how hard I struggle to get out of the car. What they don't see is how fatigued I get just walking to the door of whatever business I'm supporting. What they don't see is how a few months ago, doctors flopped me on a surgery table to slice my dura mater wide open.

I tell them the truth.

I have brain cancer. The cancer caused me to lose my mobility.

It's a very succinct way to describe the past two years of hell I have been through.

I also get a bit obsessed with vigilante justice concerning handicapped passes. Oh, you think you're going to park in one without a pass or approved license plate? Not on my watch. I write notes with my 90-year-old handwriting. I wait for people. I ask to see their passes.

I do carefully inspect to make certain they do not have the placard placed somewhere else. If I do not see the blue sign on the dash, the window, the license plate, or the floor, I get to work.

My favorite time to enact this vigilante justice is when it rains, and it rains in Boone a whole lot.

The notes are short, straight, and to the point.

Rain is not a handicap.

Running late is not a handicap.

Entitlement is not a handicap.

Part of me knows these people just don't understand. They see an open spot near the door and go for the blue. They assume because no one has used the spot yet, no one will need to use the space. They don't think about how the ramps are placed on the sidewalks next to the handicapped spots, so those who can't step onto curbs don't have to risk their lives. They don't understand how the ample space with the blue lines next to the spot provides people with wheelchairs the ability to get their chairs out of cars in a safe manner.

Another part of me feels guilty.

Once, when I was running late to campus and could not find a parking spot, I pulled my old Subaru into that blue-lined spot between two handicapped spaces. I had no idea why I would get a $100 ticket for doing that, especially because I was not technically in a handicapped parking space. I was *between* the two spaces, which for some reason, I thought made all of this better. I protested the $100 ticket, and I lost.

I should have lost.

I understand that now.

I was the bad person.

Also, not playing roller derby has made me a more pissed off person in general. Since I can't safely go to the gym by myself any longer, I have no method of getting rid of my anger. Although I'm not exactly sure why I was such an angry person before I played roller derby, I was. I would throw things, yell, and even occasionally punch myself, out of frustration. There could have been many possible reasons for this, including people who treated me poorly, people not taking me seriously, people judging me, being short, being a woman, and having a chronic, invisible illness that often made me feel like I was drowning inside of myself. I didn't have a way to sensibly control my anger, and although I rarely let anyone see that side of me, the frustration I felt frightened me.

But once I found roller derby, that anger spat itself onto the flat track and never followed me home. I skated over and over that anger until I no longer felt fear or frustration. The anger manifested as legitimate bruises on my thighs and shoulders as a visual representation that I was an absolute badass.

I finally took responsibility for myself.

I no longer had to throw cell phones, books, or remote controls. I did not have to hit my arms until they bruised and bled. (I was never a cutter because I was so sick of needles and blood after decades of diabetes; I could never bring myself to do anything that produced blood. But bruising? Sure.) Now, I had bruises that meant something. Now, I had bruises I earned. Now, I had trophy bruises I could *talk about*.

All of that evaporated like steam from hot milk during the coffee shop seizure, and now I had nothing to show for it but a bum right side and forty extra pounds of fat.

And the anonymity of being the *Handicapped Parking Police*.

I no longer cared who hated me. I no longer cared who wanted to say something to me. I no longer cared who was tired of me because I was still here.

Because I was still here, and I needed to make everything matter, even if I seemed fucking wild to some people.

the atlantic ocean

My first emotional breakdown in front of my mom happens after Sarah and Rolli leave the cruise ship rooms to hang out with their new friends in the Skywalker Lounge.

I keep rereading the messages from Lori. I have to give it to her— the woman can argue. Even in my degenerative state, I appreciate people who can stand their ground on a point that is not a logical fallacy. Lori used facts. Sure, she used facts like *your cancer is terminal, and I do not see us being friends if you are currently in this mindset and not going to get any better*, but at least she does not make shit up.

And then the panic hits.

I did not panic in the hospital, except for the moments after my diagnosis. I only cried twice, maybe three times, and one of those times was about a child who was just admitted, and another time was from joy when I took my first steps as an adult.

Now, I cry all the time.

I have these panic attacks that escalate from sobbing to howling like the coyotes who live in the woods behind my apartment. Some nights before bed, I am in my apartment alone and start screaming at 3 a.m. and cannot stop myself. No one ever calls the police, thankfully. Once I had to drive myself to an empty spot on campus so I could scream without anyone hearing me. I keep my eyes shut, and the terror comes from my throat.

I cannot get it out.

Now, I cry over lost friends and because I cannot get my blue Calvin Klein (by TJ Maxx) dress off of my right shoulder.

Getting dressed and undressed remains one of my biggest daily challenges. I am not to the screaming point yet, but I am crying.

My arm hurts, and I am sick of this shit.

I am sick of people treating me like I'm *less than* because I cannot keep up with their fucking outrageous social demands like I once could.

I am sick of them only caring about me when I can return the favor, when others can see them. I am sick of being the one who gets dropped when they realize this is not an illness that lasts a few weeks or a few months:

Glioblastoma is forever.

Friendship is not.

I am finally beginning to understand that most of my friends are actually terrible fucking people.

I hear a knock on the door, and I know I do not have time to clean myself up before Jenifer needs in. What the hell. I might as well let her see what my life is actually like; she might as well see the hell that is Suzanne Fucking Samples before I spend further time vacationing with her.

"Is your dress okay?" she asks.

I let her in and turn away from her.

"I need help," I say, and then the crying begins again.

She gets my Calvin Klein (by TJ Maxx) dress off me and, for once, does not make a comment about my weight. Maybe all the Spanx I have on is actually working. Why does brain cancer have to be a You Get Fat Cancer? Why does brain cancer have to include a shit ton of steroids? Why does brain cancer make me so fucking hungry all the time?

"What's wrong?"

My mom looks completely startled, as if the cruise ship has collided with pirates. I was always the kid who cried in her bedroom and then started reading a book when I felt better. I did not throw tantrums. I did not unload glassfuls of tears onto my parents during dinner. I was controlled. I was reserved. I was quiet.

My friends are just so mean, I say as I fall into her arms. I suddenly realize how intense this moment may seem for my mom. I did not cry in front of her at the hospital. I did not complain to her before this cruise. I did not unload all of my frustrations on her, ever.

As previously noted, the Samples family is not a touchy bunch. We sit far apart.[11] We hug at the end of a visit, but only as an afterthought. We do *not* cuddle. My family is not cold; we just do not see physical touch as a way of expressing love.

But right now, I need comfort. I need touch. I need unconditional love.

And then I actually fall on my mom, not as an act of loneliness or anger, but because I lose my fucking balance as the boat takes off back toward Florida. She pulls me off the floor and secures me on Rolli's bed.

"Are you mad because Rolli and Sarah left you?"

"Oh, god, no, no, I'm not mad at them at all. They are perfect and wonderful people. It's Lori and Ariel and Martin Christopher Goodman."

I'm crying harder now, and I am a sad little mess of Spanx and waterproof mascara on Rolli's freshly turned-down bed. I steal Rolli's mint and try to tell my mom the concise version of why I hate Lori and Ariel and Martin Christopher Goodman. I keep crying as my mom stays as steady as the cruise ship on a windless day. Jenifer may be in a shit load of denial for her entire life, but that woman is strong. She does not waver. She keeps as cool as the water surrounding our giant boat.

I tell my mom how Lori always talked a lot of smack about her colleagues and people from the derby team. She would love someone one day and despise them the next. I always laughed because well, Lori is funny, and I had no idea most of her annoyances were unwarranted.

Now I know.

My mom gives me an anecdote about one of her friends from high school who *always changes groups of friends because no one is ever good enough for her.* I dutifully listen, and I do calm down. I should have seen this coming. I should have known. Why did I think I was different than anyone else who had cancer? Why did I think all of my friends would actually stand by me? Why did I think I was special?

---

[11] As it turns out, we were very prepared for the approaching pandemic.

I toughen up as quickly as I fell apart. I have terminal cancer and am in the motherfucking Caribbean. How many others with cancer could even withstand the flight to get to the dock? I have terminal cancer, and I am enjoying the sun, the beach, and the cruise. (Did I wear sunscreen? Yes. Was I worried about skin cancer? No. I was not concerned with any other type of cancer.) I have terminal brain cancer, and I am getting a book published. My story. My craziness. My life.

I still have not told anyone about the book.

After having my insides seen by everyone, I wanted to keep this secret a bit longer. The book was the only thing I felt like was truly mine. I had created this terribly titled story, it was exactly what happened, and it was a map for me to look to when I could no longer navigate my circumstances as easily as a large cruise ship in familiar waters.

If I could write and publish a book, I could live longer.

If I could touch the ocean, I could live longer.

If I could swim without drowning in the unforgiveness of friends, then I might live forever.

part three: experiments

wake forest baptist health, the dash, north carolina

I am a science experiment.

When I finish my nine months of Temodar, the only approved chemotherapy for brain cancer since the 19fucking90s, my neuro-oncologist tells me about a device called Optune. I have already researched Optune, of course, because now that I am living with glioblastoma, I need to, I have to, know everything about it.

Optune uses what they call *tumor treating fields*, or alternating electric field therapy, to halt the progression of GBM cells from dividing. Basically, through these pads called *transducer arrays*, Optune sends low-intensity electrical fields straight to the brain. Each user has a specialized set-up to treat the location of their cancer, and the transducer arrays are taped to a completely shaved head so they can get to work on prevention and perhaps possible destruction. Optune is out of the clinical trial phase and FDA approved.

Before my doctor can even finish telling me about Optune, I know I want to try the device. He tells me Optune will *have several cords that connect to a wearable device carried on the back or hip*. As he shows me pictures, I think Optune looks kind of like a jet pack, and I immediately want to tape it to my head and see how high I can fly.

I have one concern.

There are no needles, right?

Absolutely not, he tells me.

I get that no one likes needles, but if my calculations are correct, I have had a little over 45,000 shots and injections throughout my life because of type one diabetes. It seems that most of the time, I am the only one able to remember this. I have already decided that even if I am in immense pain, I do not want to die with a needle or IV tube in my arm.

Take everything out.

I want to die free.

The *Optune People* will be in touch, my doctor tells me, and for the first time, I have a little bit of extra hope. Sure, maybe Optune won't cure me, but many people, doctors and patients alike, have said it works.

Listen, he says. *It's a commitment.*

I remind him I wore an insulin pump for many years. I find myself getting feisty when I remind him the only reason I no longer wear my pump is because my cadre of doctors collectively decided my insulin pump would be of no use to me after the diagnosis of glioblastoma. No one was sure if I would remember how to operate the pump, or if I would break it to pieces if I fell, and of course, I fell a lot.

So, they took that.

They took this, they took that, they took everything.

Maybe, just maybe the pump served as a way for me to prepare for Optune. My diabetes led me to this lifesaving moment. My diabetes prepared me for this. My diabetes paved the way for even scarier shit than diabetes, which was, actually, pretty frightening sometimes.

I understand it's a commitment, I tell the doctor, and I know he can sense my stubbornness.

I leave the office that day with a new sense of purpose. I can do this. I can wear this funky looking outer-space gear and maybe live a little bit longer. I can put these panels on my head and walk around my own tiny galaxy in Boone and not care what anyone thinks. If they ask, I will tell them. I will be open about Optune and how the Tumor Treating Fields are further saving me from brain cancer.

The cancer may not go away, but neither will I.

boone, north carolina

With the major treatments all wrapped up in a nice little *we tried but you're still not cancer free* box, I feel ready to return to part-time teaching and even to the derby team to help out with practices. I'm definitely not a coach but more of a bench supporter. I can help the newer people, who sometimes get lost in the jargon of skate terms and teammate demands to *stay with the pack!* (new skater: What the hell is the pack?) and *don't go that way to the penalty box!* (new skater: So why am I going to the penalty box again?). My coach tells me I *see things others don't see*, and I have no idea if this is true, or if he is just trying to make me feel included. Either way, I appreciate this and go to as many practices as I can.

This was, of course, not my original plan.

When I learned to walk again (which sounds so easy, doesn't it?), I immediately thought I would be able to put skates back on my feet and maybe play for the Appalachian Roller Derby Booneshiners, who is the B-team of Appalachian Roller Derby. I assumed my balance and mobility of my right foot would return.

I was so wrong.

I was wrong about everything.

After treatment and therapy, my mobility and fatigue got much worse. I completely deteriorated. I remember after radiation how I would take short walks around Winston-Salem and talk to people who were hanging out in their yards or taking their dogs for some exercise. I could walk circles around my hotel for about thirty minutes before I felt tired. Sure, my right foot still did not move, but I had learned to stop dragging the foot and rely on my calves and ankles to stay upright.

But when I got home to Boone, the actual fatigue stomped me to the ground again. I attempted to return to the gym, but I could only last on the treadmill for ten minutes. The trips began to feel like a waste of time, so I quit going. I kept doing physical therapy exercises from home, and though I still do them today, I am embarrassed by how pitiful they are.

Helping with derby, though, keeps me from dying of boredom instead of glioblastoma. After my positive attitude still led me to a highly cancerous brain tumor, I began to see positivity as a malignancy itself. No, positive thoughts did not cure anything. No, positive vibes, whatever the fuck those are, did not stop me from getting cancer. No, staying positive did not help me get through the day.

But derby did. I liked working with the new skaters. I admired them. For the most part, the new skaters were the same age as my students. I thought I had things to teach them.

Of course, I desperately missed my old derby life.

I had officially left the team a few weeks before my diagnosis, and I could not explain to anyone why.

Well, I said I wanted *to write more and travel*, but that wasn't the entire truth.

I planned to write, of course, and I wanted to travel with Chole. Derby, with the skate setups, traveling, and equipment is a costly sport. I thought if I quit derby, then Chole and I could see the world.

Well, she said she loved traveling.

When we met, all she talked about was spending more time with me. We were going to go to Maine. We were going to go to Montana, where she had lived for a short while. We were going to go to Canada.

She announced on her Facebook page we were *going to Bali in 2018!*

Then I discovered she was a huge fucking liar about every single thing in her life. The more I investigated, the more she became a counterfeit. She told an ex-girlfriend, who was also her dealer, that I *needed a lot of Xanax for a flight the next day.*

I wasn't going anywhere.

She told her sister *the girlfriend got a job at The University of Washington*, and we were moving to Seattle.

We had talked about moving out there, but I had not even looked at job searches.

I'm not leading Suzanne on.

That's exactly what she was doing.

But anyway, I started thinking about her love of travel, and I finally realized I had seen Chole go nowhere outside of West Asheville for the past two years. The last trip she took was at the beginning of her and her beloved Jackie's relationship when they went to Costa Rica for a vacation.

You have to understand: Chole talked about loving the grittiness of travel. The admiration of new cultures. The ability to see the world *just like the locals.*

But everything I had seen from her travels involved pictures of her and Jackie sitting in hammocks on the beach and drinking margaritas someone made them. They did not see the world *just like the locals*, who were serving them their cocktails. If they were enjoying a culture, it was the culture of white people everywhere. The only thing *gritty* about their travels was the sand beneath their bare feet.

When Chole and I talked about traveling to Bali, which I now admit would have been the same shit she did with Jackie, just a different person, I started saving money to pay for the expensive vacation. I could make this possible, maybe, because I quit derby. Maybe I could get another credit card. Maybe I could pick up a side hustle.

Chole was getting her way paid through her trust fund.

I did not realize this at first, and because she worked at a diner while we dated, I assumed she had saved money.

Nope.

Her way was being paid through the generosity of her dead aunt, who also paid the electric in Chole's colossal house and any bill for her pets she needed to be covered. I thought to myself that maybe Dead Aunt Whatsherface would toss a few bills my way for the extravagant vacation, but that is not how rich people work. They buy the sunshine and clear water for the ones they know and then say *good fucking luck* to anyone else who wishes to tag along. I did not expect for Dead Aunt Whatsherface to pay for my vacations, but if I had known that I was entirely on my own while Chole had her tab covered, I would have picked South Carolina instead of Bali.

But of course, we did not go, and we were never going to go.

Everyone but me knew that.

I think I knew something much more sinister lurked in my head.

I have no proof of this except I feel as if our bodies understand us better than we think. In fact, we don't have to think. Our bodies know things we only discover if we listen very, very carefully. Before *everything happened*, I would get this anxious picture in my mind (which I'm distinguishing from the brain as a major organ) of *what I would look like once I got cancer.*

At the time, I had no indication anything was wrong with me. I would go through my day as normal, and then right before I fell asleep, I would see myself as a cancer patient. I would wake up the next morning and roll my eyes for being so ludicrous. I was not anxious about potentially getting cancer or thinking I might get cancer; as if my mind was a crystal ball, I could actually envision it happening.

I find the beginning of My Cancer Story intriguing because nothing really happened until after I got my final grades turned in. My body just knew, just understood, that I could not get sick until after I got those grades finished, dammit.

I also recently found a journal entry I wrote as a 16-year-old. The entry flippantly read, *I'm probably going to die of brain cancer, or some messed up shit like that.*

Then about a month before I lost control of my body, I quit derby.

I fucking knew.

I fucking knew the whole time.

I would have never quit derby. I loved the sport. I loved the people. I loved the strategy, the subtleties, and the slow grind of the game. As soon as Chole and I split, I knew I wanted to go back.

And then I couldn't.

Still, I liked helping. I liked being around my friends. I liked stepping into that cold rink in Januarys and seeing Coach mop the floors so we wouldn't unnecessarily bust our asses. (Skating rinks are weird and sometimes defy science.) I liked joking I was like a mean dance teacher and might smack skaters in the knee with my cane if they fucked up.

I loved it all.

Until the post.

All the skaters knew my situation. Even if we weren't close, they all knew who I was and what happened to me.

One evening, I logged into social media and saw that someone from the derby team posted a meme that was popular a couple years ago and is probably still circulating today. There isn't really a picture, but the meme does not need anything visual to make its point. As far as I can tell, the meme originated as a Tweet from a Twitter account named Parker Snowflake. On Twitter, the snowflake is an emoji and it's @pmilbs, but in my head, this person is called Parker Snowflake. It appears Parker Snowflake is young and has not had anything significant happen to her health-wise, but maybe she just has a hell of a sense of humor.[12] Anyway, the text states:

ONE OF MY FAVORITE GAMES TO PLAY IS "IS MY HEADACHE FROM DEHYDRATION, CAFFEINE WITHDRAWAL, LACK OF PROPER NUTRITION, MY

[12] A deep dive into Parker Snowflake's account did not reveal any significant health issues; however, this is not to say someone must put all of their private health information on Twitter. Parker Snowflake, if you're out there, I hope you are okay. If you want to talk, find my Instagram. I don't use Twitter.

PONYTAIL, STRESS, LACK OF SLEEP, NOT WEARING MY
GLASSES, OR A BRAIN TUMOR?"

To preface my hatred of health-related memes, I have been dealing
with the "diabetes on a plate" joke for 30+ years, so I arrived at The
Brain Tumor Meme with some latent feelings. Still, jests and memes of
this nature, whether they reference diabetes, a brain tumor, a stroke, a
heart attack, or deafness, are offensive and should not be shared or liked
at the expense of someone else's reality.

But here we are, late on a Wednesday night, and I am looking at
The Brain Tumor Meme for the first time.[13] A teammate who
frequently carpools with Jenna posted the meme, and not everyone, but
so many people I knew and loved with all my heart were *laugh reacting*
at a meme they found funny whose content destroyed my entire life.

Jenna was commenting.

I can't remember exactly what her comment was, but it was
something of this ilk: *Ha ha so true! Too funny! It's us!*

No, I thought. Not Jenna. She sat right beside me in the emergency
room when the doctor said, *There is a mass on your brain.* She came to
visit me when I was staying in the Hawthorne Hotel and getting
radiation at the hospital next door. She came to fold my laundry for me
when I was too sick to sit up straight.

And now my horror had become her inside joke.

I immediately text her a screenshot of the conversation and write,

---

[13] But, oh, there would be other times. Like an unwanted ghost, this post just
keeps appearing. After debating this Tweet/meme in a Facebook group
designed to discuss ableism, I was excoriated for complaining about the usage
of "brain tumor" in the post. Other group members believed I was
disrespecting health anxiety and griped I was *tone policing* those with health
anxiety. I do not believe I was. Look, you can have health anxiety without
poking fun and disrespecting diseases and disorders people actually have. For
instance, I would never make a meme, Tweet, post, or whatever about a heart
attack and expect laughs and reposts. DISRESPECTFUL.

Please do not call me right now because I am too angry to talk. I probably sounded cranky or mean or any combination of the two. I had not been living in reality lately. I was on my own with no help, and people had forgotten about me. People had forgotten that my cancer did not go away after I completed radiation and chemotherapy.

The MRIs show tumors and not cancer, I remember my doctor saying. I tell myself this over and over again. *With GBMs, those little tentacles go out into your brain, making it impossible—even with chemo and radiation and surgery—to completely cure the disease.*

Why was I the only one to remember this? Why was I the only one who cared? Why didn't anyone seem to understand my life, in many ways, was even worse now that I was home alone without any constant help or support?

Although Feeney had initially agreed to be my roommate once I left the hospital, she backed out of that one really fast when she found a charming one-bedroom for a decent price. I don't blame her, but she should have never even brought up the idea if she was going to drop the whole thing so quickly. Now, these teammates of mine who had been so vigilant and supportive in the hospital were publicly making fun of what ruined my life with a fucking misinformed meme.

I was not a hypochondriac, and not even the type of person to take medical issues as seriously as I should have. I did not even have headaches before my diagnosis; a lot of people don't realize this. Although some brain cancer sufferers do have extremely terrible headaches, I had experienced zero.

Zero.

Zero zero zero.

If I wanted to name a symptom before I had the initial seizure, all I could say was *I was tripping a lot. I thought I was clumsy.*

People do not go to the doctor because they are clumsy.

People do not go to the doctor because they accidentally fall at a bar when they aren't even drunk.

People do not go to the doctor because they trip over the steps at school.

People do not go to the doctor because they slip on some leaves while walking their dogs.

I did not go to the doctor because, at that point, no one would have taken me seriously. I wouldn't have taken myself seriously. MRIs and neurological tests would have been an extreme overreaction for someone who just tripped a whole lot.

But now here I am, a somehow-still-alive brain cancer patient in Boone, North Carolina, whose radiation actually killed off all of my friends instead of my cancer. How could they think that's funny? I wonder. I didn't make jokes or post memes about how funny broken tibias and fibulas (one of the most common roller derby injuries) were. I didn't poke fun at people who had tumors in their lungs or kidneys. I didn't make jokes about heart attacks or meningitis or lost pregnancies.

I worried about these people.

None of this is funny to me.

Of course, Jenna tries to call.

I do not answer.

I just sit there and think: Jenna. The one who was there for me as soon as I woke up from surgery. The one whose hand I held. The one whose mom has a terrible form of cancer and was so supportive of everything I was going through. The one I thought I could count on. The one I thought I could trust. The one I thought I could believe in.

I text her a lot of things.

How could you fucking do this?

I thought you fucking understood.

This is unreal to me. I can't believe you would fucking actively make fun of the worst hell I've ever been through. I just did not see this fucking coming from you, Jenna. I did not fucking see it coming. Especially from you. You have been there through the entire fucking thing, and this hurts almost as much as my diagnosis did.

I know. I can be very dramatic. As my ex-husband once said, *you have a flair for drama.* He was not wrong.

Jenna is very sorry. I know she is, and in my heart, I immediately forgive her for hurting me. She did not mean to, and she did not post the meme. What hurt was seeing my life turned into a joke on Facebook by people who had actually watched me go through the craniotomy, the rehab, the diagnosis, and treatment. I was looking at their faces every Tuesday night when I went to practice. Shouldn't they know how awful this was? Shouldn't they realize?

What I don't immediately forgive Jenna for is participating in the conversation with no realization of how hurtful this could be to me. Part of me understands; I am not a member of the team any longer, not really. They were so sweet to buy me a new jersey so I could wear it in support, but I am not out there skating and grinding against the clock. Why should they care when I was not an integral part of the herd any longer? I ask that without sarcasm or pettiness.

Yet in my very soul, I am, unfortunately, a sensitive person.

I do not like it when people get away with hurtful comments or undeserved jests.

Because I have no other way of solving this, I post the screenshot of the meme and the conversation below the meme to the derby team's private Facebook group. I announce my resignation, say something snarky, and then I also note because I am teaching again, I probably will not have time to help with the derby team anyway. (All of this is true; however, I probably would have just faded out instead of quitting on the spot. On social media. At midnight.) This makes me feel like I am going to vomit, but I feel the need to teach people that they simply cannot post shit on social media about serious, fatal illnesses and laugh about it. It's cruel.

It's mean. It's unkind. It's unfair.

Almost immediately, I get private messages from people who feel terrible about the whole thing. Interestingly, I notice the people apologizing had absolutely nothing to do with the post. They are completely innocent, yet they are the ones telling me they are sorry. I did not expect this, and I am thankful to these teammates who still consider me a worthy friend.

The teammate who originally posted the meme says nothing.

Well, she posted something below it, but then she deleted the whole post, Jenna tells me.

She should have reached out to me.

She should have, but she thought she was doing what was best.

She should have never posted anything like that in the first place.

I don't think she was thinking about it like that.

Obviously not. You know why? She doesn't have to think about it. None of you do.

You're right, Jenna tells me. *You're absolutely right.*

I just did not see this coming, I say, and another piece of my heart drops onto the wooden rink and shatters. Why is it never the ones I expect? Why do they have to forget about me? Why are they just able to move on with their lives when I'm stuck with terminal cancer and a gaping hole in my frontal lobe?

I don't like the phrase *life isn't fair.* That's what you say to a kid in a freshman English class who doesn't turn in their paper on time because they lost the file and forgot to save it elsewhere. *Life isn't fair* is what you say to someone in a movie who survives getting abducted by aliens who later drop them on the train tracks where they get run over. *Life isn't fair* is what you say to some entitled kid on *Dr. Phil* who wants his parents to pay for his acting career while he refuses to work.

Life isn't fair is not what you say or think to someone terminal.

But these days, that's the only phrase I repeat to myself in my head, over and over and over.

157

boone, north carolina

After a single phone call and some fundraising, I am ready to meet with The Optune Lady and begin my latest treatment. Although Optune is not technically experimental, I still feel like I belong in a lab. I can do this, though. This might save my life, or at least extend my prognosis time, and I want to do anything and everything I can to make this possible.

The Optune People recommend I have a friend or loved one with me for the in-home demonstration.

I choose Dollfin, of course.

Dollfin is hilarious, loves medical devices, and is helpful. I would never feel embarrassed around her because she makes me feel comfortable, even in the worst situations. I would not have wanted anyone else to help me out with becoming a walking display of science. Experiments! Battery-operated lifesaving devices!

When she arrives at my apartment, The Optune Lady makes herself right at home and sets up all of the equipment. She plugs in a bag (yes, it looks like the bag attaches to the wall with a cord), and she hands me an electric razor and instructs me to go to the bathroom and shave my head closer to the scalp.

I knew this would happen, but it still kind of sucks.

I have worked hard to grow this hair since radiation burned most of it off in a strange crop circle ring. Sure, it wasn't long yet, but it was getting there. The new hair was becoming a symbol of my burgeoning HEALTH, and now it was gone again.

The Optune panels can only work if they stick directly to the skin of my head, so everything needs shaved, Mr. Clean style. Because of my weakened right side, I cannot shave my head by myself.

"Is your friend going to be able to shave your head every three days?" The Optune Lady asks.

"Um, sure," Dollfin says. "Shaving heads is one of my many talents."

It's sort of true. Before *everything happened*, Dollfin once shaved the side of my head in a Boone restaurant bathroom. Yes, we were a little drunk, but yes, it needed to be done. That was back when I had my *roller derby cool* haircut, and it required a lot of upkeep. CK worked at the restaurant and told us not to do it, but we didn't listen.

"I can't express enough how you need to keep your head closely shaved. If the transducers are on your hair and not your actual head, they will fall off and be ineffective."

Dollfin and I are not really listening. We are concentrating on making sure that she swipes all the new fuzz off my head. I do not look bad with a shaved head; I actually look almost trendy.

Once I have zero wisps of hair on my head, The Optune Lady heads back to my kitchen, where all of the equipment waits. I have a super clean apartment, but I still feel strange letting someone wander around my place with my friend and me. When the three of us were in the bathroom together, I felt like we were three drunk women in a bar trying to find mirror space.

The Optune Lady is a new friend who didn't quite fit in yet.

I try to make conversation. The Optune Lady is probably about my age or younger. *How the hell did you get into this?* I ask. *It's such a weird job.* She tells me she wanted to be an occupational therapist, but she also wanted better hours so she could spend more time with her family.

Then we get to the good stuff.

I have four transducer panels I will tape to my head. Those panels attach through a mess of cords to my jetpack (not a technical term), which has a battery that will need to be replaced every four-to-six hours. Yes, just like an insulin pump, I will sleep with Optune, and yes, when I am sleeping, I can leave the entire weirdo contraption plugged into the wall, so I do not have to change the battery when I sleep. During the day, I will carry around the five-pound jetpack on my side or on my back. Yes, I can use my bandanascarf to cover up the transducers taped to my bald head.

"You do have to be careful," The Optune Lady tells us. "The transducers can burn your scalp."

"Well, that can't be worse than dying from cancer," Dollfin jokes. I find the wisecrack hilarious, but The Optune Lady sees no humor in the situation.

"If the machine starts beeping, then something is wrong," she says as she shows us how to troubleshoot various problems. The transducers might get too hot. The battery might need to be replaced. The battery might start burning. The transducers need to be swapped once every few days, but maybe more if they are unhappy.

My own personal brain robot.

Our girl group heads back to the bathroom, but instead of reapplying lipstick or talking about boys, we need to tape the transducers to my head. First, I smooth a special blend of rubbing alcohol all over my clean scalp to prepare; this, The Optune Lady says, will assure cleanliness and help the transducer panels stay on for as long as they should.

And now, the moment I have been waiting for: putting the transducer panels on my head so I resemble some sort of Dollar General Egyptian queen. However, things immediately start going awry.

Because of the problems I have with weakness in my arm and shoulder, I can't get at least one of the transducer panels on the back of my head. I don't have the range-of-motion.

Dollfin helps me tape the panel to the back of my skull and promises to come over when it needs replaced. I can get the three other panels on smoothly, and before I know it, our girl group leaves the bathroom and heads back out onto the dance floor of my living room.

Still miffed by Dollfin's joke, The Optune Lady leaves, and Dollfin and I head to Basil's, where CK works, to get food. Dollfin snaps a picture of me taking a selfie, and I actually look pretty good.

Like a weird science project, but good.

Dollfin posts the picture of me and captions it #toosexyforcancer. I don't wear my bandanascarf because I want to see how the whole thing feels on my head.

In public.

For hours.

Sure, I get a few stares, but most people glance away as quickly as they look.

I can do this. I can do this. I have to do this.

The jetpack starts beeping about halfway through my dinner sandwich. This is a test. A deductive reasoning puzzle. I am good at those. Nothing feels too hot on my head, but the battery needs changed. I pull another battery out of my bag and swiftly swap the two.

Easy.

I will be fine.

I will be fine.

The only two people who understand why I'm so upset about The Brain Tumor Meme are Dollfin and CK. After I leave the roller derby Facebook group, CK decides she will leave the team entirely. I know this doesn't have to do with me, but I am a bit shocked at how quickly she makes this decision. One swipe on her phone, and she is gone from the team and the group.

This should have been a sign of things to come, but I did not pay close enough attention.

I don't really know, not at that point, that she is struggling with her friends, alcoholism, and finding her place in the world. Dollfin doesn't leave the team, and I don't expect her to.

However, she listens and understands why I am so frustrated.

These people saw me go through everything.

It's true that I was going back to school and still on chemo, and no, I probably would not have had time to entertain helping with the derby team once I got back into the classroom. Now I also had these weird hot panels on my head, and life felt a little unbearable.

I still don't understand why it is so hard for adults to think about what they post on social media, and how their words might hurt someone who loves them. I think about that meme all the time. Another friend whom I worked with once sent me a frantic message (about three days after the derby team snafu) and apologized to me for posting the same meme. I didn't even see her post, but I thanked her for thinking about other people. *I didn't realize how rude it was when I posted it, and I'm so sorry. I've had people in my family suffer from brain tumors, and I just wasn't thinking straight. I'm so sorry.* Here was someone I had not spoken to in about a year who understood how something that seems silly to other people might be hurtful.

Catrina got it.

Catrina understood.

Why couldn't everyone else?

I thanked the people from the team who apologized. As I mentioned, most of the people who apologized had nothing to do with the post in the first place. My former teammates were not bad people; they just hadn't been thinking.

Because you don't have to think about it.

You're right. We don't have to think about it.

No one has to think about this but other strangers and myself who have, unfortunately, had to go through the same thing.

More than anything, I feel misunderstood and sad.

I feel like I'm fighting every day and losing every minute. I feel like I died and am grieving the loss of myself. I have no idea how to act or react. The person I knew for 36 years passed away in that coffee shop seizure, and now a sicker clone has taken her place. I cannot connect with people, and I never know how to act. When I reexamine my life, I look for someone to blame and can find no one, not even myself. *These things just happen sometimes.* I cry all the time for the person I was, that happy, healthy, selectively angry, intelligent, able-bodied person. No, I do not mind the word *disabled* at all, and I'm learning to embrace the term and make the best of it. Still, I wish I had realized my ultimate privilege. Sure, diabetes caused me a lot of problems, but the disease never made me forget myself. I thrived *with* diabetes.

All of this *brain cancer stuff* seems nearly impossible, though.

Who the hell gets brain cancer in their mid-30s?

Who the hell plays roller derby and then wakes up the next day and can't walk?

Who the hell is this person?

I do not like my new self. I laugh now when I think about *self-love*. I had pretty decent self-esteem before *everything happened*, but I did let people treat me like shit sometimes.

Still, if, for instance, Chole talked about my *tits being too big and wearing the wrong bras*, I would laugh at her and refuse to change myself. I liked myself, but not too much. Otherwise, I would have left her after the first time she tried to stir up drama with me.

Now I was in the throes of learning everything again and trying to figure out how to move forward. I did not think about this at first; I initially assumed I would not survive this long, but once I did, I had to start thinking about these things.

Who was I without the ability to move around?

Who was I without the ability to remember someone's name?

Who was I without the ability to love the person I had worked so hard to become?

And no, forgetting someone's name is not what *everyone does*. I was always especially good with names and faces and mannerisms. I was the person who remembered. I was the person who took the time to listen. I was the person to put all of these things together upon our next meeting. It was me who remembered. It was me.

But now it's not me.

It might never be me again.

When I feel up to traveling, I visit my cousin Kyle and his wife Kelly in Asheville. Once I taught myself to drive again, wheeling my tiny Scion around all over the place made me feel powerful.

So powerful, in fact, when Dollfin asked if I wanted to meet her at the Outback in Blowing Rock, I was thrilled to say yes. It would be my first time driving myself somewhere other than the Dollar General, which is barely a half a mile from my apartment. After a lovely steak dinner, Dollfin took plenty of pictures and videos of the cop pulling me over and giving me a ticket for exceeding the speeding limit straight out of the American Australia.

I try to be more careful now, but I was just so excited.

Kyle and Kelly make me feel normal.

The Samples Family can be hard to infiltrate. Significant others always want to be a part of the family but find it very difficult to fit in with our decades-long private jokes, like putting ham in Emily's purse.

Sorry about that, Emily.

But Kelly fit right in.

Kelly did not try too hard. She just effortlessly inserted herself into pictures and plans and gatherings and acted as if she had been there the whole time. This was the only way to do it, just throw yourself in and not ask or guffaw or be timid. She was a natural missing puzzle piece. Kelly also came from a family full of siblings, and I think this helped.

The first time I met her, she touched my tits and told me how great they were. *Thank you, Kelly Samples,* I told her. *I just know you are going to marry Kyle.*

And she did.

I consider her more of a sister than a cousin-in-law.

This time when I visit, I wear my Optune science experiment panels and jetpack. I have decided to sling the jetpack around my shoulder and wear the five-pound sack on my side. It's terribly uncomfortable, but I keep telling myself that this device will save my life. I just need to keep up with it and keep trying.

It beeps *all the fucking time* and burns the shit out of my scalp. I don't see Dollfin enough to keep my head properly shaved, so everything looks very patchy, and the transducer panels keep falling off unless I use medical tape. This would not be so bad except for those places I find impossible to reach.

Because of this, my transducer panels end up in the wrong place and stuck together. (Also, this is *not* Dollfin's fault. We get together when we can, but she is 23 and has her own life and job and derby and a girlfriend, so I absolutely do not expect her to show up each time I need something else taped to my bald head.) The jetpack is uncomfortable at my side. Although I initially thought Optune would be pretty much like an insulin pump, the jetpack is about twenty times the size of a pump and a lot heavier.

I am miserable.

My scalp is raw and burned.

I have started ripping off the transducers in the middle of the night so my head can breathe.

My brain is a house, and the house is on fire.

This is fine, I tell myself. Doctors recommend patients use Optune 18 hours a day, or something like that, so taking the device off when I'm asleep will not matter. The problem is that I have to start over the next day and put it back on. I've only paid for my first package of transducers and for the first month of the machine. Just like insulin pump supplies, I can't run out before I can afford more.

"Are you okay?" Kelly asks while I'm in the bedroom. "There's a lot of beeping."

She's right. There is so much beeping, and the fucking thing won't stop. My skin is burning, and there are so many tangled cords. Where do I even start troubleshooting? I change the battery, which feels as if it's burning acid in my hands. The beeping continues after I change the battery. I unplug everything from the wall because I think that the device might have too much power. I lift my left front transducer from my scalp because the transducer keeps getting hotter.

Am I sweating?

Am I panicking?

Am I dying, finally?

"I'm just going to rip this thing off," I say from behind the closed bedroom door. "You can come in," I tell Kelly.

By the time Kelly opens the door, Optune and its accessories rest in a funeral pyre on the floor next to the duffle bag I now have to carry everywhere to keep up with the extra batteries, special alcohol blend, and transducer panels.

RIP.

"This thing sucks, and I hate it," I tell her. This is the first time in a month I have said anything.

I have tried.

I have really tried.

I toted around the jetpack.

I wore the bandanascarf over the transducer panels so the eight wires coming from my head were not totally noticeable. I tried, I really tried to refrain from complaining about the constant tingling and fire on my scalp. I tried to smile like those ladies on the brochure whose GBMs were getting smaller and smaller the longer they spent burning them out of their heads. I wore Optune to school and restaurants. I did not let the appearance of the science experiment scare me; more than anything, Optune just decreased my quality of life.

"Do you want to go get coffee and donuts or something?" Kelly asks.

Hell yes, I want coffee and donuts.

I text The Optune Lady once we settle in with our iced coffee at a new pop-up in Asheville. Unlike an insulin pump, which you can pay off in installments for the rest of your life, Optune is more of an Enterprise Rental Car. *I need you to pick up Optune and the batteries.* She asks me why and if there's anything wrong with the device, and I respond, *It's just not working out.* I sit there and wonder how people wear Optune for multiple months and years. I don't understand how it's possible. Sure, for a GBM patient, I am *active*, but I can't even think about sitting at home all day with these burning panels scalding my scalp. I just can't do it. *I can pick everything up tomorrow,* The Optune Lady says. *You can keep the bag.*

Wow, thanks.

And it's over.

I have put out the fire.

Kelly, Kyle, and I drink coffee. We eat donuts. We stay up late watching *ER* reruns. I no longer have a jetpack, and I can feel my hair growing out further with each episode we watch. I want to live. I want to live like this, unhindered by FDA-approved science experiments and jetpacks disguised as cures.

Now I feel nothing but relief.

boone, north carolina

My book needs some work.

I spend way too much time complaining about Chole and other exes.

I am not sure of some people's preferred pronouns, so I refer to everyone as *them*. I soon realize I am not Jesus, Buddha, or Gaia, and I can't make every single person in my life gender neutral. There is sort of an issue, though. JC still signs her/their emails with the preferred pronouns (they/them/theirs or she/her/hers). I do not ask JC, which would have been the best route, but I don't want anyone to know I am writing about them.

Everyone wants to be written about until they see what you have to say.

I do not want to freak anyone out, so I go with she/her/hers for JC and constantly doubt this was the right thing to do. I want to get this correct, but I am embarrassed to ask. I know better now.

The title is still fucking awful and long and laborious.

But now I have people in charge of helping me, like a savvy editor named Barbara, who gives it to me straight while still believing in me, and a publisher Lisa, who thinks others need to hear my story.

And this is actually happening.

I kind of assume that like this terrible novel I self-published (okay, I was proud of it at the time), no one will read this memoir. It's not that I don't believe in myself or my writing because I always have; it's just most people don't read anything but social media posts and web articles, and the people who were there for me during surgery and the aftermath probably have no desire to relive the hell we all went through.

Then there is this other nagging thought.

I had to start dying to make my dream come true, to achieve my biggest goal in life.

I am incredibly thankful, but I also despise this irony. My main Goal

Before Death (because what the hell is a bucket list?) was to have someone other than myself publish a novel I had written. I did not care if it was an agent signing me and then selling my book to The Big Five (the main publishers in the United States) or a small press; when I thought about it intensely, which I often did, I would have preferred having a small press publish a novel. I loved reading books from small presses because most novels published by The Big Five are typically not as cool or experimental as the small press shelves. I purchased plenty of small press poetry and fiction and thought my writing would fit in nicely with comparable titles. I was not going to write a coming-of-age story from the perspective of a middle-class white boy, and I also was not going to write a fantasy series or mystery thriller that would piss conservative Christians off until the next election.

Although Christians love cancer, my constant usage of the word *fuck* would be more than enough to infuriate them.

Before *everything happened*, I had begun compiling a chapbook of flash fiction I could submit. I read and loved collections like *juned* by Jenn Marie Nunes (from YesYes Books) that features monkeys smoking cigarettes. How fucking cool was that? I wanted to be like her, like that. I wanted to write about monkeys smoking cigarettes.

I wanted to be cool.

And I think I was on my way.

A creative writing professor who worked with me as an undergraduate and graduate student once told me he had *never seen someone so good with imagery yet so terrible at plot*. This made me mad, and I wrote a reflective essay about his eyebrows reminding me of caterpillars crawling off his face and onto the stories he was grading.[14] One of my lit professors read the reflection and made me rewrite the whole thing, but she did laugh.

---

[14] If you're reading this, professor, I hope you laugh as well. I learned so much from you, and I am, for once, not being sarcastic.

Still, the creative writing professor was right: I was terrible with plot. Thankfully, my own life gave me the very plot I needed.

I still don't know how fair this is, though. If people going through hard things profess that they never ask *why me?*, they are lying. Even if they do not express this thought aloud, they definitely have it rolling through their head on a loop. The loop may quiet every now and again, but the thought returns in the darkest hours of the night and eats at the psyche like a swollen, fat bacteria. For me, and I imagine many others, the *why me?* does not manifest as a pity party but as a search for clarity. What from my past did I do to cause this? What about my genetic makeup clicked to make this happen? What precautions could I have taken to stop those cells from dividing and dividing and dividing?

I do not know how to feel when there is an answer, but right now, for me, there isn't one.

Sometimes I wonder if people are confused as to why I'm not dead yet.

This is a dark thought, but one that persists. I obsess over people who fake having cancer.

Specifically, Belle Gibson.

Gibson, a blonde woman from Australia who looks like a model, claimed to have *incurable brain cancer*. She told people she began traditional treatment, like chemotherapy and radiotherapy, but abandoned those treatments in favor of dietary changes and a holistic lifestyle once she became pregnant. She launched a cookbook and an app called *The Whole Pantry* that shared with the world how she cured herself through all-natural methods. A version of the Apple iPhone even came with the Whole Pantry as a pre-downloaded app. She promised money to people and charities. She professed that she made herself healthy. She persuaded people through her stunning looks and ability to persist through tragedy that yes, anyone could cure themselves if they just followed her advice.

She had terminal brain cancer and brought herself back from the dark matter in the universe that threatened to take her life.

Except the only true part of her story was that she was pregnant. To this day, Gibson claims doctors came to her house and told her about her grim diagnosis. However, the only actual medical records she can produce show no evidence of brain tumors or brain cancer ever existed between her ears.

Belle was, and always has been, perfectly healthy.

Soon, her cookbook and app were ripped off shelves and phones. Of course, charities never got the money she promised them, and now the Australian courts are ripping her a new one and ordering her to pay the promised money.

We all know she's never going to do that.

Here she was, this woman who looked healthy and beat the odds. (She was healthy and did not have any odds to beat, but hey, she set a precedent!) Anyone familiar with brain cancer and brain tumors could easily spot the lies in her story. In the media spotlight, Belle consistently discussed having *stage four brain cancer*, but brain tumors are graded and not staged. She had no physical disabilities, which is possible but rare for someone with a grade four brain tumor. She was able to travel extensively and never seemed to run out of energy. For someone with glioblastoma, that would be extremely difficult.

However, this is what scares me. I am beating the odds. I am still alive. I work and write and travel. Except for all the weight I gained, I pretty much look exactly the same as I did *before everything happened*. I have hair again. Sometimes I do not need my cane or a wheelchair; sometimes I do, but not always. Are people whispering behind my back? I would like to say I don't care, but I do. I want people to know what glioblastoma means and is really like. Most people are only familiar with John McCain and how he looked after his diagnosis. (Not great.) People do not expect a smiling woman drinking cold brew to have a terminal illness, but here I am.

Raising my glass of coffee to the stars!

Some of my braver friends have asked about an *updated prognosis*. I don't really have one, but I can tell this makes them think I lied in the beginning.

Motherfuckers.

Miracles don't happen that often, so how could I be one? How could I say I had 11-13 months to live, only to make it past the two-year mark?

I do not have an explanation, but I am not Belle Gibson. *I am lucky*, I tell people, and I mean it. I've watched the months go by, and I must say that sometimes, I wish those months and days and minutes and hours would just stop altogether. Sometimes I think this is because I want to enjoy those months and days and minutes and hours, while other times, I want them to end because I am so miserable.

Often, I am grateful to be a miracle.

Often, I do not want to be a miracle.

For me, though, none of this changes that my diagnosis is still terminal. I will always have those little comets and asteroids in my brain, no matter how much chemo and radiation and surgery I have. If I had an explanation, which I really don't, it's that I've survived so long because I am young, I was healthy at the time of diagnosis, and my surgeon resected most of the tumor. This increases survival rates. However, all of this is difficult to explain in a social conversation.

I think some people sit there and wonder, *but why is she not dead yet? Is she another Belle Gibson?*

Is she one of these people who claim to have cancer but is actually totally fine?

I don't have proof of anyone suspecting me to be a phony, but I know people have questions about why I have lived so much longer than I was supposed to.

I've connected with many people and family members who have GBM, and I have received all the distraught messages of *Mum is in pain and no longer with us* and then the terrible silence of people not answering, only to find updates from family on their Facebook pages about how they *aren't coming home for Christmas.*

This is a special kind of pain, the type of pain that ties grief and the inevitable into an endless knot where I cannot even begin to distinguish my feelings. I am simultaneously saddened by the loss of my friends and terrified by knowing no matter how much longer I live, I will experience the same fate I have witnessed them all endure. The gradual slipping away. The inability to move at all. The loss of consciousness at a rate too slow to be comfortable.

I'm sure most people are happy I'm still around and not questioning anything, but I still have the paranoia of having a GoFundMe page and using some of the money for car tires so Sarah and I could make the four-hour round-trip to radiation each weekday. Was that an okay thing to do? I think so, but maybe not? Were people going to judge me for that purchase? Was anyone (besides the IRS) going to ask for receipts?

I've also traveled quite a lot, but that is thanks to my mom. My mom paid for everything except the coffee and internet package on the cruise, and I bought those with my money from teaching a summer class. And yes, I loved to travel, but it is also very fucking complicated.

There was that time when a random lady held my torso so I would not fall when trying to put on my shoe. All the benches were taken, and I was trying my best but still about to topple over. Without her kindness, I would have.

And sure, everyone sees the pictures of me in the Caribbean with me and my iguana friend Terry posing in front of a tree in our bathing suits and skin, but no one sees that after that picture, I needed to sit down for twenty minutes because posing with Terry wore me the fuck out. Everyone sees the picture of me standing on the cruise ship deck in my blue Calvin Klein (by TJ Maxx) party dress, but no one sees a picture of me falling in that same dress out of nowhere and being unable to get up until my mom helps. Everyone sees that weird but really lovely picture of my eyes turning from deep brown to light hazel after 33 days of radiation, but no one sees a picture of me fastened to the table, the screws ensuring I do not move and mess up the mesh mask that makes me look like a sporty version of a serial killer.

Travel is one of the main activities that onlookers like to criticize. *But how did you travel if you were so sick? Aren't you sick every single day? Did you throw up on the airplane? What about driving? How can you be in a car that long?*

Although I know I don't have to answer, I like to be real with people. *Yes, it's hard. I prefer to travel with a companion. I can do it alone if I have the right accommodations. I actually feel great, probably the best, when I'm driving. I feel very comfortable and secure in the car. I feel terrible most of the time, but that doesn't mean I'm puking or shitting or asleep every single second of the day. Most of the time, getting to the destination makes all of the literal and figurative headaches worth it.*

I know I should not worry about these things, but Belle Gibson makes me paranoid.

She became a *brain cancer darling* before everything unraveled.

Her knot came apart; it was not endless; it was not infinite.

Still, sometimes I will look at others and know they are trying to figure out: *Wait. Weren't you supposed to die, like, months ago?*

I sure was, but I remind them: There are two things you never see in a graveyard—a donkey or a Samples.

Also, I was given this chance by a small press to live my dream. There was no way in hell I was going to let this book get published without me. Sure, I would never reach the popularity of Belle Gibson and her fraudulent cookbook, but I didn't want that. I just wanted the opportunity to tell my story, no matter how intense everything has been. I just wanted the chance to be the voice of all those people who died from GBM too soon.

I just wanted to be heard.

boone, north carolina/harrisville, west virginia

I meet a woman named Andrea in a Facebook Brain Tumor Support group. This is the most active Facebook group I am in, but I do get annoyed with some of the posts. The group is for everyone: anyone with any type of brain tumor, a family member of someone with a brain tumor, a friend of someone with a brain tumor, and anyone with a hamster who has a brain tumor can join. I like hearing about everyone's span of experiences, but some are off-putting. For instance, I once got into a verbal sparring match with a lady named Lana, who serves as the primary caretaker for her mom who has GBM.

Lana always has an agenda: 1) Promote her own private Facebook group that deals with GBM 2) Promote essential oil she believes to be the cure for GBM from a multi-level marketing group.

I go off on Lana when a lady is asking about getting potential rides to radiation each day. The lady can no longer drive herself and has zero family near where she lives. Much like my own experience, this woman resides in a rural area and has a long-distance trek to the hospital.

Lana does not give a shit about this.

You need to join my private group Brain Cancer Survivors, Thrivers, and Jivers! We all share our experiences in that group! My mom is a 9-month GBM survivor because of essential oil I was able to get for her!

No one else has commented on the poor woman's post yet. She lives in England, and therefore, I do not know how to help her.

Thanks, the woman says, *but I'm just looking for a ride.*

Lana refuses to give up. *We are all very supportive in my group, and you won't find any negativity like you do in this group!* Then she posts a link to the aforementioned essential oil she sells from her very own multi-level marketing company.

I can't stand it.

She is specifically looking for a ride to treatment, not a poorly disguised "cure" to help you personally profit, I write.

Keyboard warrior.

Another woman in the group, Andrea, likes my comment.

Lana does not.

The original poster thanks me and does the mature thing of just ignoring Lana and her fucking oils.

I send Andrea a private message. *Hey! Thanks for liking my comment. I just get angry when people start posting random "cures" to others who are asking for specific help. It's so frustrating.*

Andrea replies immediately. *It's very annoying when all that lady needed was help finding a ride. I also live in England, so I gave her some links. xx*

I never know what happened to the lady who needed a ride. I have no idea if she found a ride, if she survived her treatment, or if she is still alive today.

However, I learn Andrea's story.

Andrea tells me she has had GBM for years. I am startled by this; she has had GBM for a very long time, much longer than most. I never ask her how old she is, but when we start messaging, she tells me her eldest child is close to being a teenager. I assume Andrea is, at the very least, in her early 30s. Her mother died of breast cancer, and she and her husband have three kids: two girls and a boy. The youngest is a daughter named Faith, who had many developmental problems at birth and requires specialized care. Andrea tells me *Faith was not supposed to live past the first week of her life, and that's why we named her Faith. We had Faith. We knew not to give up.*

I tell her Faith has the longest, most beautiful eyelashes I have ever seen. *She's never going to get any bigger*, Andrea responds. She mentions Faith is five, but *she will never grow any taller than a one-year-old.* Faith is one of the cutest children I have ever seen. Whether the pictures are of her being awake and happy at school or being at home and asleep, her eyelashes steal the show.

One of my first thoughts, though, because I know Andrea has left side hemiparesis (complete weakness, like my right side), is she must have difficulty holding Faith. Although I have never desired to be a mother, I empathetically understand that Andrea must find it so frustrating to not be able to hold and play with her child.

However, we do not discuss this a lot. We mostly talk about silly things, like why people in England put "xx" after every statement. (Most of you know "xx" technically means "kisses," but for those of you who aren't sure of the specific meaning, it's the British way[15] of saying "love you" or simply "thanks for talking to me," per Andrea's definition.)

One of the best conversations we have is when I experience a fall off the toilet. I sit on the cold seat, but the next moment, I am on the ground. It is a severe fall, but Andrea and I get a laugh out of it in a way no one else could. She calls me *a daft little puppy*, and I cannot stop giggling.

When I tell her I have decided to stop going to my scans, she gives me another opinion. *Don't you want to know? I always feel better when I know exactly what is going on in there. xx.* Sure, other people have told me this, but those other people don't know what it's like. They do not understand the concept of *scanxiety*, where you just sit for weeks ahead of the appointment and wonder if any new growths might pop up and ruin your life even further.

But Andrea understands this. She knows and has known for years, how all of this shit feels.

The longer we chat, the more I realize Andrea's GBM is more advanced than she lets on. She occasionally slips and mentions she sits in a recliner all day and waits for her husband to come home so he can move her. At first, I do not realize she is chair-bound. Although I have a lot of fatigue, I am still able to get out of the house every couple of

[15] And probably tons of other cultures as well. It would not surprise me if Americans are the only ones who don't do this. xx

days and go to work. On my days off, I can make quick trips to the store. Although I am not permitted to take my dog outside on a leash (because she might pull me over), I can still get up and open the door for her. Because she is such a good girl, Gatsby never runs away and always comes back inside.

When I ask if she has ever fallen off the toilet, Andrea tells me she has had *a catheter for a couple years now.*

I realize, without her saying anything, that her husband and oldest daughter are the only ones around to help her. When they are at school and work, Andrea sits in her recliner all day.

I know people talk about *oh she never complained*, but Andrea really didn't. Even though she was about nine years ahead of me in the disease progression, Andrea always asked how I was doing before I said anything to her at all. When I would say *not bad!*, she would respond with *now tell me the truth. xx.*

I am already writing about her in the past tense.

Sometimes Andrea mentions a nurse might stop by, but I don't think this happens too often. I get confused about how the medical system works in England., and she is equally confused about how the medical system in the United States functions. *It doesn't*, I tell her, and we both laugh.

Although neither of us can handwrite letters because of our poor motor skills, we discover Amazon provides a way for us to deliver fun gifts to one another. Andrea sends me some pickle-flavored *crisps* I can barely handle. I imagine her laughing at me as my mouth puckers in discomfort. I know she loves chocolate, so I corral a bouquet of American candy bars into my shopping cart on Amazon.uk. As a thank you, Andrea forwards me a single coaster that features a bunch of different chocolate pieces.

It does not match anything I have, but I will keep the coaster forever.

We keep sending each other random things, and we have fun.

Andrea loves *The Lion King*, so I hunt down Simba-related items to send to her.

GBM is terrible, but the disease does allow me to nurture this meaningful friendship from across an ocean.

When I apologize for sometimes not getting back to her soon enough, she says *that's okay! I know there is a time difference. xx.*

When my second diagnosis anniversary comes, I learn through her husband that Andrea is in the hospital because of an infection. I avoid bothering him, but I keep up with all the updates. He lets Andrea's friends know she is unable to use her phone, but he will be taking her phone with him to the hospital and read her all the messages she has. I type a quick note to her that I miss and love her.

xx.

I fear I will never get the opportunity to speak to her again, and I am right.

The doctors cannot figure out precisely what is wrong with Andrea. It might be an infection. It might be pneumonia. It might be something else entirely.

We all know what it is: Andrea is dying.

Her husband's updates discuss how brave their children are and how much he loves Andrea. The goal is to get her home for Christmas, if even for just two hours.

At this point, I am back at my parents' house for the holidays (this trip went much more smoothly than the trip two years ago when I never made it out of Boone), and I feel entirely helpless. I wish I lived closer to Andrea so I could have at least met her once. I wish England was next to West Virginia, so I could see how much her hair had grown back in, something we talked about frequently. I wish she was not enduring terrible frustration and pain.

We are in the same house, but I text my mom and hope the message goes through. (If you've never lived in a rural area, this might be confusing to you, but a high percentage of the time, my texts do not even make it 30 feet when I'm in West Virginia.)

My GBM friend Andrea is not doing well. Should I stand in for her tomorrow?

I do not need to translate this for my mom.

Yes, absolutely, my mom responds. It does take me twenty minutes to get her text, but I feel somewhat comforted.

Let's be real: I have pretty much abandoned religion, but I'm still not exactly sure how I feel about the whole thing. Yes, I believe in something. Yes, I was *saved* as a child. Yes, I am convinced if there is a god, she loves everyone.

I know, though, that if anyone is close to god, it is my mom and Pastor Blevins. When I *stand in* for Andrea at church, my mom and Pastor Blevins will pretend I am Andrea and pray over me. There might be some type of anointing oil involved, but no one will pull out snakes or speak in tongues.

Scientifically, I know there will be no miracle. Andrea will not suddenly be *cancer-free* and be able to hold her child again. She will not leave the hospital permanently. She will not spend any further holidays with her family.

I am hopeful, though, that my mother and Pastor Blevins' connection to the heavens will allow Andrea to be home for Christmas. *Just two hours. That's all she and her family want.* Mom and Pastor Blevins (who happens to be the father of one of my close friends, Jessica) touch my shoulders and back with their hands. Pastor Blevins asks authoritatively and efficiently that *Andrea will be able to go home for Christmas in your glory, dear Jesus*, and then he throws a quick prayer in for me as well.

A couple days later, Andrea's husband posts that Andrea didn't make it home in time for Christmas, but she might get to visit soon. *God works on his own time*, my mom says. On December 30, an ambulance whisks Andrea home for a few hours, and her husband notes that his *family is together again.*

After Andrea returns to the hospital, he begins posting stream-of-consciousness Facebook soliloquys to her about how he *remembered to put the kids' favorite show on for you* and a picture of Faith wearing an adorable color-striped jumpsuit with a funny hood. *You said she would look ace in it, and you were right.*

I get the sense Andrea cannot speak any longer, and her love begins writing these messages because she cannot respond.

A few days later, Andrea is gone.

I don't say much because her husband has not told everyone in the family yet.

A week after she passes, I post Andrea's story to the Facebook group where we met. I tell them I met her in the group, and she meant a lot to me. I include a picture of her, and over a couple hours, the post receives over 500 likes and reactions. There are over 100 comments. Andrea would be shocked by this, but it would make her feel so good. She would feel so popular and loved. I know amongst everything else in her life, a bunch of social media reactions means nothing, but I also know she would get a big kick out of being a social media star. I screenshot the picture and share the message with her husband.

A few hours later, he shares the screenshot with the world.

Still inspiring others as always xx love you babe. Fly high.

Still teaching me about British English from the grave. *Fly high.* We typically don't say that here, but I would like to start.

And then, I get a Facebook notification.

Did I ever mention to this group that I have a group called "Brain Cancer Survivors, Thrivers, and Jivers! Join us now! No negativity! My mother is a long-term GBM survivor of just under two years! I also sell essential oils that A N Y O N E with a brain tumor can benefit from!

Link.

Link.

BOSS BABE!

Link.

Andrea, you would have flipped. Who do I talk to about this now? Fly high xx, I think to myself. *Fly high.*

boone, north carolina

The worst thing about writing is that it is a business.

Only the most chosen people in the world can understand both. (Maybe not so coincidentally, the only two people I've met who understand this are both named Lisa. Just something to consider.)

The more I discuss The Terribly Titled Book with my editor, Barbara, and Lisa, the more I learn about the business side. Once published, I'm not sure how to get reviews. I'm not sure how to get the thing in bookstores. I'm not even sure how to get people to read it.

Before Running Wild Press publishes The Terribly Titled Book, I'm not even sure how to format the pages.

To look at me or talk to me, you might think I'm a pragmatic, organized person with a solid plan to get things done. You might see my apartment and notice how I vacuum every two days and despite having three pets, manage to keep the whole fucking place smelling like a cup of lavender tea. You might see my office at school and think, *Wow, this person has their shit together.*

But then at my apartment, you might open the pantry door and have seven cardboard boxes fall at your feet. You might open up the top drawer and find it stuffed with wall fragrance plugs, old playing cards, a screwdriver, some Sudafed, and a bundle of sage. You might open the drawers at my office and find an old t-shirt I slept in one night because the roads were too bad for me to return home. (The janitors had no idea. I was so quiet.) You might find a hypodermic insulin needle I dropped and put in my drawer because I did not want to throw it away or accidentally use it. You might find a couple of Pop-Tarts my friend Shannan left me.

The point is: yes, I am organized and have a plan on the outside, but when you open me up, you will find a mess of words and allusions and batshit ideas I want to use in a story someday.

Welcome to my cozy apartment where the bed is always made, and there is never any toothpaste globbed in the sink.

Open the drawers.

Comminatory, masticate, Charon, pandiculation, describing a regular person as *messianic*. Thinking about why people give Persephone all the credit when Demeter did all the work. Is this a metaphor? How can I make this a fictional metaphor without, you know, being obvious about it? Should I try to publish that weird-ass story I wrote ten years ago about a family finding a bunch of shrunken heads in the pond outside? I really liked that story, even if no one else did. I don't think there was a metaphor, but I was okay with that. It wasn't horror. Just subtle weirdness. Damn, my writing is really niche sometimes, which is not a good thing. The name Delilah is really adorable, maybe someone I know will name their kid that. STORY OR BOOK NAME THAT HAS ALLUSIONS TO THE BIBLE THERE IS MY METAPHOR! But I don't like giving my characters' names. Or genders, especially if it is a really short story. I like initials or nothing at all. Makes the story more universal. Why did I ever think I could write poetry? Poets speak their own language. I never felt like I fit in with them, although I love them. *Cancer might be endemic. Cancer is ephemeral, for some lucky people. Cancer gives me ennui.* Who were those two goddesses who guarded the Styx? Did I just make that up? I think it has something to do with going right or left, or maybe I just imagined that. How the hell does Caroline Kepnes do such a phenomenal job of nailing the internal monologue of a handsome, sympathetic serial killer? Fuck, that would be so hard. Damn, she is good. Ubiquitous. Umbrage. Underbreet.

I like these words, but I will not use them. I don't want people to have their phones in their hands to look up words while they are reading my story.

So, yeah, business, not really my thing, although I had a tarot card reading where the woman told me I *need to be more confident about my business mind and ventures,* so here we are. Thankfully, although she is a writer herself, my publisher Lisa understands the business of writing. She knows how to get shit done. She knows how to get fantastic cover art, hire the right people for public relations, and have this all done in a short amount of time.

Which is exactly what I need.

And Barbara knows how to edit, which, although I would like to claim I am also good at editing, there is this part of my brain that turns off as soon as details become involved. I don't like details as much as *the big picture.* But Barbara is excellent with these details and bonus! is a retired medical doctor. She corrects my misunderstandings about how MRI machines work and makes sure that the medical happenings I discuss are factual.

This is my dream team.

There is just one nagging problem—the darned title.

I am typically great with titles. When I was writing and submitting short stories, I had a rejection that went on and on and on about how great the title was. (It was called "The Arrangement of Skin, or the Quiet Kind," which *is* a fantastic title, if I do say so myself.) Typically, titles come to me quickly and breathlessly, and I will often choose a title before I know the rest of the story.

God, not this one.

I insist to Lisa and Barbara that the word *phrenology* be in the title. I throw around the concept a couple times in the book and, as a trained Victorianist, I think the title should have something to do with how myself and the Victorians failed at life.

I can tell Lisa and Barbara do not necessarily agree.

Lisa decides the title should be *Frontal Matter* and not *Front Matter*. We all concur on that, but then I give up. Maybe the book just shouldn't have a subtitle? No, it needs one. I really, really push for *phrenology*, but it's just not going to happen.

After minutes of debating, Lisa speaks up. "What about 'Glue Gone Wild'?"

And it is settled.

I have a book.

People I have never met are making this happen for me, and I could not be more excited, thankful, and grateful. I hope I live long enough to see the book on the shelves, which has always been my biggest goal and dream in life. I knew I was good enough, but I didn't know if I would ever have the timing and luck to make it happen. There are so many wonderful writers in the world, and there are also many terrible ones. Far too often, the terrible ones hit the shelves while the good ones face rejection after rejection. I get tired of reading books with plots that everyone can unravel thirty pages into the story. I went on a social media rant months before my diagnosis about how every single book I read with a female character went on and on and on about the necessity of having babies. If the female character could not have a baby, then OH MY GOD IT WAS THE WORST THING EVER. These were popular books, of course, but came highly recommended by peers, lovers, and gods.

I was proud my book would not do that.

Here's what I did not expect: People would actually read my book.

I posted about the book on social media and told my family and friends. I kept the secret long enough, and now it was time for me to share that I had accomplished my life's goal.

I had published a book, bitches!

I'm making everything sound relatively easy in this little write-up, but the truth is, I have no idea about what went on behind the scenes.

Yes, I wrote the book, yes, I would get a cut of the pay, and yes, I was still doing some marketing to see if I could live my other dream of walking into a bookstore and seeing *Frontal Matter: Glue Gone Wild* on the shelves. But mostly, my part in the book was done.

What I did expect: a few friends to read it.

What I didn't expect: a shitload of people actually read the book.

This does not happen over a day, but I soon realize this little project of mine has become its own constellation, and there isn't anything I can do about it.

This isn't a problem, not really, it's great, actually, except very few people know me.

Sure, they know me as Suzanne, thirtysomething teaching English at Appalachian State and playing roller derby, but they don't *know* me. They know nothing of my struggles with dating and sexuality— something I was never quite open about anyway, regardless of any orientation or lack thereof—and they know nothing about how I actually feel about my *brain fucking cancer*. They do not know how frequently I think the word *fuck*, and they have no idea what my life is actually like post-diagnosis.

I tell my mom she is not allowed to read the book.

So, you want me to buy a copy to increase sales but not actually read it.

Yes, I tell her, and she obliges.

I know she will be okay with this. Once I found my *writing voice* in college, I was thrilled to share a story, one my creative writing professor liked, with my parents. They each looked through it as I stood in our kitchen, waiting in anticipation for their rave reviews. *It's well written*, my dad said, *but I'm pretty sure I don't understand it*. Dad is a Hemingway guy, so I'm not surprised. If there isn't fish, fighting, or a tent in a story, Dad does not care. Mom is angry that the word *hell* is on the first page and won't finish the story. *It's not me, it's the character*, I tell her, but she refuses to pick the pages back up.

I am not surprised by this either.

They don't read the book, so I can avoid some difficult conversations about my parents having no idea who or what I really am.

I think we are all okay with this.

The book, though, makes people want to know me.

Although I was always quite comfortable with my job and how I fit in (I have a core group of friends who are also non-tenure track, and we mostly avoid tenure-track professors unless they directly have something to do with ensuring we all get hired next year), suddenly, people want to talk to me. They want to know me. They, at the very least, recognize me and say hello.

I realize these people who always seemed out of reach are quite lovely; I think most of the NTTs assume the tenure-track folks want to avoid us, but I discover a new galaxy when I get to know some of them. I befriend professors on the Faculty Welfare and Morale committee because they drop off food on my porch. I get to know our department head better because he tells me I do not have to do my yearly reapplication materials. (Which I do anyway because well, brain cancer did not take all of me, and I'm still one of the most responsible people on the planet. When I review them later, I am horrified at how poorly I wrote everything.) I get to know my program director better because I have to work so closely with her on securing my FMLA paperwork for the full semester I am in Winston-Salem instead of Boone.

I get to know a couple named Jessica and Zack because Jessica's dad died of GBM. She and Zack take a particular interest in my book. They arrange for me to do a reading, and I am terrified. I'm just a non-tenure track instructor, shepherding freshmen to the bathroom and back to my class every day; sure, I go to all the meetings when I can, but I never say a word and just sit in the back and vote when I am allowed. I didn't mind at all people did not know me before. Like most of them, I just did my job and went home.

Now, though, things are different.

The newly titled *Frontal Matter: Glue Gone Wild* has only been out for a couple of months, and I am doing this reading in the library. Cool. No problem. I do some practice reads, though, and...there actually is a problem.

A huge problem.

I start crying at different points in the book, but the tears never show up at the same part. I cannot predict this crying, and I begin to understand I definitely have PTSD. However, since I still don't think anyone really cares enough to come to a reading in January, I assuage my fears by convincing myself the only people to listen will be CK, Rolli, Jenna and her husband Derek, Jessica, Zack, and a few of my other NTT buddies.

CK and I get to the reading super early, and Jessica gives me a skeleton key she found in New York City. I get teary at the meaningfulness of this gift. She read the book, and she knew. She had seen her father go through this, so she understands. Although I have not spent much time with Jessica, I feel very connected to her. I put the key on a chain I'm wearing that has a few other keys I've amassed since publishing the book.

If only I could unlock the universe.

This is what I have always wanted, the ability to publish a meaningful book, in a style all my own. To share my writing with others who would have faith in my words. To pick up that book and say *I did this.*

I just didn't realize I would be trading my life for the words inside.

To my surprise, there is barely standing room during the reading. I don't feel nervous, but *shit*. I didn't expect this. I don't even know some of the people in the audience, and I can barely see over the podium. Because I'm short, we try to work out something I can stand on, but my foot, balance, and coordination issues make this impossible.

I have pre-selected all the sections I'm going to read, and I do this with great purpose. The most serious ones at the beginning. The funnier ones at the end, so everyone can laugh at my Uber driver named Ray, who jokes cancer caused him to go from *a rooster to a hen*. This will be good. I can do this.

Rolli warns the parents who are present that there is a lot of foul (*fowl*, if you're Ray, I guess) language in the reading, and they say their kids won't notice.

I didn't even think of that.

Jessica gives me a baller introduction that makes me feel like I'm about to receive a Pulitzer. I savor this moment; she discusses *hospitals*, *Sylvia Plath*, and something about my *words*. I almost cry before everything begins, but I pull myself together.

The tulips are freaking the fuck out.

Everything goes wonderfully until I reach the section about losing my ability to handwrite. For reasons I still don't understand, I cry. I do not know exactly why I cry at this part, except this *stuff* happened the day after surgery, when I finally realized how much I had lost. My handwriting might not have been such a big deal—after all, I managed to write *Frontal Matter* without my penmanship—but this symbolized everything, all the things taken from me by the tumor.

Funny enough, the loss of my handwriting also made signing books difficult, but I suppose my wonky signature made everything *more authentic*.

Although I'm crying, I don't start sobbing, and there is quite a difference. When I'm crying, I can still read, but sobbing means a good twenty minutes of panicking and screaming into a pillow until I'm too exhausted to breathe.

I talk about how marijuana got me through the worst of the chemo and joke to my department and program heads to *please not fire me*, which draws a bit of nervous laughter from the crowd. As predicted, the section about Ray provides a lighthearted end to the reading. I didn't want to make anyone feel sorry for me or believe I was weak; I want listeners to know I had been this person all along, this writer all along, and I finally had my chance to be heard.

After the event, many listeners thanked me for reading and shared different stories with me. It felt good to make some sort of impact. For people who do not write or work in the field, it can be disarming to learn how truly connected writers are to their stories, even if they don't write memoirs. Most writers believe in each and every word we use and how the combination of those words will affect those involved. It feels freeing to know that people liked my story, that they *felt* my words.

I always assumed whatever I published would be Dave Eggers' style of *thinly veiled fiction* instead of a classic memoir. I had no idea people would actually want to know or care about me finding an old man's dirty underwear when my occupational therapist and I were doing laundry one morning.

A guy in line, the age of an undergrad, approaches me after the reading and asks if he can *give me a hug*. It was so pure and unexpected, and we both nearly cried again. I have no idea who he was or why he came to the reading, but this gave me hope human kindness still exists. Sure, I had seen so much good from people I knew or sort-of-knew, but not really from complete strangers.

Kids these days are tuned in, *woke*, and able to compassionately connect with others, even if they have never met them before.

Take that, Boomer.

I leave the reading with a sense of hope, maybe not for myself, but for the message of stark honesty my story shares with others. No matter how difficult I find it to forever be that patient, etherized and dissected in front of everyone, maybe, maybe others can stop hiding from behind what terrifies the living, dying fuck out of them.

boone, north carolina

After performing a thorough and visible check that the jade sedan in the only available Starbucks handicapped spot has no pass or license, I loudly bang on the driver's side window.

The driver should always be held responsible.

"Excuse me," I say very calmly. Little do the people in the car know, I am full of explosive rage. "You seem to be parked in a handicapped spot, but you do not have a license plate or blue handicapped placard. These things are required of you to park in this location."

"Honey, we are old."

"Then you can apply through the DMV to get the appropriate pass to put in your car. If being old is a disability, then your doctor can write you a letter to prove that."

"Who gave you the right to say these darned things?" the driver, a lady in her mid-60s, says to me. She clearly worked very hard on her pink eyeshadow this morning, and a cigarette hangs like a broken bracelet from her stained fingernails.

Cigarettes are a part of this woman.

"I have a handicapped pass, and now I cannot park here and get into the shop because you have taken the only spot. I am unable to step up or down from curbs."

"You're too young to be handicapped, darlin'," she snarls back as she takes a quick drag.

"As it turns out, I have terminal brain cancer and can barely walk. Some days are better than others, like today. Today, I felt like bringing my laptop and grading freshmen writing papers at Starbucks because I need to see people. I need to be involved. I need to be reminded I'm still alive."

The driver snorts, and I swear I see a pigmented shard of her eyeshadow fly off her lid and attach itself to the dusty steering wheel.

The woman revs her car engine and accelerates out of the blue lines.

As she backs up the green jalopy, she nearly smacks into an unsuspecting college student, holding her hot white mocha she probably spent the remainder of her weekly budget buying.

We all need something.

Thankfully, the driver does not run over my foot, although I suppose it would not matter if she did.

part four: whale watching

boone, north carolina

My mom is taking me to the moon.

Well, okay, she is taking me to Alaska, but I am just as excited as I would be if she had purchased a trip to the moon. I've always wanted to visit Alaska, and I love cold weather. I'm hot all the time, so visiting somewhere without much sun is the ideal vacation for me.

Better yet, she has already talked to Nodya and David, who are coming with us on the cruise. The ship ports in Seattle, which happens to be where they live now.

It's a cruise.

Of course, it's a cruise.

Suzanne + Brain Cancer = Jenifer Buys Cruises.

This will be the longest distance I've traveled since my diagnosis, but this, my friends, will be worth all the airplane and ship germs, the wheelchairs in the airport, and the people I meet along the way who like to play the Comparison Olympics about the time they had cancer and *look at them, they are just fine now!*

Even if Jenifer has to drag me onto that boat, I will see The Last Frontier before I die.

boone, north carolina

I make arrangements for CK to watch my pets while I am gone, and I am worried.

My dear Prufrock, the cat who has been with me for over fourteen years, has shown significant decline lately. She became ill a few days after I did, and I could tell when we took Pru to the vet, Sarah thought I would be saying goodbye.

You've given her the best life, she told me. *Actually, you've given her the only life she could have. No one else would have ever put up with her.*

Sarah is accurate in her assessment. Kind of like me, Pru has always been complicated. I am the only human she pretends to notice. She does whatever the fuck she wants, and if other pets or people don't like it? Well, too bad for them.

Pru reigned over various apartments through the years with an iron paw, and no one could change her mind. I thoroughly admired her calico spunk and just let her be her; she loved me for this.

When I went to adopt her, I chose the closest pound to my address in Huntington, West Virginia. This was long before the days of classy shelters and cat cafes. I was in my first semester of graduate school and needed a companion.

I have loved cats since I was a toddler.

Cat lady for life.

Along with actual family pets, I had a cat named Henry who would visit me on the rooftop that hung like a crooked loose tooth from my childhood bedroom window.

Of course, no one believed me.

I was a whimsical child who once had an imaginary dog and two kittens, so neither Mom nor Dad was buying that there was an actual brown and black striped cat on my roof, singing his grievances to me, a happily captive listener.

Then one day, my dad was in my room, looked out the window,

and saw the chunky tabby who demanded my afternoons.

Well, shit, he muttered under his breath. *She was actually telling the truth*

On the quest for my first pet as an adult, I found the James River Road Pound, which was a few miles from my new apartment. I just *went to look*, and it was the saddest fucking thing I had ever seen.

One lady, hard in the face but soft in the heart, was trying to care for about thirty cats stuffed in miniscule cages like chickens crated in a truck. The cats yelped and clawed through the bars.

The lady jangled two little bell toys. She looked at me and said, *We don't have much. They're all so unhappy that I can't even decide which cats to give the toys to.*

My heart broke, and I wanted to open the cages and let them all run wherever they chose to go.

My car would be the ideal place.

But I couldn't do that, so I gazed past a huge black tomcat and noticed some orange, black, and white fluff hiding behind him, terrified of the male energy in that crate. When the tomcat moved, I saw these little bi-colored green eyes. I looked at the baby and said, *Are you Prufrock?* As if she was in a conversation with me, she waited the appropriate beat and then responded with a salty *meewwwww*.

The pound let me drop $20 on the counter and take Pru home that day. There was no paperwork. There was no apartment visit. There was no call to my landlord, who definitely would have told me I couldn't have a cat.

Now there was just me and Pru.

Nothing else mattered.

Although she barely weighed two pounds, Pru clawed the shit out of my Subaru before I got her home. She was scared, but we bonded very quickly. From that point on, she cared about nothing but me and food.

I shared my darkest secrets with Pru.

Pru greeted me whenever I came home, registering her daily complaints with a series of meows. She was preternaturally smart and could open doors, tear into any type of food wrapper, and read people with a single glance of those bi-colored green eyes. Pru saw people come and go from my life: boyfriends, other pets, girlfriends, friends, and a husband.

She is the only creature I can trust.

I need to die before her.

The vet notes on her chart that *Pru is a M.A.M.F.*

Thinking this is some type of actual veterinary terminology, I have no idea what this means.

It means Mean Ass Mother Fucker, the vet tells me, and I know we have found a good match.

Despite much protest, when she turns 14, Pru undergoes a series of tests to determine she is in kidney failure and has hyperthyroidism. Her blood sugar is slightly elevated, but the vet notes this could be the result of nerves, and from experience, I don't disagree. *We can treat the hyperthyroidism*, the vet tells me, *but the kidney failure is likely to get her in the end.*

For now, though, we can take her home.

When the vet tells us this, I swear I can hear Sarah roll her eyes. Sarah, also an avid animal lover, has tried to be Pru's friend for years, but Pru hates Sarah with a raging fire, burning somewhere between her extensive toe floof. Pru loves nothing more than to hiss and caw at Sarah. She has attempted multiple attacks on my poor sister, but Pru has been unable to kill her just yet.

Now they are even.

When I head to the back and bundle her into the carrier, Pru looks at me and cries *meewww!*, just as she did that day in the James River Road Pound.

Holy shit, the vet says. *I can't believe how responsive and sweet she is to you. She fucking hates us.*

She hates everyone but me, I tell them.

We have a special bond.

Sure, that bond means sometimes sitting on my chest, growling, and refusing to move. Sure, sometimes that bond means biting me and sending me to urgent care because the wound has given me an infection. Sure, sometimes that bond means scaring off any potential friends or love interests.

But it's totally worth it.

No one has ever been so close to me.

Now here we are, and much to Sarah's chagrin, we get to take Pru home so she can terrorize her auntie just a little bit longer.

I've had Pru for so long and our connection means so much to me that I ask the universe to *please kill me first*. I know I am selfish, but I cannot live without her. She has always been my ferocious little bear who protected me at all costs.

I didn't want to let her go.

But before I take off for Alaska, I wonder if Pru will be okay without me for two weeks. CK has been around long enough that Pru recognizes her as a food source. CK knows this and has accepted her fate. An experienced pet sitter and former teammate, Ash, is going to check on the kitties when CK can't.

Still, I do not want Pru to feel abandoned when I leave.

Pru did not fare well the month I was in the hospital; JC sent me pictures of her hiding behind the water heater and under the bed. She would only come out if offered turkey, and even then, she would not eat much.

JC called this *lurkies for turkies.*

I didn't want Pru to think I had died.

My friend V. offers to take Pru when I die. I feel like this would be a good match; V. is quite sassy herself, and V.'s husband loves cats. During a visit, V. said she *loved Pru and her bitchy queenliness*, so I dictated in my will that Pru could have a home with V. if I passed away first. If she did not thrive in that home, then she would likely need euthanized.

No one could give her a home like me, but I had hopes she and V. would respect each other.

And to be honest, although I should, I do not have a will. Not a real one, anyway. I have a little mustard yellow notebook with a skull on the cover that has my final wishes dictated in my 90-year-old handwriting. I do not know if this will suffice, but if you're reading this and I'm gone, the notebook is on my nightstand by my bed.

Despite my fears of Pru dying while I'm on the moon, I prepare CK for everything that might happen. *If she dies in the apartment, there is a shoebox in the closet. Wrap her in a blanket, put her in the shoebox, and take her to the vet. You know the vet is right down the road, and she will know what to do. I want a private cremation, and the ashes returned to me.*

CK understands all of this, and I am grateful.

I do not feel safe leaving Pru like this, but it's a cruise, it's Alaska, and this is an opportunity I cannot let melt away like the glaciers I'm about to see.

nowhere

I do not have a karaoke song, but if I did, it would be Reba's version of "Fancy."

Sarah thinks it might have been her karaoke song until it comes on my iTunes in the car. I start singing the words, and I can't stop. How do I know these lyrics? How do I remember them so well? I can't remember if I took a shower this week, but I remember how Fancy watched a cockroach crawl across the new shoes her mama bought her.

Maybe I always feel like I'm letting everybody down.

How could I get brain cancer when everyone needed me so much?

How do I remember all of these words?

And no, before you say, *forgetfulness happens to me all the time!* it doesn't.

If it does, it's not the same, trust me.

pittsburgh, pennsylvania

The airport is absolutely miserable.

I decide on the way to Seattle and the cruise ship, this will be my last big trip.

Time in the air does something to my mobility and balance, causing me to trip, fall, and experience fatigue that makes me feel like a skeleton pieced together the wrong way in a high school lab.

Sometimes I wonder what people expect from me; I do not think they understand how difficult it is to drive to my parents' house, and then head to Pittsburgh with my mom for another three-ish hours, all while an errant cow finds its way onto the highway and shuts down traffic for forty-five minutes.

The cow and people are all fine.

Then, there is parking the car and getting onto a shuttle, where the driver looks suspiciously like a guy in college I dated, the one with the weird nasally, high-pitched voice and obsession with football. This sports obsession eventually drove me to ignore his love letters that arrived way too long after we broke up to make a difference.

He lives in Pittsburgh, so it isn't that far of a stretch.

Thank god, my mom is with me.

I might complain about her a lot, but she is the person everyone wants when shit needs to be done. When people need help. When I need to get from a car to a hotel to a shuttle to an airplane.

There is one problem: Jenifer hates airports.

I don't really see the difference between airports and cruise ships, but Jenifer panics in airports, even after everything is in place.

HOW DO WE KNOW WE ARE AT THE RIGHT GATE HOW DO WE KNOW IF THE PLANE IS ON TIME WHERE THE HECK ARE ALL OF THESE PEOPLE GOING?

Once we get settled at the gate, Jenifer feels better. I feel exhausted. Already.

I wonder if I will see Abby Lee Miller from *Dance Moms* at the airport.

I would act like a teenager seeing Justin Bieber or One Direction or whatever the kids are into these days.

When I watched the Lifetime special about Abby Lee's cancer experience, I cried through the entire hour. As if I was seeing myself on the screen, I studied the television as she relearned to sit, stand, and walk. I know she isn't the best example of a teacher and has an extremely problematic personality, but I admired her ability to put together a team of Pittsburgh dancers after going through so much. Everyone except JoJo deserted Abby Lee, and though I'm sure the reasons were different, I still found her story relatable.

I sent her a copy of *Frontal Matter*, but I never heard back.

Abby Lee, if you're reading this, I still love you.

I check in with my Petcube, a mini surveillance system that allows me to talk to my animals, to see how Pru is doing. I see her curled up on the floor and fear that she has passed away. *Pru!* I yell. *Prufrock! Are you still there?* She wakes up and glares at me. *Meww!* she screams as she glares at the Petcube.

Pru is so smart.

I try to sleep as we wait for the plane, but I'm frustrated. Two older people glare at me because I'm in a wheelchair by the handicapped section of the boarding gate.

Sometimes I don't think I'll ever sleep again.

boone, north carolina

I have been falling a lot lately.

I think about what falling means to me.

In roller derby, people frequently fall. The important part is not that you get back up, but that you get back up quickly.

When I played derby, I fell all the time, but I wonder now: how long did I have Alecia, my brain tumor? Was she causing me to be the type of roller derby player who fell all the time? Or did I just fall too much? Sure, I always got up quickly, but I still caused my team hardship because I was on the ground instead of helping my pack stop the jammer.

I didn't want to fall.

I often tell others I had no symptoms before the seizure in the coffee shop, which is true.

However, looking back, I remember falling all the time. I fell when I walked Gatsby. I fell in the shower one day. I fell in the parking lot at school.

But I was always able to get up quickly.

Clumsiness is not a reliable symptom. I cannot imagine going to a doctor or to the emergency room and saying *I have been clumsy lately. Can you please give me an MRI?* Everyone would have laughed at me and sent me out the door with a $500 itemized bill.

Now, my falls happen without warning and without wheels.

One second, I am standing, and the next, I am on the ground.

Most of the falls thus far have been benign, until now.

All I want to do is go out to the car and see if I can find my missing watch.

The last thing I remember is trying to put on my slipper. I should have just waited for CK to get to my apartment, but I wanted to do something for myself. The last thing I saw was the corner of the wall.

I scream, and the river outside stops moving. I don't know how long I am out, but it's likely just a few seconds. My neighbor in the apartment next to me recently moved, so I know no one can hear me.

My first concern is my eye; I use my good arm, the left one, to touch both of my eyes, and they are still there.

There is no blood on my hands, but my face is smashed into the rest of my shoes, and they smell like dog shit.

How many little things go to the wayside once you get brain cancer? Although there isn't actually any dog shit on my shoes, they smell terrible. I have not washed any of my shoes for two years now. I can do my own laundry, but CK can do it faster and better. I never ask her to do it, but she does it anyway. I can take care of myself, and if she wasn't coming over, I would figure this out.

Somehow.

I try to make myself comfortable because I will be here for a while. I count my shoes. One, two, three, four. Stay awake. My right leg feels bruised but not broken, thankfully.

Gatsby is sniffing me and whining.

I start to scream. I cry. Maybe the upstairs neighbors will hear something alarming and check on me. Their pug peed on me once, which really pissed me off, but I would learn to love them, even if they didn't help me.

I scream louder, and I swear I can hear the noise echo back to me from the river, which moves along again beside me. I imagine I'm in the river, and it's just going to carry me to a new life where I can wash my shoes again.

Gatsby crawls onto my back and cries. She thinks if she sits on me and keeps me warm, I will magically stand up and feel better.

The pup tries to help me, but there is nothing she can do. She licks my face in an attempt to get me moving, but I can't even reposition myself.

I am hurt, scared, and tense.

Even the parts of me that usually work are no use now. I know this fall must be bad because when Gatsby has seen me topple before, she has not given a fuck.

The last time I fell, I was outside with a bunch of mail. I was trying to open the door and lost control of the envelopes and the prized coffee in my hand. Gatsby dashed out to use the bathroom—which is fine because she goes out without a leash all the time—but then she started sniffing some flowers and didn't care her mom was splayed on the cement and a two-dollar royalty check was blowing toward the river in the wind.

I have no choice but to wait for CK, but there is another problem.

CK has this habit of bursting through the door like a superhero. It doesn't matter if it's a typical day—she pushes the door as fast and hard as she can to show that she is always here to help. This is completely unnecessary, but I've learned an important cancer lesson— people have to put on a show they are helping. If you don't see it and it's not ostentatious, it doesn't seem to count for them.

I know once she arrives—will it be ten minutes? Forty minutes?— CK will swing open that front door with the force of her strength she uses to lift 170-pound kegs at work.

My body positioning means if she crashes the door open, she will crush my entire right side, which is already a piece of shit.

I try to push myself away from the wall and my shoes, but I do not have the power.

Gatsby settles in on top of me, and we wait.

I do not know why I don't have my phone with me. What was I thinking? Was I seriously going to go out to the car in the dark without my phone? I could yell at Alexa, but I was probably too far away for her to understand me.

How the hell did this happen? How did I end up somehow falling and being completely unable to get up? My head hurts so badly. I check for blood again, but there is none. I typically fall on my weak side, but somehow this time, I ended up on my stomach.

This is why my doctors did not want me to keep my insulin pump. The fall would have crushed the expensive artificial pancreas, and then I would have nothing. Nothing to save my life. Nothing to keep me going.

Absolutely nothing.

Sometimes I feel like I have nothing anyway, but I try not to feel too sorry for myself.

I wonder if I actually died in the fall.

Maybe I am dead, and Gatsby finally cares about my wellbeing because her food source is now gone.

No, she is sweeter than that.

She just gets distracted.

Maybe I am dead because I feel as if I am watching all of this happen from my ceiling.

I remind myself to tell Angie the Apartment Cleaner that the fans need dusted. My right side looks as twisted as an ornate skeleton key; my spine is straight by my limbs are gnarled and mangled.

Maybe I am dead because I feel so separate from my physical body. I can no longer feel everything that hurt when I first fell.

And then I hear the car.

I hold out my right arm as far as I can, which isn't much. I know as soon as CK flings open the door, I will not be able to hold or push back for long. My arm is so weak I can barely hold the limb above my body. When I hear her approach the porch, I start yelling. I have no idea what I'm saying, but I just need to alert her that she cannot open the door.

She hears me, and I can hold the door in place, so she does not crush my side.

All she can do, however, is peek through the door, where she sees my legs. I have been wearing the same pajamas for four days now. I managed to get one slipper on, but my right foot is bare and twisted.

Gatsby refuses to move off me. She is warm. I feel safe.

I'm afraid I won't be able to get in, CK says. *Can you move at all?*

I cannot.

CK pushes the door as softly and slowly as she can. My right side creeps closer to my spinal column as she continues to creep the door closer to my body.

Finally, CK manages to slip through the entrance like a ghost.

I am dead.

I know it.

Okay, don't panic, she tells me. *Everything is going to be okay.*

But I do panic, and everything gets worse. My entire right side vibrates in a focal seizure that makes my left side a captive, shaken by memories of tragic tumors and symptomless nights where something so dark and dangerous lurked into my body, just out of sight. I cannot *calm down*, and instead, all I do is scream and wish I was actually dead.

None of this is worth it.

I should have just died on the table.

I should have just died.

Whenever CK touches me, I tremble harder. *Just wait*, I tell her. *I can't move right now. Whenever I try, I just start having a seizure.*

She sits with me on the floor, and we wait.

Something about my body's fear response causes the seizures to get worse. This doesn't always happen. Sometimes, the seizures occur without warning, an attack of my brain on itself that renders me unable to walk or move for a half minute or more. Other times, the seizures occur in response to the feeling of tenseness already in my body. Stress seems to exacerbate the seizures, but I cannot simply tell them to stop.

They do not like to listen.

My body fights against itself constantly; right versus left, and although the left side is stronger, the right side always wins.

Always.

Finally, I stop shaking enough so CK can roll me onto my back and gently pull me onto the carpet. Once on the carpet, I need another break.

My right arm won't stop seizing.

This is new. Usually, except for the initial seizure that led to my diagnosis, my right arm does not tremble like this. The arm seizures have happened once or twice, but not like this. It won't fucking stop. Each time I try to move, my arm just starts shaking again.

I instruct CK to give me another minute, but nothing helps. I begin crying again, which, of course, makes everything worse.

I might die on this floor.

I always imagined dying here, the river by my side, still flowing forward while I slowly faded away.

Now I'm just dramatic.

I need to get my shit together.

I slowly roll over to my back, and then CK picks me up and lifts me onto the carpet. Because I haven't been able to exercise for two years, I weigh as much as her kegs at work, and this has become a joke between us. With all the weight I've gained since my diagnosis, I can't do much anymore. I keep saying I need to lose weight so she can still lift me, but she is powerful—even when she was a fresh meat roller derby skater, CK hit me so hard I thought I might lose a kidney.

We decide she should drop me in front of my futon so I can relax a second before I try to stand. I feel as if I've run twenty miles in the snow.

I am exhausted.

I am terrified.

I am alive.

the pacific ocean

Unlike Caribbean cruises, Alaskan cruises are quiet and relaxing. There is no Cardi B constantly blaring all over the public areas of the ship. There is no cadre of hairy sasquatches in the pool, piña colada in one hand and a tanned, twentysomething in the other. (I do wonder, though, if we might be lucky enough to see an *actual* sasquatch from the balcony of our boat, the wild hairy creature just wandering around the Alaskan wilderness, unaware of the lurkers on the cruise ship. Is that a moose? Is that a bear? OHMYGOD IT'S A YETI.) Dining areas are quiet and full of mobility aids.

I feel right at home.

In a last-minute switch, David could not accompany us on our adventure, so Nodya asks her friend Holly to come. My mom was initially convinced this would never work; how could they get the paperwork done in time? Did Holly have a passport? Was it valid? We could not pass Holly off as a man named David! Despite the initial concerns, Holly makes it onto the boat with Nodya, and everything works out. Holly and Nodya are content to do their own thing and meet up with us when I am able.

Problem: The elevators are always crowded.

I stumble as quickly as I can onto an elevator so my mom and I can make it to the dining room in time to meet Nodya and Holly for dinner. We have a server named Jelena who calls us all *Madam* and makes certain that Madam Jenifer and Madam Holly have all of their intolerances and allergies addressed.

Nodya and I, immune from these things, devour every piece of seafood, pork, and peanut put onto our plates. We all wish that Jelena could come home with us; she takes her job very seriously so that Madam Holly and Madam Jenifer never fall ill. We all look forward to seeing Jelena and friends at dinner. It feels nice to be heard, taken care of, and addressed as Madam.

Madam Jenifer takes the steps to the dining room, so I am in the elevator alone. Another lady with a cane looks at me and says, *Did you have hip surgery, too?* I look her in the eye and say, *No, I have brain cancer.* The elevator gasps. *Well, you're doing pretty well then!* The lady says.

I could be offended, but I'm not.

I've realized if I just say *I have brain cancer*, people tend to shut up and leave me alone.

Tomorrow, we are taking a shore excursion to visit sled dogs, so I remain focused. I can't wait to see these dogs and how they work, how they play, and how they live. Part of me wonders: Is this okay? Are these dogs being harmed? Does someone need to rescue these pups?

As I get off the elevator, I wave to the cruise ship barista. He winks at me. Stanislav was actually the barista on our last Caribbean cruise, and I bet he never thought he would see me again.

boone, north carolina

When my friend Lisa from grad school comes to visit me (why are the people who visit always coming from so far away? Why don't my friends who live down the road ever stop by?), we go to Foggy Pine Books, the local Boone bookstore that agreed to carry *Frontal Matter: Glue Gone Wild*.

Foggy Pine is my favorite bookstore of all time; just like it sounds, it's a bookstore you might find if you were wandering through the forest on a gloomy night. The wooden floors creak as you browse the newest in fiction, and the owner Mary tells me *there is definitely a ghost*. The fuzzy gray Nebelung kitty, Jane, blinks her jade eyes at me in agreement as she licks a paw from her spot atop the cozy fireplace armchair.

I am nervous. What if it's not here? What if the owner just decided to shove it *in the back somewhere*, and if people came in and asked for it, she would begrudgingly drag it out and make a reluctant sale?

Lisa finds the book first; it is with the memoirs and biographies. I didn't know if it would be there or with the regional authors, but I am happy as long as it sits on the shelves and gets dusted or moved around every so often by the bookstore employees. I don't even care if no one picks it up and reads the back. The important part is that *Frontal Matter* is here. I wrote the book, Running Wild Press published the book, and now it is amongst the other commerce on the shelves.

It's all I could have ever wanted.

Lisa takes my picture and then begins selling my book to a girl in the stacks who is looking for a work of fiction to give to her friend for her birthday. *Okay, so this isn't fiction, but my friend over here wrote this amazing memoir that I know your friend would really love.* Lisa is fantastic; she has also believed in my writing and sold me to anyone and everyone. If she is ever interested, I know she would be a baller agent.

The girl says *uh, thanks, maybe I'll check it out sometime,* and although we know she won't *check it out sometime,* we feel as if we have both done our jobs.

I miss Lisa.

She was with me the only time I ever got blackout drunk. We went out to eat and then to a party thrown by a guy named Tim. I was in my first semester of graduate school at Marshall, and I had no idea what the fuck I was doing. I was performing perfectly in all of my classes, but I had problems, or what I thought were problems at the time. There was Kris-with-a-K, the woman who hated me because Kris-with-a-K liked me, and the people she was paying to take me on dates.

But at some dude named Tim's house—an actual house (who in grad school had a real house?)— I drank glass after glass of white wine and pretended I was classy.

I can tell this isn't your first rodeo, Tim told me, and we both laughed.

What he didn't know was that it actually was my first rodeo, and an hour later, I would be asking Lisa to pull over on the interstate so I could vomit. I lost my favorite shoe on the interstate that night, and Lisa went back and got it for me the next day.

She has always been a true friend.

What I'm leaving out is that Lisa also had to deal with me puking all over myself and my belongings once she finally found my apartment. I had never invited Lisa over, and it seemed I could not remember just which apartment was mine in that huge Victorian home on Jefferson Ave. that once belonged to a single family and now belonged to another single family who rented out five apartments to responsible college kids and graduate students.

I was once a responsible graduate student, but I had finally reached my limit.

Lisa somehow got in touch with Bill, a guy who lived in the same house who was also working on his English degree. Bill was an ingenious poet, a nice guy, but I hadn't had a lot of interaction with him since I broke up with his friend Ryan, the kid from Pittsburgh, whom I swore was driving our shuttle to the airport.

Bill was home and helped us find my apartment, where Pru waited to judge.

He was also game for an interesting night, and he and Lisa undressed me and watched me vomit on all sides of the toilet until they had no choice but to toss me in the shower.

I always wondered what she looked like naked, Bill solemnly said, *but I never imagined it would be like…this.*

Poor Bill.

Poor Lisa.

I become obsessed with Ashley Judd while I'm in the shower. *Please don't tell Ashley Judd how drunk I am. I really don't want her to be disappointed in me. Just don't tell Ashley Judd. She means so much to me.*

To this day, I can't drink white wine.

To this day, I have no idea why I was so obsessed with Ashley Judd.

Lisa forgave me, I think.

I'm not sure about Bill, though we are Facebook friends. He has a lovely wife and child now, and sometimes I wonder if he still writes.

When her father became very ill, Lisa moved home.

I feel badly she is visiting me in Boone, because I'm scared that something might happen to her dad while she is with me. I'm paranoid about death all the time now. If I don't hear from my sister for two hours? Dead from a drug overdose and probably raped by some dude she made eye contact with in a Brooklyn alleyway. If I don't hear from my dad? Parkinson's has made him fall, and no one is there to help him. If I don't hear from JC? Random vegan food allergy, and who would be there to help? Who?

Lisa buys me a hat and a necklace at a craft fair in Boone.

I tell her I am lonely, and she tells me she would date me if she lived in Boone.

We both know that we are not *like that*, but she means she would spend a lot of time with me and make me feel loved.

I am very sad when she leaves.

I know she will always be there for me, though.

the pacific ocean

My mom and I keep waking up around 4:30 a.m. because of the time change.

I don't care. I toss the pristine white bed cover off my battered body.

It's Alaska, motherfuckers, and I never thought I would be here.

Mom is already on our balcony with the binoculars. In the early morning fog, the view looks like a vintage postcard. The mountains in front of us have pure snow on their peaks that resemble the color of my bed cover. I do not know for sure, but these mountains look untouched by crampons and other human devices created to traverse this type of majesty.

Because it's May and getting closer to summer, there is no snow or ice at the bottoms of the mountains, only at the tops.

This creates a halving effect; one mountain looks like two totally different pieces of geography with the snowy white caps and the blossoming green bottoms. More interesting to me, though, are the miniature archipelagos that run alongside the mountain range. Some of the islands are too small to stand on, but others are big enough to at least put up a tent, maybe even a tiny house that Americans are so obsessed with these days.

Sometimes, the little islands show signs of life.

There's even a birdhouse on one.

I imagine what life might be like if I just had the cruise ship maroon me on one of those islands and let me live out the rest of my days alone in the middle of the sea. Would it really matter if I died in a matter of days instead of a matter of months? Two-year survival was nearly unheard of on the island of GBM. I still could not figure out how I was still actually alive. My tumor, because it was MGMT negative, was not supposed to respond as well to chemo as it did. I thought, much like the others I had come into contact with, I would be gone within a matter of months.

216

But now here I am, on a cruise ship headed to Alaska, kind of able to walk and imagining myself on an island in the chillier parts of the Pacific Ocean. Would it be more or less painful to die of starvation and exposure to the elements than it would be to die from brain cancer?

I had read so much research on end-of-life indicators for GBM patients; I had also seen countless posts on social media from caretakers who described what the last minutes were like for their loved ones with GBM.

1. Inability to swallow liquids.
2. Inability to hold urine or bowel movements.
3. Inability to move.
4. Seeing objects that aren't there.
5. Describing upcoming travel and using phrases like *I need to get a bag packed for where I'm going.*
6. Talking to loved ones who have already passed on.
7. Finally drifting into unconsciousness forever.

In a way, this did not seem too different from other death stories I had heard. I had never actually seen anyone die, but the thing that scared me was Death by GBM seemed a little more drawn out. If I had my choice, I would just have the MRI machine shoot millions of miniature swords into my body once it recognized I had another tumor, but sadly, this was not an option.

In my island fantasy, though, death might be the same way. Slow. Painful. Unable to eat or drink liquids, even if I had them. Maybe I could convince someone from the cruise ship to give me a decent tent and tender me off to one of those islands where I could live out the rest of my days, gazing upon the breathtaking mountain scenery. That would be much better than looking out at a parking lot of a hospital, which was undoubtedly my fate, if not today, then soon.

Everybody wants to die at home, but that's never the reality.

My island life fantasy is interrupted by the ship's cruise director, Dirk, who has been providing info on where to see wildlife and other fun Alaskan sights.

Do not look to the left! I repeat, do not look to the left! It appears that a seal is dying giving birth. There is blood everywhere. Oh, this is bad. Oh god, there is so much blood. Do not look to the left.

Although I am on our room's balcony, I can hear the ship collectively gasp. Most people are also on their balconies, and we are on the left side.

I close my eyes.

I do not want to know.

boone, north carolina

Your dad and I are moving, my mom tells me at the end of 2019, almost exactly two years after my diagnosis. We have sold our house and Nana's house to Mary Beth next door. She wrote us a check.

The Selling of the Houses on High and West North Street has backgrounded my entire illness. When I was in the hospital, my mom would call my dad constantly and ask what on earth the guy painting Nana's house was doing? *This was supposed to be done months ago, and he's still not done! Is he using the Copen Blue or the Nantucket Blue? We decided on the Copen Blue, but from the pictures you sent me, it looks way more like Nantucket Blue! Ted! I told him to not use the Nantucket Blue, but the house is half white and half Nantucket Blue! He needs to start over! What are we paying him for?*

My father is completely colorblind, so I know he does not give a shit about any of this. It's also the middle of January, and below freezing in Winston-Salem and West Virginia, so I have no idea why anyone is worried about painting a house Copen Blue (what is a Copen?), Nantucket Blue, or any color at all.

I finally have to make a rule.

When in my hospital room, no one is allowed to discuss anything dealing with paint.

My mom laughs, but I am not quite there yet.

In her world, she and my dad are the stars of their own romantic comedy, and my sister and I are mere extras in the film. Sometimes, I'm not even sure why they had us.

Along with all the beeps and whirs and alarms of my hospital bed and the realization I am completely trapped in this hell hole, hearing my mom yell at my dad about the paint color of Nana's house is not something I can withstand.

I cannot get away.

For once, my mom acquiesces and never talks about the paint in front of me again. During Christmas of 2019, I catch myself asking, *who painted Nana's house?* I had forgotten about the whole debacle entirely. When my mom reminds me of how irritated I became when she talked about paint colors in the hospital, I suddenly remember.

And now the house is as Copen Blue as it could possibly be.

When my mom discusses moving, I assume she and my dad might try somewhere different. My mom grew up in Harrisville, where they live now, and though she had short periods of living in various places around West Virginia, she has never lived outside of the state. I immediately think she will tell me they are moving to Myrtle Beach; after all, she is retiring, my dad is already retired, and Jenifer loves warm weather and pools.

And everyone from West Virginia eventually ends up in Myrtle Beach.

If West Virginia is almost heaven, then heaven must be Myrtle Beach.

We bought a lot near South Side, she tells me.

South Side is maybe a mile from where I grew up.

Neither of my parents like change.

I think you should come live with us once we move, my mom tells me.

I suppose I don't like change either.

I don't think that's a good idea, I tell her. *There's no way that my cats will get along with Princess Peppermint* (the cloud of a cat my sister asked them to watch for two weeks and has now been living with them for seven years). *And Gatsby is absolutely terrified of Princess Peppermint.*

My dog Gatsby will not even walk in front of Princess Peppermint to get a drink of water in the kitchen at my parents' current house. Instead, she loops the long way around to the water bowl by slinking through my parents' bedroom, the living room, and the kitchen.

That's true, my mom says. *Princess Peppermint does not like visitors.*

If I moved in with you, I say, *neither myself, Pru, Duffles, or Gatsby would be visitors. We would live there.*

That's why we are building you your own apartment attached to our new house, my mom says. *It's called a Generational Suite. You, Pru, Duffles, and Gatsby will have your own space, and that space is connected to your dad and me through a barn door.*

I stop to consider this: a barn door? I know nothing about how to build a house. I've always rented, so I do not care about *granite versus marble countertops* or *vinyl versus laminate flooring.*

I know Harrisville is a one-stoplight town, a town that, as a child, I could not wait to escape. My dream was to attend college somewhere in the South near my cool, single uncle (who later in life had five children) and get away from Harrisville and never look back to that small town, a place figuratively suffocating me with its incessant rumors about anyone and anything, and the chemical plants half-an-hour away literally suffocating all of us and what probably gave me glioblastoma in the first place.

I sensed there were other rumors to hear in the world, and though I was grateful to grow up in a community like Harrisville, I never wanted to come back to this commixture of 19th-century buildings and Dollar General stores that lived life from one holiday to the next. My friends and the boy-next-door, Dave, were the only people who gave me something to look forward to while I lived there. Once Dave moved while I was still in high school, I would stare next door toward the little red house at the missing spot where his green truck once idled. My friends all dispersed to different places, all red dwarf stars in bigger galaxies.

After realizing I needed to attend a four-year in-state university to use my scholarships, I accomplished all of those goals I had as a kid.

I went to graduate school in Auburn, Alabama, and then moved to North Carolina to live and work.

People told me it wouldn't happen. It wouldn't be that easy.

I would never get into an English Lit grad program on my first try.

I did, to my top pick.

After that, I would never find a job.

I did, on my first try. I didn't see any postings for Appalachian State, but I blindly sent them a CV. Two days before I moved, they called me. Sure, it was a non-tenure track job, but the focus on teaching suited me.

I did not dream of ending up back at my parents' house.

This was not for me.

As much as I loved the good people there, I wanted to be myself, and I could not be myself in Harrisville, West Virginia.

I'll never forget when Sarah and I were in high school and decided to dye her blonde hair dark purple before attending a baked potato benefit for a sick person in the community.[16] I would have done it, but being a blonde, Sarah was the more natural choice. The gasps and whispers could have kept a solar system moving as we sat and licked the butter and sour cream off our spoons. We didn't really say much to anyone; we couldn't because they were all talking about *the Samples girl with the colored hair.*

Everyone readily accepted Sarah should not and would not live in West Virginia, but I always felt as if I was expected to stay. When my dad got sick from Lyme disease, my phone would not stop blowing up about how much my mom needed my help.

What people didn't know was that I was already on my way home, grading papers at rest stops and replying to students' texts about their final portfolios as I took the exit for Route 50, knowing I would not have phone service for however long I was in town. No one saw me sit with my parents in the hospital, my dad on a ventilator, and my mom having a stress-induced Crohn's attack in his tiny hospital bathroom.

No one saw me sit for hours with my dad in the nursing home,

---

[16] Little did I know that one day, I would be the person needing the baked potato benefit. Thank you, Robeyn. Also, I hope someone showed up with purple hair, or perhaps something stranger.

watching Westerns and explaining to him that no, I would not go get him a candy bar and a Diet Coke because he was having problems swallowing, and just because he was my dad did not mean he could boss me around, especially if it meant not following hospital protocol.

Sounds familiar.

They tried to make me go to rehab, he said in a hoarse voice. *I told them, no no no.*

Ted! my mom scolded. *You have to do what they tell you!*

He's quoting a song, Mom.

I am forever my parents' interpreter.

I knew he would be fine.

No one saw me raking the dead blue jay with the three-inch-thick layer of leaves in my parents' yard that my mom didn't have time for, and my dad could no longer do. I had to hold my breath when I saw the red-stained blue jay feathers blowing out of my pile and into the unraked leaves of the past three months.

No one saw me deciding to fix (and later understanding this is something a person cannot *just fix*) my dad's small-time hoarding problem once and for all as I threw away prescription bags from 1982 and pencils that had not been used since he was a full-time 6th-grade social studies teacher.

Of course, I did not mind doing these things at all, but who was calling Sarah? Who was asking her to help out her parents? Who was calling her hair salon and asking if she could take a few days off?

There have just always been things expected of me.

And then suddenly, I could not do any of those things.

Then, Sarah was called upon for me, and she answered.

Once my dad received the diagnosis of Parkinson's, he started taking a *magic pill* every morning and claims he *feels great.* I believe him, but I also notice the little tics he has; he sways back-and-forth like a sky dancer when he stands up. It's not dramatic—you have to be paying attention to notice it, but I am always paying attention.

Although he shouldn't, he tries to help me.

It would just be more manageable, my mom says, *if we all lived in the same place.*

What she means is that *it*, whatever *it* is, will be easier for her if we all lived in the same place. She would not have to worry that if my dad fell in West Virginia, she would not be able to come to North Carolina if I had another brain tumor.

Sure, she signed up for this with my dad. He is eight years older than her, and though that's less than a decade, I'm sure my mom expected that one day, she would need to take care of him as a doting spouse would.

What she did not expect was her previously healthy 36-year-old daughter would silently develop a highly malignant brain tumor, requiring her to worry about me as well. (Of course, I still worried about my diabetes every day, but that was a worry of years long ago for my parents. They stopped asking me about my blood sugars when I was a kid and then seemed to forget I dealt with it every minute of each day.)

I remember when I called my mom to tell her I *had a mass on my brain.*

Are you sure it isn't a sinus infection? Maybe an abscessed tooth? I know you were saying you needed to go to the dentist. It's probably that tooth acting up.

I just had a CT scan at the ER, I said to her. They told me there is a mass on my brain.

Still, it took about a week for my mom to understand that no, I was not fucking around, no, I could no longer move my right side, and no, my tooth was not abscessed. I remember my sister getting tanked after she heard about my diagnosis and calling my mom at midnight, telling her *your oldest daughter is in the hospital ready to have brain surgery, and you're still at home with dad? What the fuck is wrong with you?* My mom put the phone down and let Sarah yell. *I mean, what was I supposed to do about it?* she told me later when she finally arrived in Winston-Salem right before surgery. *She was drunk.*

So yeah. Moving home does not sound so enticing to me. Not at all.

I tell my mom *I will think about it*, but a small part of me knows the thinking has already been done for me.

I will be moving home.

wake forest baptist health, the dash, north Carolina

I start going to scans and appointments again.

I cry at every single doctor's appointment now.

All that crying I never did in the hospital, well, here it is. All the time. I can't stop myself.

This is the hardest part, my very kind neuro-oncologist tells me as he hands me a tissue. *You likely feel that because you're not in active treatment, you're not trying. That you've run out of options. That you need something to focus on that just isn't there anymore.*

He's done this a time or two before.

This is normal, he says, and I do begin feeling a bit better.

I refuse to go to my other doctor, my radiation oncologist, because she never tells me anything different than Dr. Stroupe, and I don't have $180 for both appointments.

I make enough to live, but I don't make enough to save my life.

I always skip her appointments unless Dr. Stroupe really thinks I need to go. It's pointless, I think, to have two doctors tell me my scans look good, there are no open clinical trials, and all we can do is *watch and wait.* I do have the brainpower to allot my finances and my time accordingly, and my finances and time do not have another hour or another $90.

Dr. Stroupe wants to know a little bit more about how I am.

I have about four good hours per day if I'm generous with myself. Now that I'm back to teaching, those hours are mostly spent in the classroom. Otherwise, I'm in bed. I'm not always asleep, but my body can't take much more than a few hours upright. After that, *Wheel* and *Jeopardy!* is on, and I'm checked out. I quit writing after the publication of *Frontal Matter: Glue Gone Wild,* and now the focus is on the promotion and getting the book into stores.

You need to give yourself a break, he tells me. *You're a very active GBM patient.*

I laugh. Active? Active my ass. I don't do shit anymore.

His response to my laughter tells me I need to give myself a little more credit. Most GBM patients aren't even alive by this point, and here I am, teaching and shit. Getting in-and-out of my car three days a week. Going to meetings. Grading papers. Letting my dog out to use the bathroom.

I AM ACTIVE.

Because this is what active means now. Active no longer means getting up at 8 a.m., taking a shower, going to Starbucks, driving to school, teaching all day, getting back in my car to drive home, taking Gatsby for a walk, eating at some point, getting ready for derby, driving to derby, skating for about three hours, going out afterward for a snack, driving home, taking another shower, and then finally, answering some student emails as I fall asleep watching *Dateline: Secrets Uncovered.*

Active simply means *getting out of bed sometimes,* and I have to get used to this.

I realize most people in my position certainly do not live as long as I have, and most are not able to continue working a full-time job. I think quite frequently, *I am one of the lucky ones,* which sounds absurd, but things really could have been so much worse.

However, this does not ease the anxiety, depression, or hopelessness.

I often feel I have nothing to look forward to. One of my MRI reports says *cerebral volume loss that is advanced for patient's age,* and this confirms to me that in my mid-30s, I am really fucking old. I've always felt like an old soul, but this—this is not what I was imagining or going for. When I later look up *cerebral volume loss* on the internet, a lot comes up about dementia, Alzheimer's, and memory issues. *Neurocognitive deficits.* My accommodating doctor explains they would all expect this from someone like me, someone who has had a brain tumor removed and has GBM.

But I didn't expect this.

I didn't expect any of this.

I realize now I have to make the best of what life has given me. I'm not ready for the *live, laugh, love* pillows or to post fake Mark Twain quotes on Instagram, but I do have to get out of bed, and I do have to make every second count. However, this comes with a different type of anxiety: *How* do I make every second count? Now that I've exceeded my life expectancy, how do I change the world? How do I know for sure I'm doing the right things at the correct time?

Suddenly, my achievements cease to matter. Now that I've met my goals of writing a book and getting it published, I need to stop fixating on that.

Is it too late to make sure I'm a nice person? How can I be compassionate when the most I can do is smile at strangers and offer a quick hello? How do I help others meet their goals and feel good about themselves?

Although I know I shouldn't, I sometimes see myself as powerless.

Once my sister and I made putty for patients who were in the Sticht Center about a year after I was released. I felt good then. I felt like I was giving back. A week later, Sarah and I got a letter explaining they could not give the patients the putty because there was the possibility of spreading illness.[17]

Dammit.

My doctor says something about potentially extending my time between MRIs, and I finally start paying attention. *We can go for a few months*, he tells me. *I know it's hard to pay for MRIs every month, and I know the anxiety must be maddening.*

I love Dr. Stroupe because he listens to all his patients but does not claim their experience as his own. He does not say, *I totally get how you feel.* He says, *I know this must be hard, and I want to help.* He asks me how much I pay, and I tell him that although Wake Forest Baptist

---

[17] Pre-pandemic! I must commend them for being so careful.

wants $700 for each MRI, I am on an extended payment plan, where they just keep adding on to other payment arrangements and payment plans I have made. It's the payment payment payment plan that I'm never going to be able to pay pay pay.

Unfortunately, because our medical system is as broken as a tibia/fibula after a rough roller derby bout, Dr. Stroupe can do nothing about this; however, he is informally collecting information from his patients to get an idea of how dire their financial ruin is.

I have to admit, I don't even worry about this anymore. I did at first, and then when I realized there was no way I would ever pay off approximately $20,000 of hospital bills (after insurance), I just stopped worrying about them and stopped paying them. I would need to have a few great days as a *Jeopardy!* champion to even begin. I only paid for what the hospital demanded I pay for: doctor's appointments, the down payments on MRIs, and my chemotherapy, which I had paid in full. I knew if I did want further treatment in the future, those were what I needed the most.

I am still clutching a tissue at my appointment.

I do this now, grip items with my right hand, my bad hand. Part of me thinks I do this because if I am grasping something material from this world, I can never leave. I will never die, and I will never have to say goodbye to anyone I love.

I move the tissue to my left hand so Dr. Stroupe can shake my right hand. Perhaps I hold on a bit too long, but he does not seem to mind.

He seems to understand I just want to stick around for as long as possible.

ketchikan, alaska

In Ketchikan, I like walking around the town a bit with my mom. I use my cane, but I am ambulatory enough to be a tourist for the day. Because Boone is a tourist town in the snowy winter months, I love getting the experience of leaving my localness behind and wandering around somewhere new, somewhere that I am part of the crowd instead of bitching about *goddamn tourists* when they take too long at a red light.

Unfortunately, as soon as we get off at the port, my mom and I notice that so many of the shops are owned by the cruise ships. The jewelry and t-shirt stores are land versions of the floating mall on our boat.

To see the real Ketchikan, we are going to have to do a bit more walking.

I will pay for this tomorrow, but I don't care.

Thankfully, this area is relatively flat, unlike Boone, West Virginia, and other parts of the vast territory that is Alaska.

We find some totem poles and learn that some of them were raised for the Tlingit chief before all the white people came searching for gold.

My favorite, though, is a totem pole that shows how some bad bitch called The Fog Woman created salmon so everyone could eat.

To be perfectly honest, the red, blue, and brown faces on the pole look nothing like a Fog Woman, but I commit to using my imagination.

I can see the Fog Woman swirling misty, stratus clouds around herself until ice crystals consolidate to become a silver fish. I can visualize the Fog Woman parsing that silver fish out to everyone like Jesus, and then before anyone knows what is happening, bam! There are thousands of tourists walking through the Ketchikan mist and eating little salmon patties pasted onto crackers in a store owned by a cruise ship.

I still don't have any tangible religious beliefs, but I'm starting to like this Fog Woman. I do not have anything against religion, and I so badly want to believe in something, but I just can't get there. I wonder if maybe seconds before I die, I will decide on some belief and then go with it, but often, this doesn't even seem possible. For one, I want a woman to be in charge, and for two, if I decide on something, then I fear I will quit wondering and searching. What's the point then? I was raised a Christian and still have some considerable Christian beliefs, but I just can't stand there in front of the Fog Woman and claim that Jesus has healed all my problems and forgiven me for my transgressions.

The Fog Woman would not buy it, and neither would I.

I look over to my Mom, and she claims she can see an image of Jesus in a jewelweed flower,[18] but I see something else: a bookstore.

There is no better way to understand a place than to find a local bookstore and visit the Local Authors section.

My mom indulges me, and we head into the store. Like any bookstore, the atmosphere is crowded coziness; sadly, there does not seem to be a bookstore cat, which does not go unnoticed by me. I immediately find the Local Authors section and look for something fictional but based in Alaska. I don't really care about who climbed what mountain when they were here on vacation. I want to know the down and dirty, the how-to-survive Alaskan winters, the ups-and-downs of being a townie.

Sometimes you can learn more from fiction than from nonfiction.

I find a book called *Point of Direction* that seems to do just that.

After I take the book to the counter, the woman working the register seems to walk the entire length of the state getting to her post. When she finally arrives at the old-fashioned machine, she lifts her jeweled red glasses to her face and tries to figure out what I want. I put the book in her hands, and she blankly stares at me. *Oh, you want to buy something!*

---

[18] At least she's not seeing Jesus in a piece of toast?

she says, and we both laugh. *Most of the time, people just ask me questions about Ketchikan. No one ever wants to buy anything!*

Naturally, this makes me a little sad, so I add three stickers to my purchase.

My mom and I stop a few other stores so she can purchase souvenirs for her young nieces and nephews, and I take a moment to admire the unique Ketchikan architecture. The houses and buildings are so close together they can barely breathe. It's what you would think a small fishing village would look like, except this small fishing village caught tourism on a heavy line and reeled it right on in.

Not many white people may have found gold in the Klondike Gold Rush of the late 1800s, but they indeed found gold later on. The buildings look like brightly colored crayons with a rust-colored one melting and getting all over the rest of the bunch. Every house I see has an abundance of steps, which means no matter how badly I might want to, I will never live here. If I had more time, if I had more energy, if I didn't have an uncooperative right side, I would move here and work at that bookstore. I would find a calico stray and create a bookstore cat, and no one could stop me.

My mom interrupts my fantasy of living in Ketchikan; she has an armful of bags, and it's time to head back to the ship, where I will sit on our balcony and gaze at those crayon-colored houses, read my new book, and wonder what it might feel like to be someone else.

boone, north carolina

Everyone has read *Frontal Matter*.

Everyone.

Except my mom.

Much like I would never let her watch my competitive baton twirling performances in high school, I still do not allow her to read the book.

This is what happens when you write a memoir.

Everyone.

Knows.

Everything.

I did not think of this when I wrote it; I honestly did not believe more than a few people would read the memoir. Of course, I am grateful people did, but I'm also terrified of discussing the book.

A part of me does not even remember what the hell I wrote.

I guess the book served its purpose; I wanted to write it to remember all the weird shit that had happened to me.

However, a few months later, I cannot even look at *Frontal Matter*. I hide my copy at my apartment for a while, and eventually, I take that copy to my office at school, so I do not have to remind myself every single moment of why I wrote the book in the first place.

I think of the tragedy of this: I had to trade my health to make my dream come true.

Lisa from Running Wild Press, though, has made this more than a dream come true. She somehow manages to get my book into the swag bags for Golden Globe nominees. A local paper does a story on this, and everyone keeps asking if *there is any talk of a movie*. I tell them no, there is not. Just because high-profile actors and actresses have copies of my book does not mean I am automatically tossed into the Hollywood crowd. It is SO FUCKING COOL, though. Never in my life did I imagine that something I wrote would be included as a gift for Golden Globe nominees.

I want Diane Keaton to play me, my mom insists as if I actually have any say in 1) the book becoming the movie and 2) the casting choices. I just laugh and say something like *I'll do my best. I think I have Diane's number in my contacts.*

I would choose Moira from *Schitt's Creek* to play my mom. Not Catherine O'Hara but the character Moira. With a very slight Appalachian accent, I think she would be perfect.

Lisa also sets up a radio publicity tour with a firm in New York. When I go to visit Sarah, I get the chance to meet the representatives from the firm, Steven and Brian. They are very kind, literate, and easy to talk to, even though I spill soup all over my seahorse sweater. (Sea horse, sea hell?) *This* was my dream. I did not care about movies or shows or actors and actresses; I cared about books. I cared about discussing books. I wanted people to read my book, and Brian and Steven push me to open up about the book's subject once again, so I am not closed off when the radio interviews begin.

I *have* to talk about what happened to me, or there is no interview.

Brian helps me with this and teaches me some *bridging techniques* so I'm always selling the book when I'm on the air with the radio hosts. The more coaching I receive, the more I can discuss the surgery, learning to walk again, and how I managed to write the book.

After our lunch with Brian and Steven, I tell Sarah *this is my dream. Not hailing cabs in the middle of the city or hiking some mountain no one's ever heard of. I have always wanted to meet someone in New York City to talk about my book. That was my dream.*

And it was.

Because I obviously never take the straightest path to anything, I got my first taste of *making it* in creative writing while I was working on my Ph.D. in Victorian Literature. Why did I pick Victorian Lit and not creative writing or even Contemporary American Lit? Because I like a challenge, and most Victorian novels clock in at just around 800 pages.

I loved the books; I loved the process of how they were made (most are so long because they were sold in serial sections by newspapers), and I loved these writers actually got paid for their work, even if they had to do so under a pseudonym.

Weekly, even.

Perhaps more interesting? The authors would just write and write and write, and the newspapers would publish and publish and publish until the general public lost interest and moved on to the next vampire story or tale of forlorn love.

This fascinated me.

I loved that the writers got paid and people actually looked forward to reading their work.

Yes, of course, the end result was a Ph.D. student like myself poring over multiple copies of Dickens' *Little Dorrit*, poolside at my apartment complex in Alabama, trying to distinguish a dissertation topic no one had attempted before, but I appreciate the novels to this day, although they have nothing to do with what I teach.

However, I got bored simply reading and crafting seminar papers and a dissertation. I was a creator; I needed to be writing to keep my sense of identity.

During that first semester of graduate school, I wrote a short story called "Present Imperfect," and my creative writing, something I had only considered a hobby at this point, blew up in a matter of weeks. A now-defunct-but-once-very-popular website published the story and nominated "Present Imperfect" for a Pushcart Prize, which is the best of stories published by small presses.

A few days later, I received an email from an agent at a well-known New York City agency.

Did I have a novel? she wanted to know.

I did, but it was nowhere near ready for anyone to read or publish. But since I had this opportunity, I told her I did, in fact, *have a novel called Generational Sin*, but it was in rough shape. It was a family drama, much like all the other family dramas out there: The book had religion, misunderstandings, affairs, and a dead baby who no one in the family wanted to remember.

I worked with this agent for months.

I edited.

I had dreams of flying into New York City and meeting her so we could discuss how to sell the book to one of The Big Five publishing houses in NYC.

The Ph.D. could wait, I told myself before I went to bed at night. Sure, I was still writing academic papers and excelling in my classes, but all of my professors knew I was not made for scholarly publishing. My papers worked fine in a classroom setting. Still, they did not have the panache of papers that achieved the ultimate goal: publishing the work in a scholarly journal before graduation, so I could get a goddamn job.

I oddly always placed in the school's scholarship poetry contest, though.

I told everyone I had an agent interested in my work; this seemed like a sure thing. She edited with me, discussed with me, and tweaked sentences with me. She wanted *Generational Sin* to hit shelves. We would do this together, she promised me. We would sell this book and go to the top.

After about eight revisions and hundreds of emails between us, the agent wanted one more revision before she would sign me.

No problem, I told her.

At this point, *Generational Sin* looked nothing like the original family drama I had created. There were two affairs now, so the husband and wife could be equal. The husband and the wife were both sleeping with other men, which was not in my original outline, but I liked it. There was an extra middle sibling who had her own chapters now, and I enjoyed how the middle sibling seemed to have a more straightforward point-of-view than the other family members.

Still, this wasn't my book.

The only thing I had left was my dead baby narrator, who was cut out of the middle sibling's chapters but still very real to the reader, if not her own family.

I surprised myself by how willing I was to change everything about My First Book. The final draft looked nothing like I had envisioned, but I was still very proud of how the story materialized. The agent had taken a wacky family drama and turned it into something saleable and shelve-able. I daydreamed I would still finish grad school but rely on my writing to make money. I could still teach if I desired, but writing family dramas would be my career.

After I sent her the final version of *Generational Sin*, the agent emailed me back the next day.

It was so fast, I assumed it had to be good news.

Great news.

It was not.

Suzanne, I am sorry to say that I cannot take this book on. I thought it had a lot of promise, but in the end, it's just not for me. I know you have worked so hard.

She didn't sign me; she didn't even sign her name to the email.

I curtly thanked her for her time and effort, then dissolved into the brown carpet of my rental apartment. While I was on the floor, a scorpion scuttled across the floor and nearly stung me. I grabbed a glass from the kitchen and trapped the scorpion, so I could put it back into the Alabama heat where it belonged.

I took movement for granted back then.

After freeing the scorpion, I sat on my couch, which I constructed myself; the couch sunk in on the left side and always had the appearance of being a broken piece of furniture I found alongside the road instead of a DIY project I finished on my own. I sat on the right side, so I could take a few minutes to cry.

The right side promptly cracked, propping the left corner back to where it belonged.

Now my body is so much like that terrible couch.

I would not be flying from Alabama to NYC to meet this literary agent and speak of my book over a lunch of strawberry salads with a fancy vinaigrette dressing. I would not see *Generational Sin* on the bookshelves of airports when I was flying to-and-from book signings. I would not be browsing a library one day in some big city I hadn't been to yet and see *Generational Sin* on the shelves, ready to be checked out by teenagers who were willing to move on from the YA genre to something more adult.

I read and reread the email about sixteen times. *Suzanne, I am sorry to say that I cannot take this book on. I thought it had a lot of promise, but in the end, it's just not for me. I know you have worked so hard.*

Suzanne, I am sorry to say that I cannot take this book on. I thought it had a lot of promise, but in the end, it's just not for me. I know you have worked so hard.

Suzanne, I am sorry to say that I cannot take this book on. I thought it had a lot of promise, but in the end, it's just not for me. I know you have worked so hard.

I could not believe this shit. It was worse than being led on in a romantic relationship. Of course, I had worked so hard! I had worked so hard to make the revisions she suggested, and she had worked hard to make them. Why did she waste my time? Why did she waste her time?

I never got those answers.

I also never won the Pushcart.

My creative writing career was in worse shape than my couch, and there was nothing I could do about it.

I kept trying. I emailed other agents. Because the first agent contacted me, I never had to go through *the proper way to write a query letter for a novel.* I attempted to follow all the rules, but I only got *no thanks*, and *this novel is not for me.* At least I did not get strung along in a series of revisions that now covered the carpet of my bedroom in disarrayed stacks of paper I stole from the English department.

I submitted other short stories, still hoping for that Pushcart, but nothing worked. It seemed my shot at being a writer had dissolved faster than the sugar I put in my coffee to get me through teaching, going to class, and starting this new sport called roller derby that seemed pretty badass.

I would not be published again for years.

Things happen, as they always do. I kept writing, but nothing made sense. I joined a writing group, and they hated the story I wrote about my friend's toxic marriage. They were right; I gave too many *old-fashioned descriptions* that *jarred with the current nature of the marriage.* I stopped submitting anything for publication. The writing group never met again.

I finished my dissertation and graduated with a perfect academic record.

I became super involved in roller derby.

I got married and then divorced.

I came out, sort of.

I played more and more roller derby until I finally moved up to the A-team and was a consistent, offensive blocker.

I dated nice people.

I dated toxic people.

I dated an addict who refused to see how her issues hurt others.

When I found myself alone, that's when I finally started writing again.

After all, I had so much to say.

And then, everything went to shit the day I had that seizure in the coffee shop. When I woke up at 5 a.m. every morning in the hospital, all I could think about was writing and walking. If I could do both, I could be myself again. Without a choice, the hospital had me on a strict schedule, but I absorbed everything because I wanted to get better. I needed to get better. I needed to do this for myself.

I had no idea how far this would go.

juneau, alaska

When the boat docks in Juneau, our sled dog tour begins. I still doubt the decision. As someone who very much supports animal rights, is this okay? Are the dogs being made to run the sleds? Are they abused? Are they howling at their wolf ancestors to save them from this terrible fate?

However, as soon as we arrive at the camp, we are greeted by happy yips and barks. There must be over a hundred dogs at the camp, and they all cannot wait until it is their turn to jog the tourists' sleds.

I assumed they would all be Alaskan Malamutes or Siberian Huskies, but they are myriad breeds and sizes. A newspaper-colored puppy named Gordy takes a liking to me and wants nothing more than to be in my arms and lick my face.

I welcome every second of it.

Our group gets a guide named Brittany, who is a total badass. The dogs at the camp all have a different guide in charge of them, but Brittany is the only female. She tells us how she runs with her dogs all day during the sledding season, and she sleeps with them at night in her tent. She has no family in Alaska, no kids, and no real friends except these dogs.

I might be in love with Brittany.

No, I'm not in love, but I am in awe. Brittany's dogs watch every flick of her fingers and listen to every crunch of her boot on the gravel. When she starts gearing up the dogs to do a quick run with us, the pups start to howl and freak the fuck out. Finally, someone asks Brittany, *Why are they so upset?*

They're afraid of getting left behind, Brittany tells us. *They love to run.*

Of course, none of them get left behind. Every once in a while, Brittany tells us, she can sense one of her dogs does not enjoy running. That dog, she says, will typically slow down a lot and not follow the rest of the pack. The pup will drag behind the rest of the pack and get distracted, kind of like a roller derby teammate who joined for the cool fashion but didn't realize skating takes work. Those dogs get adopted to families, she tells us, and I secretly hope that Gordy hates running and can come home with me.

After learning all about the dogs, we get our sled ride.

I have zero sense of balance now, and I am surprised how terrified I feel of letting happy dogs control my fate. My mom helps, but I struggle to get onto the sled. I want to be tucked in the middle so I can't fall.

When we settle into the sled, and the dogs begin to run, the ride is exhilarating. I am reminded of skating and miss this feeling: the wind biting my face and a little bit of danger. The dogs go full speed down a hill, and I am reminded of rolling outside in the winter, which was one of my favorite activities. I would put on a coat and hit the concrete bike trails and not give a shit about the cold. It invigorated me as I skated and listened to sad indie songs during those mornings by the river. If it was snowing, I couldn't do shit, but the cold did not bother me.

I watch the pups follow their route. Although Brittany guides them, they don't need direction. The dogs know exactly where to go and what to do. This is like a roller derby pack; the animals move together toward a common goal.

They are a team.

The hounds stop for a break next to a puddle and drink what they wish. Then their personalities come out; a goofy pup starts smiling for the tourists' cameras, and a big brown dog takes a quick nap. Brittany walks down the line of wolf descendants and strokes all of their ears. They love her, and each one can't wait their turn for affection. Brittany invites us to pet all of the dogs and give them attention; they *love* people she tells us, and they certainly do.

When the break ends, Brittany gears up the dogs again, and we head back up the hill. I know from seeing previous tours while we waited, at a certain point, the other guides come behind the sled to give the riders a final push up the hill. I don't think the dogs realize this, which makes the overall experience endearing as fuck.

During those last few moments of the sled ride, I close my eyes and remember the days when I could run. When I could push. When I skated beside the French Broad River with no one but the wind and moody tunes guiding me along. I treasured those mornings, but maybe not enough.

I miss flying down hills, totally unsure if I would hit a rock and go tumbling or come away unscathed.

I miss jumping over the curbs on the trail; if you didn't jump, then you definitely fell.

I miss being powered by eight wheels and a sense of adventure.

I miss it all.

boone, north carolina

I am actually really good at talking on the radio.

The interviews begin early and happen rapidly. Some only last seven minutes, while others go for an hour. Brian prepared me well for the discussions, and answering the questions feels natural. The more interviews I do, the easier it feels to discuss the sudden and complete loss of my right side, the craniotomy, learning to walk again, all the chemo and radiation, and this.

I don't have a name for what happens to me now.

This.

I do not feel as if I'm *in recovery*.

I'm definitely not in remission. The tumor has been removed, but the cancer is still there.

I do not feel like I'm back to *my normal life*.

I'm stuck in some liminal purgatory that honestly makes me, on my worst days, prefer death. I do not like going to bed at 10 p.m. and waking up at 1 p.m., still feeling tired even though I missed all the a.m. hours. I do not like the way my right leg feels completely unattached from my hip and won't listen to my brain when I say *walk just fucking walk you piece of shit leg*. I do not like forgetting what words I have at my disposal and calling dumpsters *really big trashcans* in brief moments of aphasia. I do not like how my seizure medication and big black hole in my brain make me experience moments of psychosis.

I don't mention any of this on the radio.

Some of the radio personalities are exceptionally prepared, while others have my story thrown at them seconds before I'm on the air. *Hi, did you write a book?* one of the hosts asks me during his commercial break. *Yes*, I say. *Frontal Matter: Glue Gone Wild*. I can hear him scratch down the title on a notepad. *Um okay great.*

That was my worst interview, naturally.

There is one question that continually throws me. The question is in my press packet, and I have practiced the answer in my head, but I'm still befuddled by it.

Reviewers have said that you use short sentences and phrases to convey meaning. Why did you use that technique?

I'm confounded by this question because...well, that's how I've always written. Some writers can pen these beautiful, long sentences and paragraphs that still manage to keep the reader hooked, but I'm prone to sentences that stab people in the skull. I like moving on with the story before they notice what has happened.

This is just how I write.

This is how I've always written.

I finally understand: This is the first thing I've written that people have read.

I do not apologize for my style. Sure, I can write long sentences that are grammatically correct, but writers don't always need to do that. Sometimes, short sentences work just fine.

On the air, though, I say, *The short sentences and phrases convey my message of shock and disbelief at what I was going through.* Finally, though, I start adding in later interviews, *I have always written this way, and I suppose it's a format that works well for this story.*

I tried other ways of writing. I tried to mimic my classmates' short stories about eating disorders and self-harm. I tried to write those long, beautifully daring sentences that described the side panels of housing developments and intricately carved Amish wood.

It just didn't work for me.

Nothing sounded authentic until those short sentences came along and changed my life.

I stop for a moment between interviews 16 and 17. I never imagined I would be on the radio discussing a book I wrote. This is surreal; this cannot be my actual life.

Sadly, as soon as I have that thought, the inevitable following thought occurs: You are dying of brain cancer.

This is also your actual life.

But I get myself together and speak jovially (but without faking anything) to the radio hosts. Even if they did not read the copy of the book sent to them, they find themselves amazed at the story. *You had a seizure out of nowhere, and it turned out to be brain cancer? Do you have warnings for people everywhere?*

I don't, not really. I attributed most of my silent-ish symptoms to 30+ years of diabetes, so it was a rare situation. However, I give a spiel anyway, because it's absolutely true and important for people everywhere to hear.

If you think something is wrong, it probably is. Many doctors have a history of not listening to women, so keep pushing. You deserve to be heard.

Mic drop.

If I can't save myself, then maybe I can help someone else.

british columbia, canada

The final stop on our Alaskan cruise is not actually Alaska but Canada. I've been to Canada before but never British Columbia. My mom and I sign up for a whale watching tour. I've never seen a whale before, but I really want to. I cannot imagine being big, powerful, and living for so long.

A whale flew upward from the waters during lunch today, but I was too short to see its wondrous, natural arc beside our gaudy cruise ship.

It takes forever to get off the boat, but once we find our tour group, I immediately realize this excursion is not as friendly for disabled people as advertised. We have to walk a long way to our Orca-viewing tour, and because it is late, I already feel entirely deenergized. I have to give myself a pep talk on the walk; my cane helps, but my mom and I lag behind the rest of the group like two lost schoolchildren. I know the group won't leave us behind, but it doesn't mean they won't sit on the vessel and watch me struggle to get there.

And they do, with every step.

When we finally make it to our tour boat, I have difficulty getting onto the plank.

Everything shakes.

I really wish the cruise's tour descriptions gave better details of not only the physical aspects of these excursions (lots of walking!) but also indications of which disabilities would be accommodated. That little blue wheelchair by the excursion list, for example, could mean *safe and accessible for those with visual impairments but not safe for those with severe balance issues.*

When my mom and I finally make it to the boat, all the Carols and Stans are already seated and ready to drift off into the Pacific for some whale watching. Although I'm (barely) standing there with a cane, no one offers to move.

CAN SOMEONE PLEASE OFFER ME A SEAT?

I have no problem asking people to move, but that isn't the point. Our group is about to take off in a small whale-watching canoe onto some windy waters. Why, when there are plenty of seats but all of them taken, should anyone with a cane need to stand?

It's because I'm young.

Although I'm nearing my late 30s at this point, I look like I'm in my early 30s, at least. Because of this, people think I'm either faking the need for mobility assistance or using the cane as a fashion accessory. (I mean, my cane is trendy, because why not? Remember it's purple, blue, and silver with compasses and nautical symbols all around the base. Have compass, will travel, bitches.) The same people taking up all the seats watched me struggle to get on the plank and then the boat. They should have been moving before I officially made it onto the small ship, but they all just sat there. Was I the whale? Were they sitting there to watch me?

Apparently.

Not all people are bad; some are just clueless.

I think my question scares my mother. My assertiveness has always frightened her a little. I'm not even that assertive, but I'm more forward than she is. She and my father (both Pisces, if anyone has an interest) taught my sister and me to be polite, fair, and diplomatic.

Unfortunately for our parents, I found words, and Sarah found hair dye.

My mom is assertive at work but in public? We should be quiet. We should be polite. We should never say anything to anyone unless asked.

Embarrassed, a lady and her husband quickly move so I can sit. My mom goes to the tiny indoor cabin because she finds the B.C. wind too cold. Because my mom went inside, I invite the lady to sit beside me.

"I'm so sorry I didn't move at first," she says. "It's just…kind of shocking to see someone so young need assistance."

Called it.

Although I could take this lady's comment as offensive, I do the opposite. There is no reason to make enemies on a whale watching tour in British Columbia.

"I totally understand," I tell her, because I do. "I never expected myself to be in this position or requiring so much help. It really shifts your life in unalterable ways."

The boat is packed, so the woman and I sit close. This makes me feel secure, like the wind won't knock me off into the water.

"I'm really nervous that we won't see any whales," I tell her. "I missed the one at lunch today."

"People saw one at lunch today?" her husband asks me, completely bewildered.

"Yeah, the whale did a nice little flip for everyone. My friends saw it, but I was too far back."

"We will definitely see a few tonight," the lady tells me. "We've done this tour before, and they do a good job. They know exactly where the whales will be. They've even named them."

I had no idea this was how the whole whale thing worked. I imagined my mom and I paid roughly $100 just hoping to see some tails flipping around in the distance.

They have names?

Damn.

These whales were loved.

As we venture a greater and bluer distance onto the ocean, the husband dips down into the covered room where my mom takes shelter. He comes back out with a three-ring binder that has a picture of the whales above their names. The guides know roughly how old the whales are, how far they travel, and what pods they belong to. They know each and every scar and nick on each whale's body, specifically the tails.

I can't help but think of my first semester at Auburn, where I took an American Lit class. I met my future neurologist, Ben, in that course.

We read *Moby Dick* at the egregious speed of this boat. The professor had us write a single-spaced page-long response for each class, which meant I knew far too much about whales. Of course, Moby Dick was a sperm whale and not an orca, but nonetheless, I feel a literary connection to these animals.

Finally, the boat stops, and we wait.

There are no whales here, not even the smallest blip in the calm sea, but the view is a gorgeous spectacle of a luminous sunset meeting the gleaming turquoise water. I convince myself if I actually do see a whale, it is a sign from the Fog Woman I will live longer. I know no one is supposed to make deals with transcendent beings, but at this point, I figure, why not?

We see nothing, not even a ripple in the water at the first stop, and I am discouraged.

"Don't worry," my new friend tells me. "They will find us some whales."

I wish I had her faith.

At the second stop, my mom ventures out of the covered section of the boat to join my new friends and me. Jenifer, who has always had an eye for detail and miracles, spots the tail first.

"Look!" she scream-whispers, so as not to scare the monstrous, gentle creature. "A whale!"

A crowd gathers around us to see what we all paid for: whales in the wild.

This one, whom the guide tells us is named Thomas, is around my age and typically puts on quite a show for people.

She is not wrong.

Thomas flips and flops and shows off his magnanimous tail to our boat. He is egregiously extroverted, and we love it. My mom takes pictures while I gaze at his beauty and personality. If Thomas would sit down with me and let me give him the Myers-Briggs personality test I am so fond of, he would definitely be an ESFP.

Thomas is the Elvis Presley of whales.

He shakes his hips. He entertains. He even sings us a cute little ditty, which the guide tells us she has only experienced one other time in her nine-year career of whale watching. This whale *knows* what we came here to see. He is in a safe Sea World, and he refuses to let this opportunity to be seen pass him up. Thomas shows off his tail, his face, and all his sides. He seems to be about three times as big as our boat, and I finally wonder if he might get under us and flip us over.

I would be okay with that.

Death-by-Thomas-the-Whale.

Much better than Death-by-Brain-Cancer.

After Thomas frolics along to a different patch of ocean, we witness around thirteen other whales in the Pacific.

This is not a sign from The Fog Woman, I understand; this is a cold slap of Pacific Ocean water in my fucking face.

I have more time.

The ocean swallows the sun until tomorrow, and we get to see some fancy homes and hotels on the banks of B.C. I feel fine, I tell myself. I'm not even that tired.

And then without warning, the boat speeds up.

At this point, I am standing to stretch my legs. I needed to walk around the boat for a moment, but I picked the wrong time. The problem with falling is not falling at all but getting back up. Since my right side constantly betrays me, I can only be lifted very carefully from my left side. No matter how strong I am, it is very difficult to get myself up from a fall.

This terrifies the shit out of me.

I start screaming, right there in the middle of that peaceful whale watching boat.

I AM GOING TO FALL I AM NOT OKAY.

Before my mom can rush to my side, my new friends run to catch me and assist me back to a seat. I didn't fall. I had friends. I *am* okay.

I enkindle this quick fantasy I will exchange email information with my new friends. They caught me. They saved me from possibly breaking my arm, hip, or leg. Of course, this never happens, but I am grateful for them, nonetheless.

When will this experiment end? My brain is a whale, and the doctors have been watching the organ splash around in my skull for two years now. Have they taken notes? Are they still discussing my progress? Have I proven myself yet? I am tired of being on display.

On the way back to the cruise ship, I close my eyes and let the wind slap my face.

I've always been a little strange.

What writer isn't?

part five: return to the beginning

nowhere

I have this recurring dream where I am in a hospital.

This is not a hospital I recognize. The building is small and more like a campus hall. I come here late every week, and a janitor named Shell unlocks the door for me and the others. Occasionally, I see patients who live here rolling down the dimly lit halls in their wheelchairs or using their canes to walk to the bathrooms. I always greet them with a smile and hello, and they do the same for me. I do not know any of their names, but this doesn't seem to matter. We are familiar; we are friends.

Lush green shrubbery bookends the building and obscures the sign, and the weather is always slightly cold and menacing.

Wind.

Threats of snow.

A lot like Boone, but this is somewhere completely different.

Depending on the dream, sometimes I will walk to the hospital after I hang out with friends at a bar, while other times, I come straight from home. I'm always walking in the dreams, but I need to use my cane.

Shell always stops sweeping or mopping to help me down the two steps that separate the foyer and hallway from the room where we all meet. I always get there just a few minutes early, and the first time I have the dream, I am the only one there. I check my phone to see if my executive functioning problems have caused me to mess up the date, but I am right.

There is a meeting tonight.

Soon, others join me in the chairs, which Shell has haphazardly spread into a circle. I still don't know why I am here. Is this an AA meeting? Am I taking a class? Why the fuck am I here? Did I join a cult?

I study the others and soon figure out exactly why I belong.

A guy who appears to be in his early 30s walks in with a limp and sits across from me. Although I still have trouble recognizing my right from my left side, I can tell he has the opposite problem. He experiences left side hemiparesis.

A woman in her mid-20s appears through the door, now propped open by Shell, and the woman has a bandage wrapped around her head.

She's fresh out of surgery.

Sharp wind gusts through the propped open doors, and I look at Shell.

Sorry, sweetie, she tells me. *We gotta get everyone in first.*

Although maybe I should be panicking, I am calm.

Cold but calm.

Woman with the Head Bandage and Guy with the Limp already know each other. They don't seem to notice me at first; however, when they do, they point me toward the snacks of saltine crackers and oranges. I skip the orange (too sticky) and pour myself a cup of hot water. If I'm chilly before bed, I'll often take a couple swigs of hot water, so this makes sense.

As I hobble back to my seat, I see others have joined us. Just like I have my cane, and the other two had a head bandage and a limp, there is something visibly wrong with all of us. The woman beside me is in a wheelchair and swollen from steroids. The guy who just came in and sits next to me holds a catheter in his pale hands.

We are all roughly the same age.

I should freak out, but as I tally the feelings in my dreams, I understand this is the calmest I have felt in quite some time.

Shell closes the door, and The Woman with the Head Bandage gives us a quick speech.

Thanks for coming to tonight's support group. We have a new member tonight, so let's welcome Suzanne. I smile and try to wave, but my right hand is too heavy. I don't hold anything; I have already attacked the crackers and hot water, so I have nothing weighing me down. Still, my right hand won't move. I imagine they call me Heavy Hand Suzanne.

I hope my smile will be enough, and it is.

After surgery, an attendant in the hospital always told me he *loved my smile*.

Without anyone saying much, I finally feel like I belong somewhere. After my diagnosis, surgery, and treatment, I searched high and low for an in-person brain tumor or brain cancer support group. Living in a small mountain town made this problematic, but I was able to find a brain tumor group in Asheville. However, a hospital did not run the group, so they did not have regular meeting times.

Their last meeting was in 2016 at Carrier Park, where I used to skate.

I tried contacting the woman who seemed to put together the meetups, but her Facebook profile was so private, she was impossible to message.

But here I was in some weird campus-like building with a brain tumor support group that had come to me in my dreams. I was not ready to share about my experience yet (common for new group members, Catheter Guy tells me. I can open up whenever I feel more at home, which would hopefully be soon), but listening to the others in the circle helps me feel like I finally have people in my life who can understand. These aren't just any random group of people with a brain tumor; they are all young adults with GBM. No one here has a meningioma or a craniopharyngiomas; of course, all brain tumors are terrible and life-altering, but these people have been through the worst of the worst, the most malignant, terrifying brain tumor of them all: The Eraser, The Destroyer, The Goddamn Glioblastoma.

I finally speak up.

Yeah, it just sucks that so far, I haven't had anyone be able to understand what I'm going through. Most GBM patients are old men or children. I mean, it blows for everyone, but I feel like a lot of people ignore young adults with cancer, especially ones like glioblastoma.

Oh, exactly, the group echoes. *It's like we don't matter. It's like not starting our careers, not having the opportunity to get married, and not having the chance to have kids is lost on everyone.*

I mean, I never wanted to have kids, I say. *But yeah. It's like no one cares about my goals and aspirations for the future. It's all about honoring the old and the very young. No one gives a shit about the needs and wants of someone between the ages of 20 and 40.*

I would never say this to a regular group of people. All cancers are terrible, and there is never a right age to get one. However, the public tends to pay way more attention to babies and the elderly who get brain cancers. Sometimes, it seems they are the only ones who truly matter.

Catheter Guy looks at me. He has dark brown eyes and black hair with a winding scar on the side of his scalp. He's kind of cute. I take a second to stare at him. Stop it, I tell myself. This is not why you are here. You do not meet romantic interests at a GBM support group. That's absolutely ludicrous. Still, I feel like we have some sort of connection, and I blink my long eyelashes at him when I finish my grandiose claim that no one cares about young adults with cancer.

When I look back up at the circle, Wheelchair Woman has wholly disappeared. When I shut and reopen my eyes, The Woman with the Head Bandage is gone. *See you soon, Heavy Hand Suzanne,* Catheter Guy tells me, and then, I am the only one left in the room. I grab my cane so Shell can help me out the door.

See ya next week, sweetie, she tells me as I walk out to the windy street.

I stand out there, zipping my coat, my cane leaning against the sign, before I finally realize what just happened.

All those people in the support group are already dead.

I am meeting with them to prepare for what comes next.

Still, I do not feel scared. I am comforted knowing they are there for me, I have support, and people understand what I'm going through.

When I wake up, I realize the people in my new support group likely died at various stages of GBM. The Woman with the Head Bandage likely passed in the hospital after surgery. Woman in the Wheelchair, full of steroids, probably made it quite a few years, just like my new crush, Catheter Guy. Guy with the Limp probably passed away before he got his strength back to walk.

Jesus.

They are waiting for me.

The dreams recur, and I start looking forward to the feeling of ultimate relief, of talking to people who actually understand. I do not have to explain anything to them; I do not have to explain why I'm angry, why I'm mean sometimes, or why I'm so fatigued and unbalanced that Shell always has to help me down the steps.

They just know.

They just know, and they understand.

I feel isolated when sleep prevents me from seeing my fantastical support group. Especially after Andrea died, I quickly discovered I was not in frequent communication with anyone else who had the same issues.

Except in those dreams.

In those dreams, I can be me.

Sure, it's very likely some weird purgatory; I don't think heaven or anything like heaven has someone on the support staff named Shell. (Also, why is she there? She is so nice, healthy, and seems able-bodied. Did she secretly kill a husband? Did I ever see her on *Snapped*? I don't know, but I'm grateful all the same.) However, I don't care what it is. I know they are preparing me. I know they are waiting for me.

I know they are anxious for me to end my story.

boone, north carolina

I cannot keep my eyes open.

All I can do is wail like a feral child.

I am alone in my kitchen when the feeling hits. I am sitting at my table that Lori and Martin Christopher Goodman gave me.

Hate them, love the table.

The table is falling apart, but it is my favorite place to sit. My body does better in structured seating; I can't get up from super comfy couches and chairs, because they do not give me enough support.

I can't stop screaming.

The same word loops through my head on repeat: *Glioblastoma glioblastoma glioblastoma.*

I am tortured by this word. I had never heard the word *glioblastoma* until two years ago. However, years before my own diagnosis, I did once share an article with a freshmen comp class about Brittany Maynard, the young adult who decided to legally terminate her life (with the help of a doctor), after her own glioblastoma diagnosis. Back then, the articles just said *brain cancer.* I remember passing out printed copies of the article because I felt this was important. I wanted my students to pay attention to this. I wanted them to see her power, to view her decision as brave and as proof the choices we make should be our own.

For college freshmen, this is a concept most have not considered.

I remember reading the article and thinking I could not even comprehend the difficult nature of Brittany's decision, but I supported her choice.

So did most of my students, though her decision did not require any of us to agree.

*

I remember sitting on a beach with my friend AMo when I had finished my treatment. She did all the planning, picked me up, and paid for everything. I met AMo when I started graduate school at Auburn, and she was assigned to be my graduate student mentor. A year ahead of me in the program, she took the mission seriously, and a decade later, I still look to her for guidance.

The beach was not crowded that day, and there was still enough sun to make the trip enjoyable. AMo and I sat in the sand, watched dolphins frolic through the spring ocean, and discussed the decision to die. If we can euthanize our pets when they are sick and hurting, why can't we euthanize ourselves? Eventually, we reached the topic of mental health and came to the consensus that if a person is hurting so badly mentally, they should also be given this same right…but only if their brains had fully developed, and they had undergone significant counseling to make sure this was the right decision.

Later, we witnessed a bloated, dead alligator on a river tour; I found the alligator oddly symbolic as it floated in the river like a forgotten novelty raft. Soon, I would be inflated with steroids and dead in a hospital somewhere, a forgotten human raft of skin, bones, and disease.

*

I felt certain this was the decision I wanted as I screamed in my kitchen.

I was not thinking about my neighbors; no one called the cops on me, which I was thankful for. This would be their second trip to my little apartment, and I did not feel like they would just let me sit at home and cry this time; they would likely take me to some sort of psychiatric services, which honestly, probably would not do me any good.

There's no fixing a brain that has a mind of its own.

I don't realize this at first, but my hands and face are wet. I'd just checked my blood sugar before the panic attack hit but hadn't stopped the bleeding from my finger before losing my shit.

Later, when I look in the mirror, I notice I still have blood and tears dried together on my face, as if I was just part of a brutal attack.

But right now, I still can't open my eyes.

If I open my eyes, then everything is real.

I ask Siri to call Chris.

She might be my only hope at getting back to reality. I'm out of it, sure, but I'm alive and awake enough to realize I need help.

When she and I dated, Chris had severe panic attacks related to the sudden death of her brother. I had no idea what I was doing, but I tried to help her out when they happened. More than once, I found myself frustrated. How could I fix this? Why was this something I couldn't fix? What the hell could I do to make this better for her? The answer was not much, but I did my best. I tried, though. I really did.

All I can do on the phone with her is scream and tell her, *I can't open my eyes.*

Chris worked as a counselor before *everything happened* with her brother, so she knows what to say to someone like me. Well, as much as anyone knows what to say.

She listens for a few minutes to my crying and screaming and then offers some advice: *I need you to open your eyes just far enough that you can find the Klonopin bottle in your purse and just take one whole pill for me. Do you think you can do that? You just have to open your eyes for a little second. Then I'm going to draw you a Medicinal Native American tarot card, and that will help.*

I start laughing uncontrollably.

Wait, are you laughing? she asks.

Yes,

And my eyes are open. I find the bottle in my purse and dig for a pill. My motor skills still suck, and it's hard to secure the tablet in my hand. I wet my finger and finally connect with a yellow tablet. I wash it down with my ever-present coffee.

I took the pill, I say, and then I start laughing again.

Why are you laughing?

For one, I tell her, I know I must be in bad shape for her to ask me to take medication. Chris is not a fan of psychiatric meds because she knows what pills can do to a person if abused. She has had multiple friends die from Xanax and alcohol overdoses, and, of course, her brother died from a tragic drug accident.

I'm also laughing because you're the only person on the planet who would offer to give me a Native American medicinal tarot card reading in the middle of a panic attack.

I'll only do it if you want me to, she tells me.

This is working, I think, as I slowly open my eyes again.

Nope. Too soon.

I close my eyes as she tells me she pulled the wolf card for me.

The wolf tells us to trust our instincts, Chris says.

I don't know if she's reading from an actual card or making all this shit up. I also don't know if this is cultural appropriation.

Within a few seconds, I'm sure this is cultural appropriation, but maybe not. I'm open to receiving the wisdom this card has to offer. I have nothing else to rely on right now, and I would love to have some kind of guidance.

Any kind of guidance.

When you feel like you do not have confidence, Chris continues, *Wolf is there to guide you. Wolf can help you find belonging, especially if you do not feel as if you have a pack. You may feel uneasy, but Wolf will give you the energy to move forward in the coldest of winters. Wolf is focused and calm.*

I have stopped crying.

I have to ask.

Where did you get these cards?

I found them on eBay, she says, and I say she did a good job.

You're doing a pretty good job is something Chris says all the time when things are rough, and someone needs encouragement.

Maybe if you're good tomorrow, I can pull you another card.

She also does this often; as a counselor who worked in many group home settings, Chris promises prizes for good behavior. I think it's funny; it's a habit she just can't break.

I feel my muscles tense and am afraid I'm headed toward another blackout.

I ask Chris if she remembers our first date.

The Klonopin is definitely kicking in.

Our first date was the weirdest first date in the history of first dates.

We were on the same derby team, but I did not really know how I felt about her yet. She was intriguing, for sure, and from our previous interactions, I could tell she was an eccentric genius. With her sharp jawline and asymmetrical haircut, she had the look of being a lifetime lesbian, and that scared me. Still, she had good taste in music and was funny.

We met at a coffee shop in Asheville that seemed to disappear after our date. We parked separately but found each other outside. She had her guitar slung on her back, which confused me. I would later learn she has a lot of safety mechanisms in place, so if she begins to feel ungrounded or suddenly misses her brother, she has something to help. Chris never planned to play the guitar at the coffee shop, but she needed the instrument with her.

We went inside, ordered, and sat across from one another on some mismatched couches.

Is that what I think it is? I asked her.

There was a woman sitting on some scaffolding in the window of the coffee shop where clothed mannequins once lived. The shop must have been an old department store; the woman lounged at a small table with another chair across from her, and it was easy to imagine her completely still and dressed in unpurchased clothing. There was a tapestry strung over the card table, and gold and red glinted in the sun. The woman wore a long, flowing purple skirt and, every once in a while, shuffled something around in her purse.

Is she a fortune teller? Chris asked me.

I can hear you, and yes, I am. Forty dollars for a reading.

Chris and I tried not to laugh. So much for being quiet.

If we had known then what we know now, we would have asked her for a reading. She would have said something like *tumultuous times ahead, but you will never stop learning from one another.*

But instead of talking to her, we talked about ourselves.

As soon as I began discussing my childhood, Chris pulled out a notepad and pen from somewhere. *Is it okay if I write a few things down?* she asked me. *Of course*, I said. I mean, other people might have found the notetaking thing strange, but I found the habit endearing.

I told her about how I always played a responsible role in my family while my sister got to do whatever she wanted. I told her about how I was diagnosed with type one diabetes at the age of five, which pretty much obliterated any hope I had for being irresponsible or carefree. I told her my mother is *really into religion* and my dad rarely speaks.

I had, and still have, no idea what she wrote down on that notepad. She did show me, but I could not make sense of her circles and lines and connections she made between abbreviations and designs.

Can I come to your house? she asked me.

No, absolutely not, I told her. The main reason? I had papers strewn all over my kitchen table; the mess looked like a bloodless crime scene. I was embarrassed. There were probably over a hundred pages on the table, along with two or three notebooks. I was working on transcribing my handwritten materials to the computer, and the process was daunting. I did not even know what to call the mess. Was it a novel? A group of short stories? A disaster?

Probably all of those things.

So I told her no, she couldn't come to my house, and I think she took that to mean I was not interested. We briefly hugged and walked back to our cars. I knew she and I had similar taste in music, so I send her the Youtube video for Phantogram's "Don't Move" as soon as I put my seatbelt on.

She said that's when she knew she had a chance.

I knew she had a chance the whole time.

The Klonopin is kicking in harder now. I need to eat something and get in bed. I'm in bed about 17 hours a day now. I'm not always sleeping, but moving has become so difficult and painful, I prefer my hospital-grade bed or even my futon. As long as I have my computer or my phone, I'm fine.

I'm so sorry, I tell her. *I never meant to put all of this on you.*

I think you're doing a pretty good job, she tells me.

Lob you, I say.

It's a mispronunciation we picked up from following so many pet accounts on Instagram.

Lob, she says, as she ends the call.

I feel as if I am breathing again. I do not hear the words *glioblastoma glioblastoma glioblastoma* on a loop in what's left of my brain.

If I hurry, I can still make it to bed in time for *Wheel* and *Jeopardy!*.

It's incredible how many petty things one can do from a laptop.

I order a copy of *Frontal Matter: Glue Gone Wild* and have the book sent to Chole's address.

I mark that the book is a gift, and yes, yes, I would like to include a message.

The most famous you'll ever be, I write in the text box before I click *Purchase.*

I would do anything to see her face when she opens the envelope.

boone, north carolina

Everyone but my mom has read *Frontal Matter*, though I did see on her Amazon page she purchased the audiobook.

Clever woman.

Without the label of fiction, I have nothing to hide behind.

My endocrinologist has read *Frontal Matter* and knows how terrible I am at taking care of my diabetes.

My boss has read *Frontal Matter* and knows I relied on a marijuana tincture to get me through nine months of chemotherapy.

My grandmother's sweet best friend has read *Frontal Matter* and knows I am sexually attracted to women.

I don't know if my dad has read the book, but I wouldn't be totally shocked at this point. He might have made it through all of his fishing magazines, his West Virginia *Goldenseal* publications, and his worn copies of everything Hemingway ever wrote. That man knows more than he ever lets on; he was the first to tell my family about an affair happening in town when no one else knew, and he has the observation skills of a hungry owl.

Dave's mom posts on my Facebook wall and tells me she has purchased the book.

I alluded to Dave in *Frontal Matter*. He was the *guy who wrote me letters when he was 25, and I was 16*. Until my mom gave him my phone number when I was going through treatment, I had no idea what happened to him. I knew he had a daughter, and if I had to guess, he lived somewhere in the Virginia area.

I was right.

When he asks to see me, I don't respond.

Why should I? I haven't spoken to him in over 20 years, and he made me feel absolutely lost inside my own mind. I felt so connected to him when I was a kid, but I knew he did not feel the same about me. But still, I can never push out of my brain (no matter how damaged it gets) that day he handed me his new mailing address before he left town. I loved getting mail—as I still do—and I remembered the advice my mom gave me. *If you want people to write you back, you have to write them first.* Sure, she gave me this advice when I was seven, but it stuck with me.

I have no idea what I wrote to Dave in that first letter, but he wrote back, always on a yellow legal pad. My cousin Emily and I analyzed those letters like I would later close read poems in college. What did he mean, exactly, when he signed his name *Love, Dave*? Was this love like a friend-love? An older brother? A pen pal?

Or did he really *Love, Dave* me?

Emily and I investigated every syllable.

I did not see Emily that often, but throughout our childhoods, we would do this thing we called The Cousin Exchange Program, where I would go to Kentucky for a week, and her brother Kyle would come to West Virginia to hang out with my sister. The next year, Emily would come to West Virginia, and Sarah would go to Kentucky.

We did this without fail for the majority of our childhoods. Emily and I would enjoy morbid activities, like picnicking in the graveyard and summoning the ghost of W.W. Thompson, the millionaire and past property owner of their gargantuan farmhouse.

Legend said W.W. buried his riches all over the farmland and then hung himself in the front yard; there was a mirror that was unable to be moved, and if you looked in the left corner of the glass, you could see the same tree where the lifeless W.W. swung like a banjo strap in the Kentucky breeze.

Phones called themselves in that house. Radios spoke to sleeping family members, one time telling my uncle he was going to *leave that woman*. My cousin Megan somnambulated too closely to the steps until they eventually moved.

But anyway, during the less exciting moments, Emily and I read one another's journals. At specific points during the year, we would also meet up at my Grandma Samples' tiny home that raised seven war-torn boys and a single sister who smoked Virginia Slims and loved miniature poodles. When Emily and I did not visit our grandmother's on the same weekend, we would hide letters behind a kitschy 70s owl painting; this was cheaper than a stamp, and no one would try to find our letters.

If we mailed our correspondences, Emily and I had two siblings close enough in age who spent their entire childhoods trying not only to read but also hear and record our conversations with a TalkBoy and TalkGirl device. These might have been inspired by the original *Home Alone*, but they didn't work very well. The Owl Picture, though, worked until our aunt was dusting, and a sheet of notebook paper flew out from under the birds like a little leaf from the tree where the owlet and its mom perched.

We had names for everything.

We called Dave *The Old Man and the Sea.*

Once Dave and I started writing to one another, I immediately romanticized those legal pad letters. Boys *loved* Emily, but I didn't get the same attention. Was it because I was queer but didn't have a word for it yet? Was it because I was a little heavier than most girls my age? Was it because I was in love with Dave and just didn't have the heart space for another mediocre guy? I eventually dated a mansplainer named Josh Rutan during my senior year of high school, but I had to break up with him when I could no longer handle his love of Mariah Carey and Destiny's Child that he insisted on blaring from his truck whenever he picked me up to go somewhere.

I didn't feel jealous of Emily.

We had so much more to do than be jealous of one another. We had new Counting Crows' albums to deconstruct. We had new Christopher Pike novels to devour. We had legal pad letters to close read.

Once we graduated high school and went to college, we would leave twenty-minute-long messages on our dorm room answering machines and beg our parents for phone cards so we could call one another. It didn't necessarily matter if we talked or just left the pertinent information on the answering machines.

Green is getting on my nerves, one message she left said. *He's just so…uninspired. He wrote me this letter that just talked about how nice and pretty and sweet I was. Could he not even use a damn thesaurus? Anyway, let me know if you're still down to see Pete Yorn at that festival. I can definitely get you a ticket.*

Oh, the early aughts.

Emily and I still visited one another throughout college. I would put all of my money into gassing up my green Subaru Impreza to hang out in her dorm room for the weekend.

Of course, The Old Man and the Sea eventually washed up onto the campus shore.

I had emailed him once since I had been in college.

It was a lengthy *yeah, I'm fine without you and dating lots of older men* email, which was true. Were those older men always dating me back? Not officially, but things were *going on*, like nights spent together after bottles of wine and Steven Stills records. Dave did return the email, and the only thing I remember him writing was *so you're seeing older men now, huh?*

I took that as a win and felt somewhat vindicated.

But there was still so much unsaid.

We have to find him, Emily said one day in her dorm room at Western Kentucky University.

We booted up Emily's desktop because laptops weren't a thing back then. A simple Google search did not provide much information; we found quite a few people named Dave with his last name, but they were all older than TOMATS, as we abbreviated him.

He is nine years older than I am, so at that time, he would have been around 29. I had heard rumors of girlfriends through comments his family made, but other than that, I knew nothing. His last email address was registered through some generic email provider and not a university or organization.

Emily and I finally find something worth investigating: a concrete contractor in rural Virginia.

We consider this before we take any action. Would he be the type to work in concrete? Who *was* the type to work in concrete? This was the only lead we had, so we went with it.

The problem: I was nervous.

Yet this is how Emily and I worked; whenever one of us faltered, the other one took over. I probably had more *bad ideas* throughout the years—like the time I wrote secret admirer emails to Green so he would be pushed to break up with her—but we would do anything to see that the other got what she deserved.

We deserved the world.

Okay, if we didn't deserve the world, then we at least deserved to be free of boys who didn't know how to use a thesaurus.

I whipped out my phone card like I was making a considerable purchase and handed the plastic to Emily.

She knew what to do.

The phone rang twice before a lady, out of breath, answered.

Allo?

Hi, I was just seeing if Dave was available. I have a concrete job that I would like to get an estimate on.

ALLEN? I could hear the lady yell.

Okay, we did not plan this out very well. If this was actually TOMATS, then what the fuck was she going to say? *Hi, I have Suzanne here, and she has some things she would like to clarify with you?* Should I just pretend to need concrete and feel satisfied we figured out what type of person worked in the concrete industry?

Uh, he's out on a job, the lady said.

Well, I was just wondering if I had the right person. Do you happen to know how old Dave is?

This made no sense, but we were wet with cement and needed to see this through.

For whatever reason, the lady suspected nothing.

ALLEN? How old is Dave?

Emily holds out the phone, so we can both hear the response.

I think he turned 53 last year?

Okay, thank you so much! Emily said before we both burst into a pile of legal pad laughter and confusion.

About seventeen years after that phone call, TOMATS/Dave returns to my life with few texts and three Facebook waves.

Only old people wave on Facebook, I say.

I can't be mad forever.

Maybe I'm still in love.

I'm sure I am.

boone, north carolina

When I return home from Alaska, I immediately notice Pru has lost more weight.

The poor baby looks like a street cat who survives on bits of sardines and mice heads.

While I was gone, Pru also decided to shit and piss in front of a bookshelf, so CK and my patient pet sitter, Ash, started putting down puppy pee pads for her.

CK tells me Pru has *lost her mind*; CK does not believe Pru suddenly hates her litter box or has some kind of issue with it. After all, I have one of those litter boxes that looks like a UFO and self-cleans. The litter box was one of the first purchases I made when I returned home from the hospital. There was no way I could safely clean a cat litterbox, and there was definitely no way in fucking hell I was giving up Pru or Duffles.

Both cats love(d) the litter box because they feel (felt) as if the other one does (did) not use it.

And then Duffles actually gets the entire box to herself because Pru loses her goddamn mind and decides to start shitting in front of T.S. Eliot.

Part of me thinks Pru is smart enough to understand words and wants to shit and piss in front of her namesake.

Besides doing her business in front of my bookshelves, Pru also loves to stand in front of the Lazy Susan in the kitchen and meow for hours.

And hours.

At nothing.

She weighs just over four pounds, but I cannot let her go.

Throughout our fourteen years together, Pru is the only living creature to truly get me. We are both temperamental, and we understand that about one another. She might bite my finger and give me an infection and then lick my face in sorrow seconds later, asking for forgiveness that she knows I will provide without a second thought. Pru has always had a strong personality; what she wants, she gets.

I can identify with this.

At the end of every night, no matter if I choose the futon or the bed, Pru purrs herself into dreams of swatting mice beside my face. When I have insomnia, which I do every night, I pet Pru's head until we both fall asleep.

Although I can feel the sharp pricks of her spine and have to cut off mats in her fur daily, I cannot see past those nights spent together, head-to-head, both of us sick and codependent. I give Pru her hyperthyroidism pills after I take my seizure medication; our routines coincide, and I don't think I will survive glioblastoma without her.

I always hoped I would go first.

Selfish but true.

I can't help myself.

I mull over The Decision for days too long. Weeks too long. Months too long.

I consult all of my friends who have vet office experience. My old derby buddy Wrex, dealing with a cancer diagnosis of her own, warmly tells me *saying goodbye is one of the kindest things we can do*, but I keep pushing forward. Pru continually slumbers by my head at night. She purrs when I touch her ears. She is the first of my babies to greet me at the door when I return home from school.

Mom! Mom! Mom! You were gone for so long! Guess what I did today? I sat in the closet and wrote academic articles about string theory! I started a cult! I catfished a woman on the web out of all her money!

Pru would do all of these.

Pru knows everything: She had seen me beat the shit out of myself when I got a B on a paper in grad school, an old teacher's words looping through my head. *If you get a B on a paper in grad school, that teacher is sending you a reallll strong message that your writing is not good enough.* I never cut, and I dealt with blood often enough that I had no desire to break the skin but seeing purple and red blossom on my forearm like fireworks made me feel as if I was getting the punishment I deserved.

Pru would leave me alone at first but then comfort me once I had settled down.

She still sits on my chest and growls whenever I try to move, and I take this as a sign Pru still needs to be here. She still has enough sass to blame the dog for every single thing that goes wrong. Dropped plate? Pru swats Gatsby. I fall? Gatsby gets a scratch. A noise in the middle of the night? Pru hisses at the poor pup.

But she keeps losing more weight, and the mats in her fur grow like a wet Mogwai. She stops bathing herself. She vomits at least twice a day. When Suzanne writes at the kitchen table, Pru screams at Susan for being so lazy.

I call the vet and the end of November and finally schedule Pru's last moments.

We have a late-afternoon appointment for December 2. Before we go, I sequester the other pets in my bedroom and give Pru and entire can of Tasty Treasures. I give her a whole slice of Swiss cheese. I give her the Christmas present I got her, a little tube of stinky wet deliciousness from Japan that vaguely smells of fish. I give her an entire spoonful of whipped cream cheese, which she devours with noisy licks I will never hear again.

I hate myself for this; I am her equal. I am in no position to schedule her death.

She's so light in the carrier that I have no problem schlepping her to my car without help. Pru can't weigh more than three-and-a-half pounds at this point, and I hate myself for waiting too long. I hate myself for doing this. I hate myself for everything.

She makes no sounds on the very short drive. If I was healthier, I might have walked, so I could spend more time with her. When we arrive, she remains silent; this is so unlike Pru. Since I had her as a tiny kitten, she has done nothing but express herself through meows and purrs.

Pru knows.

She always knows.

We wait for a few moments before Gail and my favorite vet tech, Sarah, take Pru into the exam room. This is the same place where when her hyperthyroidism was first discovered, another tech tried to give her fluids. Once he got the intravenous line in, Pru bit me and dashed off to hide under Gail's desk.

This time is so much different.

Instead of bossy and demanding, Pru stays quiet. I can feel she is fearful; she would prefer to stay in this crate and pass away on her own. Gail and Sarah unscrew the top of the crate, so they do not have to dig Pru out of her safe hole.

When they pick her up and remove the bottom part of the crate, she does not make a sound.

I'm right here, I say, not crying yet. I want Pru to feel loved and not frightened. I pet her head and scratch her chin, just like I do at home. *I'm never going to leave you.*

I think I am more scared than Pru; she is so brave. I signed and dated all the papers. Couldn't they euthanize me with her? Couldn't I sign my own papers and go beside of my one true love?

The short answer is no matter how many times AMo and I discussed it, no, they can't.

I pet her head as the needle slips into her spunky calico fur. Pru has always had little tufts of hair sticking out everywhere; even when she was healthy, she was not a fan of bathing herself and would rather me dunk her in a bathtub once in a while and do the work for her.

I've never seen her so calm, Gail says. *She's ready.*

Sarah doesn't get a third of the scheduled pentobarbital into Pru before I know she's gone.

Pru dies with her eyes open; those double-green peepers turn shiny like sea glass. No one warned me that some animals die with their eyes open. I am not prepared for this, but seeing her sick, old body limp in the cozy pink towel makes me feel better that her spirit has moved on.

I am sure she is a lion now.

Although Pru went within seconds, Gail keeps petting her. This gives me permission to do the same, and I am thankful that Gail, who had accepted Pru in her sassy, discourteous days, is the one to help her say goodbye.

The one to help me say goodbye.

The problem is I am not taking the whole *goodbye thing* as well as Pru.

It's always harder for the ones left behind.

I am not okay. I can't do this. I am not okay I am not okay I am not okay.

I see why they schedule euthanasia appointments for the end of the day.

I'm loud. I'm terrified. I'm screaming.

Hey, hey, hey, Gail tells me. Oh god, I think with guilt, vets also have to be counselors for people like me whose pets are their children. *It's always harder for the special ones, and I know she was your favorite.*

I'm seconds away from screaming again.

Look at this, Gail tells me as she shows me a picture of a shiny, happy dog. *This was my favorite.*

I don't remember the rest of the story but seeing pictures of Gail's special pet does calm me down. I wasn't around when my two cats from childhood were attacked and murdered by a pack of dogs. My parents unfortunately had to deal with that bloody mess. I was sad, of course, but something about not seeing the incident made their deaths feel so far away.

I hold onto the table where Pru died so I can steady myself. I feel like I'm slipping into something familiar, something that happens when I start hearing the word *glioblastoma glioblastoma glioblastoma* on the loop in my head. Everything is dark, scary, and unavoidable. I might have screamed again, but I'm not sure. I just can't understand why she went before me or why we couldn't go together.

I don't think I'll survive much longer without her.

Gail tells me I can pick up the crate later, which I am thankful for; there would be nothing worse than taking home an empty crate. I manage to get into my Scion, alone this time, and I start driving. No one will be looking for me; no one will know where I am or care.

Instead of driving toward Asheville, I head toward Boone. I pass the auto insurance sign that's updated yearly.

The billboard features the face of a kid who was likely a student of one of my colleagues not that long ago. Each year, though, the kid's face looks wearier. This year, he did not even bother to shave the stubble off his face before the portrait.

I always joke with myself that the kid is Insurance Agent Thomas J. Eckleburg, Boone's own version of Doctor T.J. Eckleburg from *The Great Gatsby*. Each year, Thomas J. gets a little more tired of App students fucking up their lives and their cars. Thomas J., who once drank with his buddies before big football games, now has to clean up the messes of those he once was.

At first, he's okay with this.

He still has friends in undergrad and *gets them good deals, man*. But as the years go on, he sees Boone as a wasteland of more student housing and drunk ski tourists who can't drive in the mountain fog. He becomes jaded and wants to move to Florida, but he's a Millennial and could never afford Florida, more or less the actual move. So he just sits for his portrait each year, his smirk shrinking as his stubble grows. He has seen it all, and he is fucking sick of it. Sick of students, sick of tourists, and even sick of townies like me.

Although it's really not an appropriate place to do so, I pull my tiny Scion onto the curb and park under the billboard. Cops frequent this area of Highway 105, but I just don't give a shit. I sit under Thomas J. and cry. I cannot go home; my other pets do not greet me like Pru did, and now Pru is in a freezer at the vet office. I am doing a private cremation, so I can always have her ashes with me. I could drive to JC or Rolli's; they would both not be terribly surprised if I showed up.

Instead, I call my dad.

He, of course, can't understand me. When I finally gasp long and hard and tell him, *I had to put Pru down*, he says, *Your mom told me you were going to do that. I know how hard it is. I've had to say goodbye to so many cats and dogs throughout my life.*

But not like Pru, I demand. *She was different.*

He sighs because he knows I am right.

She was pretty old, you know.

I know.

I settle down a bit and try to breathe. My dad has such a calming presence that this happens naturally. I knew this would happen, and goddammit, that's why I called him. Dad always makes dandelion greens taste like candy and pencils seem magical. I could never wait for him to get home from school and give me all the broken, extra writing utensils his students left behind. He had seen all of his older brothers go off to war and come back hardened and tough. I would say that some came back criminals, but a couple of them already were before they left home. My father has seen so much shit that his face no longer forms expressions. Then I hear my mom burst through the door, and she wants to talk to me.

She's gone, I say. *My baby. She was all I had.*

Although my mom fucking hates cats, she does understand what it feels like to lose a child. It hasn't happened yet, but despite her chainmail of denial that I'm absolutely fine, somewhere inside of her, she knows the truth.

I know, she says, speaking to me like I'm a child again. *I know.*

When we get off the phone, I sit under Thomas J. and cry until I have to open the door to throw up. He stares down at me, perhaps a little judgmentally, and seems to say, *We're all getting older and sicker and tired of this bullshit. You're no different than the rest of us.*

And he's right.

Traffic on 105 tonight is much lighter than I expect. I whip and flip the Scion back on the road and do not have any idea where I might go next.

boone, north carolina

I walk into my rental property's office on a Wednesday afternoon.

I regret everything.

The weather is windy and icy, and I forgot my cane.

The office is tucked into the corner of a plaza like a misplaced postage stamp, and I carefully make my way from the handicapped parking spot to the stone masonry, so I can hold onto something and prevent the wind from blowing me over. This sounds ludicrous, but my palms barely grasp the stone pillar to avoid falling.

What if I did fall?

This is a question I ask myself before I go anywhere.

If I fell in this parking lot, I would not be able to get up, and I would be fucked. Absolutely fucked. I forgot my phone in the car, and I don't have an Apple Watch or anything fancy like that. I refused to get a Life Alert button, and I want to do this all on my own.

However, if I fell in the parking lot, what would happen? Would people see my iconic pink coat and avoid running over me? Would someone realize that no, I actually could not get up on my own and help me?

Fuck.

I have no idea.

This dreadlocked white dude (welcome to Boone!) at the realty office seems to read my anxiety and rushes outside to help me. Despite my judgment of his cultural appropriation, I am thankful for this guy and his assistance.

Since *everything happened*, I have learned to read people better; I can always tell who has had a friend or family member struggle with mobility. They are the first to rush to help, and they don't ask questions.

Once inside, I approach the lovely lady at the desk.

Hi, my name's Suzanne Samples. I live at 9311 in Apt. D. I've been there four years and re-signed my lease for another. Unfortunately, I have terminal cancer, and I'm going back to my parents' house in West Virginia to die. Should I just get a sublease when all of this goes down?

My new dreadlocked friend stands next to another desk and listens to me in awe. Two Yorkie puppies dash around the office, clearly in charge.

Oh, how cute! My sister has a Yorkie! I say.

The Apartment Complex Lady, her red lipstick and pixie cut still fresh at the end of the day, looks at me without blinking.

Yes, she says. *We can just…set up a…sublease.*

Amazing, thanks, that's all I need!

My dreadlocked friend opens the door for me and makes sure I get out to the parking lot without falling and breaking a hip, femur, or wrist.

Everything has been decided for me.

I will miss Boone.

harrisville, west virginia

Christmas in West Virginia is a disaster.

On the six-hour drive to Harrisville from Boone, I have to stop twenty minutes into the trip because my leg feels like it's falling off. I park at an abandoned storefront in Mountain City, Tennessee, to stretch and know that this simple act is foreboding. I keep thinking someone might shoot me or call the cops and tell them I'm trying to break into this place that once sold junk and broken dreams. I peek into the window and see a weird clown; I need to get the hell out of here.

By the time I make it home to West Virginia, Duffles has broken out of her crate. This surprises me; always the good girl and quiet during travel, Duffles has never staged an escape from her temporary prison. Instead, she usually preferred the crate and still liked sleeping in it once I delivered her to wherever we were headed.

And now here we are in my parents' driveway, right next to the road, and Duffles is roaming freely around my tiny Scion. This might have been fine if I was mobile enough to grab her and put her back in the crate, but I am not.

Instead, I see my dad at the door and yell to him that *Duffles escaped in the car.* He does not hear me, but he sees me pick her up under her little paws and walk as fast as I can to the door of the house. Duffles, a solid 18-pound Maine Coon who has *gone viral* more than once in a Facebook group called THIS CAT IS C H O N K Y, should not be lifted by either of us, but here we are. I cannot make it up the tallest steps to my parents' side door, so I hand my dad Duffles. Thankfully, she is scared, so when he drops her, she runs straight back to my childhood bedroom and waits by the door.

Duffles is a gentle giant.

Look, here's the thing. I do not know why my parents never built standard steps to the side door of their doublewide. I do not know why they use the side door instead of the front door, except it's closer to the driveway. I do not understand why they just cobbled together a bunch of cinderblocks instead of making a safe entrance. The cinderblocks, like a mouth full of old teeth, are loose and dangerous. They could have at least tried to do something else with these once my dad fell ill with Lyme Disease and Parkinson's, but nope: Each time my dad came home, he had to hope for the best as he climbed that rickety, rotting mouth.

My parents are moving, I tell myself. I am moving with them. Things will improve.

I hope things will improve.

Because my mom is still at work, my dad has to help me up these teeth steps. The problem is he is not strong enough to pull me up the concrete stairs,[19] and I am not strong enough to make it on my own. He wants to do his best and claims *he's got me*, but he drops me onto the ledge, tearing my pants and skinning both my knees.

At least Duffles did not escape.

I crawl to the couch and know my knees will look like a watercolor in the morning. However, I do not have another choice. I inch across that 25-year-old carpet and perch my elbows on the couch. I have found this is an easier way for me to get up rather than using my arms.

But I need to rest.

I know my dad feels embarrassed, but he shouldn't. Although I can see he is in better shape than I am, neither of us is doing very well.

Are you going to be able to get up? he asks me.

I just need another second, I tell him. I need a lot more seconds. I need minutes, I need hours. Gatsby, who is a very good girl, followed me inside and began drinking all of Princess Peppermint's water.

Princess Peppermint hisses at us all.

She hates everything and everyone but my dad.

---

[19] At this point, I kind of wish I had the number for the Dave who works in concrete. What kind of people work in concrete again?

I totally understand this.

By the time I've hoisted myself onto the couch, my mom comes through the door. My dad and I sit and watch Discovery ID as if nothing happened. Duffles remains secured in my bedroom (far from her nemesis Princess Peppermint), and Gatsby lounges with my dad on the couch. Gatsby looks at my dad as if he is Saint Roch, the Patron Saint of Dogs. She stares at him with hearts in her eyes and complete trust in her soul. She's met my dad only a handful of times, but he seems to have that effect on all creatures.

You know how I feel about dogs on the couch, my mom says. She's holding dinner from The Pizza House, or what I have started to call The Ritchie County Country Club. My dad goes to get a sheet for Gatsby so they can continue their snuggle session on the sofa. He acts annoyed, but I can tell he loves it.

Discovery ID keeps playing the song "Scarborough Fair" as they show scenes of coworkers shooting each other up, and wives stabbing their husbands in the back.

This will become the soundtrack for my month-long visit home.

I am fussy at dinner; I can't really eat, and nothing tastes right. Mom brought me my favorite food from The Ritchie County Country Club—a grilled chicken salad—but I sneak my chicken to Gatsby and Princess Peppermint under the table. If there's one thing those two can agree on, it's chicken.

When I tell my parents I'm going to bed, Saint Roch looks at me as if I just announced I'm running for president. My dad is—or he was—always the first to go to bed, but my life is different now.

I am older than both of my parents.

I am exhausted from the drive, and I want to cuddle with Duffles in my old bedroom, which now boasts pictures of my mom and her *Cozumel Girls* with an IT IS WELL WITH MY SOUL sign instead of my Beatles and Jimi Hendrix posters.

But whatever.

I still have the green carpet she let me pick out.

I fall asleep around nine, but I wake when dizziness and nausea simultaneously attack my body. Although the bathroom is right next to my bedroom, I'm not sure if I will make it before vomiting all over the floor. Sure, my parents have sold the doublewide, but I don't want to soil the carpet and make things more difficult for the next owners.

This, perhaps, might be the most complicated part of having *mobility issues*. I take a long time to get up from my bed, and there is absolutely no guarantee I'll make it to the bathroom in time before I vomit.

I do, but barely.

Puke sprays from the fountain of my mouth: Bile stains the wall, the top of the toilet, and the shower curtain. I can't stop. I keep projectile vomiting until the small room looks like a scene from *The Exorcist*. I don't have time to stop and wonder what might be wrong with me, but I keep wondering why no one comes to help.

My mom, preferably.

Love my dad, but he is kind of useless in these situations.

I'm alone and can't get up to make my way to the living room, where my mom sleeps. My parents have a great marriage, but they do not sleep in the same bed. I totally get that; I don't want anyone in my sleeping space either, except cats. Their bedroom and living room are on the other side of the house, and I have no plastic bags or trashcans to carry with me when I start puking again. It is hopeless for me to get up and get help.

I keep flushing each vomit, and then everything turns fluorescent yellow.

My insides, the toilet, my head, and the wallpaper.

Am I in a Charlotte Perkins Gilman story? I wonder. I always loved her in undergrad and didn't mind a bit when I had to read "The Yellow

Wallpaper" for nearly every single class. I remember people in my class (non-English majors, obv) complaining about the story and saying things like, *But why does she crawl around on her hands and needs at the end of the story? No one does that.*

Why *wouldn't she do that?*, I challenge them.

Now here I was, crawling around my own bathroom where nothing was actually yellow, but everything had turned a bright shade of mustard. What the fuck was wrong with me? It had to be the new seizure medication I was taking. I just started taking it yesterday, so I must be having some reaction. I don't have any time to think more about this, though, because I start vomiting all over again. I don't even try to clean up after myself anymore; it's just going to keep purging out of me like an angry demon.

I sleep on the bathroom floor that night. I'm pretty sure there is black mold in the shower. Whatever. We're getting out of here soon enough.

I rest for another hour before I start puking again. I have no nausea medication and am in the middle of nowhere. I roll to the bathroom counter so I can attempt to pull myself up. I could yell for my mom or dad, but they won't hear me. I do not have my phone.

I do not have anything.

I finally yank myself from the carpet by grabbing onto the sink. I consider that the entire thing might fall out, but I don't care.

I make it to my bedroom and find my phone.

Does anyone in Ritchie County have some prescription anti-nausea medication? Not doing well.

I then walk out into the kitchen, slowly and carefully. I sit down at the table and tell my parents I need help. They are unfazed; my family is now no stranger to medical emergencies. At this point, my phone is my only hope.

"I thought I heard you getting sick last night," my dad nonchalantly says as he reads *The Ritchie Gazette*. "Wondered if you were okay."

"What is wrong with you both?" I ask, but neither one of them answers.

Within minutes a few people have responded to my post.

Can you meet me at the Ellenboro McDonald's? a sweet girl I know from high school asks. I have not spoken to her in probably 20 years, but that's the fantastic thing about small towns like Harrisville: If you're from there, you're always from there. Even if you talked some trash about your neighbor's church dress last Sunday, she'd still meet you somewhere in town to give you some clothes because the meth trailer beside you exploded and burned down your house.

They are always there.

The kind people and the meth trailers.

I ask my dad if he will meet my friend in the McDonald's parking lot to get me the Zofran. I take down the post so no one gets in trouble. What a lovely friend, I think, as my dad drives the five miles to meet her.

As my mom says, I *give my dad purpose.*

What's wrong? my mom finally asks. She's still in her nightgown and has an eyelash curler attached to her face. I explain to her, as I hold a yellow Dollar Store bag below my mouth, I've been vomiting all night and can't keep anything down, not even water. The nearest hospital is an hour away, so that is not an option right now. It's also three days before Christmas, and I'll be damned if I spend another fucking Christmas in the hospital.

Where did your dad go? she asks as I vomit into my bag. *Gross.*

I tell her he went to go do a drug deal in the Ellenboro McDonald's parking lot. She doesn't answer me but tells me she will get me some Sprite on her way home from work. It's her day to go to the pharmacy for her and my dad's medications anyway, and she needs to get some gifts for some children she's sponsoring for Christmas.

*

By the time Sarah and Blaze Danger arrive, I am still sick but not as much. The McDonald's drug deal went well, and I am on the mend.

But once Blaze Danger and Sarah enter the house, everything explodes. This is our own meth trailer of noise and confusion. Sarah's little circus dogs start running around on top of our straight-out-of-the1990s couch, and my mom can't stop them. My mom doesn't like to touch animals, so the only way to move Jared and Claire is if someone else picks them up. I'm not accustomed to seeing my mom give up, but I recognize the look in her eyes as Claire, the eight-pounder, dances across the top of the couch like it's her own personal high wire.

Meanwhile, Jared, the four-pounder, frenetically runs across the couch like a little circus clown. Gatsby is happy to have friends arrive, but she knows and abides by the rules: You can't be on the couch without a blanket. Gatsby might push those rules a little by sticking her front paws on the fabric, but she does her best. However, she either can't hide her excitement or wants to claim her territory and pees on the living room floor as soon as she sees her little cousins.

Claire and Jared have never lived by rules.

My mom, who has Christmas Eve off, is in the kitchen making stromboli, Sarah's favorite food. "Scarborough Fair" plays in the background on Discovery ID, which my dad and I haven't changed since I got here three days ago. We have watched *Forensic Files*. We have watched *Snapped*. We spent three hours yesterday watching a car chase that ended up being curtailed by a tractor in a field. *What an ending*, my dad remarked.

We have heard "Scarborough Fair" at least fifty times.

And Blaze Danger and his size 22 red Chuck Taylors have arrived to spice up the Christmas peace and quiet.

My family does not make noise. Sure, we talk, but we are all mouse-like and polite. We respect each other's space. We don't pick food off each other's plates. We don't push or scream. If we have a question, we don't interrupt. Although Sarah's life is undoubtedly wilder and more boisterous than everyone else's, she's still a Samples. Only speak when you have something important to say. Mind your own business. Only make unnecessary noise if you're going to be terribly funny.

Blaze Danger did not grow up like this.

Maybe Sarah did not tell him, or perhaps she is performing an experiment.

It's hard to say.

I can picture Discovery ID featuring a story about Sarah and Blaze Danger. At this point, I am not sure if he and Sarah are dating, but well, she brought him home for Christmas. When they were for sure dating, Sarah broke up with him. I had not yet met him, but I assumed he was just another casualty in Sarah's tumultuous dating life. Why did they break up? I asked her. *Because he said I did not bleach my butthole enough. So, when he told me that, I pulled down my pants and underwear to show the security guards who stood outside. I said, DOES MY ASSHOLE LOOK BLEACHED ENOUGH TO YOU ALL BECAUSE THIS GUY HAS A DIFFERENT OPINION. They laughed and said my butthole looked terrific. Then I had a guy over from Tinder the next day, and Blaze Danger tried to get in the building so he could beat the guy's ass.*

Of course, I had to ask.

How did Blaze Danger get in?

He ordered Chinese food for everyone in the building so he could sneak in when the delivery guy got here.

What the fuck? Why wouldn't he just order Chinese food for one person in the building?

I guess he wanted to make sure that someone was home and would buzz the guy in.

What happened when he got in?

He tried to open the door, and I told him it wasn't a good time. The guy I was with came out, and they went at it.

What happened to the other guy?
Never heard from him again.

Are you going to Scarborough Fair? Parsley, sage, rosemary, and thyme. Remember me to one who met Blaze Danger, for he was once a true love of mine.

Blaze Danger tries to shove some sort of white chocolate truffle into my mom's face as she finishes the stromboli. I guess Sarah forgot to tell him about my mom's dietary restrictions. He offers some to my dad, who looks as if he's watching an absolute apocalypse happen in front of him. My dad's brown eyes, the same color as mine, do not blink. Blaze Danger finally makes his way to me with the truffles, and I decline because I'm still not able to handle anything but Sprite and the parade of tiny dogs on my lap. (Which, of course, I do not mind. I love the dogs and don't care what animals jump up on the couch that my parents are going to get rid of in a few months anyway. My only complaint is that the dogs need more outfits.)

Sarah puts the truffles on the table. I will eat most of them when I feel better and damn, they are good.

But Blaze Danger isn't done.

Now he has golden Donald Trump coins to give the Samples family. I'm so confused.

You have a sense of humor, right? Blaze Danger asks me as he hands me the coin.

I don't answer. I feel as if only people without a sense of humor would respond yes to this question. It's the same on dating profiles. If they say they *have a great sense of humor,* they are usually as dull as a freshman research paper about marijuana legalization.

I take the coin and toss it into my Kavu bag; I want to see how the rest of this goes down.

Next, Blaze Danger tries my dad. I have to admire his chutzpah; Blaze Danger lets nothing deter him from offering the bizarre gifts. He is an unwise man, and we are all baffled babies in a manger. My dad mutters a confused *thanks*, and my mom simply says *you can just put it on the table*. She's making stromboli and doesn't have time for truffles and Donald Trump coins.

Claire, Jared, and Blaze Danger follow Sarah to the backend of the house. Gatsby senses strife and stays with me and her grandparents. I hear Sarah give Blaze Danger the grand tour of the doublewide, and I finally realize why Sarah booked Blaze Danger a room at North Bend State Park instead of letting him stay at the house.

I can actually hear my dad roll his eyes as the four of them make their way back to the living room.

Sarah must also hear him because she announces she and Blaze Danger are going to North Bend to get him settled in. Sarah asks if she can take my car so she can drive back alone. After her driving me back-and-forth to radiation, I am skeptical, but I do want her to return to our house, so I give in.

If you hit a deer, you owe me $500, I tell her.

That must be your deductible, my mom adds as she stuffs some sausage into bread and cheese.

When I was in New York and had to listen to Blaze Danger's diatribe about how he was going to marry my sister, I sat at the table in Jimmy's Corner just like my dad sits at our kitchen table now. I did not blink or move as Blaze Danger explained to me how he and *Sarah Rachel Samples* were going to walk down the aisle to Savage Garden's "Truly, Madly, Deeply." He went on and on about how much he loved her and would never hurt her, and I guess just expected me to forget about the whole bleached butthole incident. Sarah and Blaze Danger made me take a picture with Jimmy[20] (who has some close connection to Muhammad Ali) that night, and we both proudly displayed our canes in the photo.

---

[20] Rest in Peace, Jimmy. COVID-19 got a good one.

You know what he's thinking? Sarah asks me as she zooms in on Jimmy's eyes. *I just met a bitch with a cane!*

They leave the dogs when they go to North Bend.

I remember Sarah telling me while I was in New York that Blaze Danger was coming home with her for Christmas, even if they weren't really dating or doing anything at all. I asked him if he felt comfortable driving on curvy roads with deer, and he laughed in my face. *I'm from Wisconsin*, he said, as if that meant something.

Sarah returns about two hours later without Blaze Danger. She tells me he drove to North Bend at the approximate speed of seven-miles-per-hour and stopped for at least twenty seconds whenever he saw a deer in the distance.

I thought he was from Wisconsin? I say, and she rolls her eyes.

I know then she tried to warn him like I did.

Something bad happened when we were there, she tells me. *We decided to jump on the beds like we were kids. Blaze Danger stuck his leg out and punched a hole in the wall with his massive foot. We put the fire escape route sign over it and are just hoping no one notices.*

My mom yelps from her bedroom.

Girls!

I haven't moved from the couch, so I know I didn't do anything. My mom knows where everything in her home is located. She can tell if anything anywhere has been touched or moved a single centimeter. She knew I used her hairbrush the other day, and I thought for sure I put the brush in the exact spot where I found it.

An animal did something in here. In my bedroom. One of your animals.

I know Gatsby, the prized grandchild, did *not* do anything. Yes, she did pee a little when Jared and Claire first got here, but I got that cleaned up as soon as it happened. Plus, my dad has been increasing the times he takes *Gats* out, so neither of them gets bored. On day one, he took her out twice. Day two, three times. Today? Four, all before I woke up.

Circumstantial evidence, my mom says, *shows Jared committed the crime.*

Too much Discovery ID.

Sarah's dogs do whatever the fuck they want. Their piss is infinitesimal, and their shit is gravel-sized; they might as well be mice destroying her $2500 a month Brooklyn apartment.

Jared does not get in trouble. How could he? He is wearing a Santa Claus suit and barely weighs four pounds. Sarah cleans up the poo, and Dad, always the helper, sprays some disinfectant.

Who knows where else Jared has performed his business in the doublewide.

I ask Sarah what Blaze Danger is doing in the afternoon, and she says he is watching movies.

He loves movies, she says. *That's all he does. Downloads movies and gives them to me. Are you dating him?* I ask.

No, she says. *I'm not dating him, but we did bring matching sweaters for Christmas day. The sweaters have holiday shrimp on them, and there is a pouch on the front for actual shrimp that is leftover from dinner!* Later, when we have Christmas dinner at North Bend State Park, Sarah and Blaze Danger wear the shrimp sweaters, and a former teacher approaches our table to talk to us. *Now, you don't know this because you married into the family*, she says as she points to Blaze Danger, *but…* I have no idea what she says next because I can't stop watching Blaze Danger's beaming face. You can't bring home a male friend to Harrisville for Christmas and wear matching sweaters to dinner. You just can't do that. *My favorite vegetable is popcorn*, he says, and I want to be tucked into a shrimp sweater and disappear.

I've had innumerable talks with my sister about using men. Do they deserve to be used for rides home at Christmas, alcohol, money, and whatever else? Sure, some of them. But this has been her pattern for so long that I am concerned. Boys drop everything for her. They fall in love. Then she tosses them away like a used holiday shrimp napkin.

So, what does Blaze Danger think is happening? I ask.

I ask because Blaze Danger has already given the entire family truffles and golden Donald Trump coins. I suspect he has more presents in his car for all of us, which worries me. He drove Sarah all the way to Harrisville, West Virginia, and now he is sitting in a lodge room with a hole in the wall at North Bend State Park. This would not be fun for anyone.

I don't know, she says. *I think I've told him we aren't dating.*

You think you've told him?

I mean, he gets it.

I don't think he gets it at all, I say. *From the texts he sends me, he thinks you are getting married and walking down the aisle to Savage Garden's "Truly, Madly, Deeply."*

It's a joke, she says.

Well, I would certainly hope the song is a joke, but I'm pretty sure he thinks he's walking you down the aisle, or i-s-l-e, as he spells it.

He can think that all he wants, she says before she takes her adorable circus animals outside so she can smoke. Everyone knows that Sarah smokes, but no one talks about it. If I smoked anywhere within 1,000 feet of my parents' house, they would tie me to the carpet and let Princess Peppermint maul me to death. But Sarah? She can do whatever she wants.

She always has.

I don't know why she even attempts to slather on Bath and Body Works hand sanitizer before she walks back in the door.

Where is your sister? Did she go back to North Bend already? my dad asks.

She's walking the dogs, I say.

I play my part in the charade too, I guess.

I can smell the cinnamon apple hand sanitizer before she walks through the door.

boone, north carolina

I can't stop myself from talking to Dave.

When he texted me while I was going through radiation, I was mad. I was angry. I was not ready to talk to him. It had been 20 years since I'd last heard from him, and now I was fighting for my life.

I didn't think I would survive.

I sat in the Hawthorne Hotel with my loyal cats for a month, Ubering to radiation, and writing all afternoon.

I did have a few visitors: Jenna, Feeney, and Nodya, but there's only so much energy I had to entertain others in a hotel room. They understood this, of course, but I always went back to the day in the hospital after I accepted the reality that yes, I did have brain cancer, and yes, I was going to need to have at least 33 days of radiation in Winston-Salem.

One of the first things I did was try to set up a driving schedule for the people who said *they would do anything they could to help.*

I sent out a group text and tried to be as careful as I could. I read about people on the internet whose friends drove them to radiation; of course, no one could do it every single day, but at that point, I had plenty of friends with various schedules in the local area who could volunteer for different days. If everyone just did one day, I could even stay in a hotel for a couple nights if necessary.

Hey! I wrote. *I have to have radiation for 33 days, and it has to be in Winston-Salem. I would like to create a driving schedule so that people can help where I need it the most. I don't have the money to stay in a hotel for an entire month. My sister is even going to be here for some of those days, so it should be easy enough to set something up. I'm not saying that the same person needs to drive me all the time, but whenever people have weekdays off, can we figure something out?*

Here's the only response I got, from Lori, the Queen Bitch of the friend group: *Uh, something isn't right here. The hospital should set something up for you.*

There was no one setting up anything for me.

I had a social worker, and she tried her best. But she was the only social worker in the unit, and she had a shitload of arrangements to make for a whole floor of people. Her face drooped a little further each day I saw her, and I feared she might need medical help herself. *Oh, just ask the hospital's social worker!* is a default answer, sure. But what if the social worker is trying to get Bill from room twelve his Medicaid card he should have gotten years ago but never did the paperwork? What if the social worker is trying to figure out what nursing home Larry needs to go to after his release? What if getting the 36-year-old rides from Boone to Winston-Salem for radiation just isn't a priority for the social worker?

I can help with anything! Just let me know!

What if I let you know that you're a fucking liar, and you don't mean anything you say?

I think this was the beginning of my friends in Boone ignoring me for a good time. No one stepped up to the radiation call except for my sister, and she was in fucking New York. JC and Dollfin did take me to a couple early appointments, but the word RADIATION seemed to scare everyone away. Did they think they were somehow going to get exposed just by sitting in the waiting room? Hell, Sarah sat in my car and chain-smoked the whole time, and that was totally fine. No one was getting hurt.

But all those days when people had time off? Seemingly not enough time off to drive me to radiation. I'm sure Skully would have, but she lived too far from me at the time. It might sound like I was selfish and expecting a lot, but I guarantee I would have driven any friend to radiation on Tuesdays and Thursdays when I didn't teach.

Motherfuckers.

But back to Dave.

It's not surprising to me that I started talking to Dave again. He showed up and was there for me. He started listening when no one else did or would. He asked how I was doing on days when I didn't hear from anyone else.

We also have unfinished business.

Maybe I am living in a fantasy, but I start imagining what my life would look like with him. I had loved him for so long; when I heard through my mom, who heard through his sister, that he was married and expecting a baby, I was in college and single. The news devastated me, so I started dating outrageously incompatible people in rebellion. If Dave was married and starting a new life with someone, then what was I supposed to do?

I dated people I could not love back.

This is the thing about love; it's not reasonable, and you can't help it. You hurt people, but hopefully, you do it in the gentlest way possible.

The problem is that no matter how gentle and kind I try to be, my words come out like flaming asteroids. I've tried to stop this. I've tried to be better. However, I've come to understand that maybe I'm just not the type to speak softly and carry a big fucking stick. It's just not me.

But why mess with brutal honesty? Yes, it can hurt. Yes, it can illuminate terrible things about anyone involved. Brutal honesty, though, gets everything out without leaving any lingering questions. Everyone I've broken up with has known how I felt about them before the actual breakup happened.

I can't help my feelings, but I also cannot help the feelings of others.

I tell CK as soon as I start talking to Dave.

I have to. I can't hide this from her. I know I will hurt her, but I value honesty more than hiding shit. Dave and I are just catching up, but because I have had feelings for him in the past and I'm not sure how I feel now, I know I have to tell her.

Because everything I write seems to make someone mad, I'm sure she will say I was hiding shit, but here's the problem: When I tried to tell her about things with Dave, she shut me up and said she didn't want to hear about it. So that left me stunted and unable to give her the complete honesty she deserved.

The other thing: Because I have already outlived my prognosis, I've decided to do anything I possibly can to make myself happy. Nobody except family members and a few friends seemed to care if I was happy or not during and after my diagnosis and treatment. It was all about them and how they felt.

So, who could blame me now for wanting to feel happy?

I finally decided to say *FUCK IT* and say whatever I needed to say to people. Live my life the way I wanted to. Was I having psychotic breaks from reality? Yes. Was I refusing to leave my apartment for weeks at a time because I did not want to experience the outside world? Yes. Was I avoiding texting my mom because she stresses me out when she won't stop talking about her swollen ankles and high blood pressure? Yes.

But I finally deserved to be happy.

I lived my entire life trying to please other people. Did this work for you? Great. Were you happy with this outcome, even if I wasn't? Super! Did you feel you got everything you needed from this experience we just had? Awesome!

Maybe people didn't like my new terms, but maybe I did not care.

Dave still loved me, I think, and I was still that 16-year-old girl, staring out my family's sliding glass door the day before Christmas to see if his truck had pulled into his parents' house yet. Once he moved, Christmas was the only time I got to see him, and I looked forward to it all year.

Was it maybe a little weird for both of us?

Yes.

Was it maybe something I shouldn't have indulged in?

Yes.

Was he maybe my soulmate?

I needed to find out.

I should have allowed Dave to see me the first time he asked, when I was in the middle of radiation. He would have probably saved me from a lot of loneliness, but I just wasn't ready. I didn't know if I was going to live or die, and at the time, everything seemed pretty black-and-white. Now there are plenty of gray areas, and I am trying to navigate those gray areas like an astronaut in a solar storm with a cancer albatross around my neck.

I really think people should give me more credit.

Yes, I loved CK, really just as a friend, but the *thing* with Dave was something she could not understand. I feel terrible about this, but it is a situation I can't stop from happening. I have to take this chance, and I have to take it now.

I would not cheat on her, but I have to end this before I get to know this Dave.

Present Dave.

I never stopped wondering about him. I always hoped I would run into him someday; maybe like in a movie, he would see a poster for a book signing I was doing and magically show up.

I mean, sure, I looked him up on social media instead, but maybe this was better. I could ease into it instead of being shocked. I could take my time getting to know him again and see what happened.

He loves me.

It's the kind of love that stays with you for over twenty years, for over a lifetime.

I need him, and I can't help it.

He loves me.

He really does.

I hope.

boone, north carolina

My dog goes feral when the UPS driver leaves an Amazon envelope on my step. Although the weather has cooled, I have been leaving my door open to let in some sunlight. Isn't sunlight supposed to help with depression? With expressions of despair? With feeling low and *bummed out*?

I did not order anything from Amazon because I am poor. When I was in the hospital and first diagnosed with the tumor and aggressive brain cancer, people sent money. Lots of money. Sadly, after purchasing a hospital-style bed, tires, a litter box, a shower chair, a wheelchair, some chemo, and 33 days of radiation, all that money was gone.

Forever.

Unlike many glioblastoma patients,[21] I valiantly returned to work, but I still lived that paycheck-to-paycheck life, much like everyone else I knew. As a Xennial, I did not have a chance at saving money. Even with a good job and a cheap apartment, I could barely afford the insulin needed for my diabetes and the seizure pills necessary to keep my right leg and arm from constantly trembling and freezing into paralysis again.

My right arm and leg still convulse, though, so I definitely wonder just what, exactly, I am paying for and popping into my mouth twice a day.

The seizure meds manage to rot out one tooth and create four other cavities, so there is that. Or maybe it was the radiation? All except for one of the cavities were on the side of my head where the tumor lived, so who knows.

I finally get up from my futon to grab the package at the front door.

It's a bag of dog treats and a book of essays called *The Rib Joint: A Memoir in Essays* by Julia Koets. I don't need to look at the receipt to see who the present is from, but I do anyway.

---

[21] I am not suggesting I am better than anyone else who has glioblastoma. Rather, I am suggesting I am lucky I had the opportunity to return to work.

FOR YOU AND GATBSSBY.

JC and Miriam, the dog.

I smile and feel remembered.

This is not a friendship I imagined lasting, but I'm so glad it did.

I don't really see anyone but CK anymore; I have become more and more of a hermit. It's not that I refuse to leave my apartment, but I started teaching online this semester and have no reason to go anywhere. The miles I once put on my car sit untallied in the driveway. I no longer have to get oil changes. I go to meetings at school, and every once in a while, I go to Chris' for a *weekend retreat*. This actually doesn't happen on weekends most of the time, but I go to get a change of scenery. Her backyard looks like a national park, and I feel safe with her. She and CK, who share the same birthday, had become close recently and even spent New Year's Eve together when I was with my parents.

Little did I know that I was actually setting up a friendship that would eventually leave me behind. I was just trying to *do the right thing*. CK got jealous, and I thought if they spent more time together, we could all be friends.[22]

Evenings once filled with derby practice and drinks at The Cardinal have morphed into a strict schedule of waking up around noon, writing, grading, physical therapy exercises, dinner by 5:30, and back to bed at 6. All of this occurs to the soundtrack of constant anxiety about *when I'm going to die* and *if I will make it home in time*.

Home as in West Virginia.

I do not want my parents to build this *generational suite* only to have the apartment remain empty throughout my parents' final years.

CK comes over when she can and does her best to keep me happy. It's hard, though, dating someone who has all the things I once had: derby, a social life, goals, and dreams. I do not resent her, but I wish I

---

[22] It turns out the old saying is true: Two's company, three's a crowd. I became the crowd.

still entertained those intangible, amorphous activities I once took so much for granted.

I don't really have any goals or dreams anymore, but I am writing again, feverishly, and can't stop.

I collect Pru's ashes at Gail's office and make a shrine to her in my living room. Gail writes me a beautiful card that expresses how, more than anything, she could tell that *Pru knew it was her time to go.* I put the card in the typewriter and set the box of ashes beside the heirloom. I surround the ashes with some crystals Chris gave me; I don't honestly know what she's talking about, but she says she *programmed the crystals for healing.* CK buys tiny flowers each week that we put around the box of ashes like a crown.

I'll never get over this.

I was supposed to go first.

She was never *just a cat.*

Pru was my equal and never failed to remind me.

Hey, I message JC. *Let's get together soon. I miss you.*

harrisville, west virginia

Blaze Danger buys me all kinds of Christmas presents.

I feel terrible because I bought him nothing, but Sarah says it's okay.

Last night, they went to City Perk, the local gambling joint cleverly disguised as a coffee shop. Sarah won a couple hundred bucks, and Blaze Danger lost the same. They returned smelling like smoke and the 1980s.

Merry Christmas.

boone, north carolina

CK has tried to silence my writing for months now.

Whenever she does something that might make her seem unfavorable, she threatens if I write about it, she will break up with me.

I write a short story called "Mercury Is in Mayonnaise," where I discuss how she trashed my cousin Kyle's house after a drunken rage. Then, when I thought I was safe back at my own apartment, she showed up at 3:30 in the morning, blazed off her ass, threatening me, and destroying anything that got in her path. I needed to sleep and get up for work the next day, but she was stumbling all over my apartment floor, trying to read a letter she wrote about how she was *terrified of me*.

Confused, especially because I had done absolutely nothing to *terrify* her (we had never even had a fight where we yelled at one another at that point), I tried to get her to sleep on my futon or my bed, but she would have none of it.

I was scared and helpless.

I couldn't even walk, and I had a person stronger than me falling all over herself and smelling stronger than the brewery where she worked.

I finally convinced her to get into my car, and when I was driving her back to her apartment, she attempted to exit the vehicle multiple times. I quickly locked the doors. After pulling into a parking lot, she tossed her own keys into a wooded area and disappeared into the night.

Trying to keep her safe didn't work. Trying to keep me safe didn't work.

It just wasn't working.

I contact Dollfin because I don't know what else to do. We discover CK called the police on herself that night and checked herself into a psychiatric ward. I'm glad she's keeping herself safe and getting help, but I don't feel like it's a good idea for me to be involved. Plus, I barely have the energy to care for myself.

I don't tell a soul.

Later when she's released, she's furious with me for not contacting her on her burner phone. I don't know what happened to her actual phone, and why I should have the number to the burner phone. This entire snafu is my fault, and how could I not contact her while she was sick in the psych ward?

I have never felt more manipulated.

Somehow, she convinces me to get back together.

I mean, she's 24. I get it. Sort of. I also wish she understood that I am much smaller than her and can't control her when she gets rowdy and violent. Because of my disabilities, I am at a constant disadvantage. I can't hold anything up with my right arm or steady myself with my right leg.

I can't hit back.

I can't fight.

I just have to sit and hope nothing worse happens next.

But I have my words, or I think I do. I write that story about that night, and I send it out for publication. I know it's good. I leave out some super personal parts I know would upset her. The story immediately gets picked up by a cool literary journal. I also submit the story to the West Virginia Writers annual contest, which is an event dear to my heart. I've always placed but never won.

This year, I win.

I never show CK the story. I know it would make her mad, even if I did leave some parts out.

Because I didn't show her, she went through my phone when I was sleeping and opened my email until she found the story. She read the whole thing and when I woke up said, *Is there something you want to tell me?* I had no idea what the fuck she was talking about, so I told her no, I did not have anything I wanted to tell her. I was truly boggled, because at that point in our relationship, everything was good. I had not reconnected with Dave yet. The drunken rage and psych ward were months behind us. I had written the story ages ago and forgotten about it. We had our issues, but CK was much better than Chole, so I considered myself lucky.

You mean you don't want to tell me about Jesse?

Jesse? I thought to myself. What about Jesse? Jesse was a girl I matched with on Tinder after my diagnosis, way before CK and I got together, and met once. Sure, we liked each other, but it was more of a friend connection. I had no romantic interest in Jesse at all, and there was nothing in my phone that would prove otherwise.

I, uh, texted her yesterday about a Netflix show. There's nothing...

I guess I believe you, CK said as she pretended to do laundry. CK does more laundry than anyone I know. Sure, she does my laundry, but I never leave the house, which means I wear approximately six items of clothing per week. I could get away with doing my laundry once a month, but CK seems to do hers every day. She wears my underwear, which I find gross. She has zero boundaries and does not respect mine. She doesn't understand why I worry about being a good person. She also leaves comet trails of socks and sports bras around my apartment, which I can't stand.

Everything has its own space.

That's the way it should be.

This is my only sanctuary.

I'm super confused about why Jesse would make her mad.

Are you sure there isn't anything else you want to tell me? she asks.

No, I say, completely sure of myself.

I spend most of the day feeling as if I'm living in a different galaxy. The Millennials I know love to accuse people of gaslighting them, but when they gaslight other people? I guess that's perfectly fine.

I don't know until days later: She is furious with me about the story. A story about her actions that put me in danger. I'm a writer, I try to tell her. That's what I do with everything. But as it turns out, I'm an excellent writer, so I share the things I write with the world. And you know what? The world likes it. They love it. They want to know what I'm doing next.

This doesn't work for CK.

You know that story was hurtful, so why do you want to hurt me? Why do you want to make everything worse?

I explain to her that the story was not meant to hurt her. I had, or at least I thought I had, left out enough so no one would know I was referring to her. The point was I had entered the story in one fucking contest, and one literary journal that actually never got off the ground. So, basically, three—four—people had read the story: CK, the contest director, the contest judge, and a person who started a lit journal that folded before anything was published.

I do not understand why she is mad.

I never posted the story online.

I never showed the story to her current derby teammates and my former teammates; I never told any of them what happened because I didn't want to make her look bad or tarnish her place on the team.

If I did find a place to publish it, only about three people would read it anyway.[23]

I'm not making anything worse. I'm expressing myself. You have to know that when you date a writer, they are going to write about you. That's just…how it works. I'm a creative person. And only three, four counting you, people read it.

She wants to know why I didn't put my thoughts in a journal or something. (Which, likely, she would have read the journal and still been mad, so this doesn't matter.) Why couldn't I just process everything like everyone else?

---

[23] After the first draft of this manuscript failed to merit publication, the story won the 2020 Prime Number Magazine Award for Short Fiction, sponsored by Press 53 in…Winston-Salem. The Dash! "Mercury Is in Mayonnaise" can now be read on their website at https://www.press53.com/issue-181-pnm-award-for-short-fiction#Samples.

Because I'm a fucking artist, I tell her. *Because my work fucking matters.*

CK wants to know if I love writing more than I love her.

Yes, unequivocally, I tell her.

She hates this answer, but I am truthful. I have been writing short fiction since second grade. Writing is not just a way for me to process my feelings; it is a method for me to share the madness we all collectively face, not just me. I feel like people need my writing. They need to laugh. They need to cry. They need to experience all of this with me.

I wouldn't care if you got mad at me and painted a giant mural in Boone that says I HATE SUZANNE. I would actually be honored. I wouldn't care if you went to my sister in Brooklyn and had her shave the words SUZANNE IS A CUNT into your hairstyle. It's a means of not only expression but also connection.

That's different, and you know it, she says.

But I don't think it's different, and I don't know it.

We will stay together after this, a little while anyway, but her attitude toward art will always bother me. Art does not come from the mundane; art does not come from the ticks of a clock or the fuzz on the side of a vent, unless you are Virginia Woolf or something.

Art comes from pain, madness, and anger.

Destroying yourself makes art.

I mean, what did she think I was going to do?

Make some candles or something?

That's just not my style.

Before we *break up for good*, we get into a fight one morning. She starts unplugging shit, throwing items onto the floor with gusto, and slamming things around. I wake up and am already mad at the way she is acting. We yell at each other, and I try to stand up, but I am shaking and unsteady. I am attempting to get the hurdy-gurdy music box she gave me for Christmas and throw it somewhere, just like she is hurling items everywhere in my apartment. I do wing it toward her feet, but I also fall backward into a basket where I keep extra blankets. I start screaming because I twisted my arm, and everything fucking hurts. CK rushes over, not to help me, but to put her hand over my mouth.

I try to stand, and she pushes me into the wall.

When she finally takes her hands off me, I look her in the eye and say, *I hate you.*

She will never silence me again.

Instead of just going our separate ways or seeing if I need help getting up, she rushes to where she works and begins to tell everyone her side of the story. *Suzanne is going to say this, but this is what actually happened. She was trying to hurt herself, and I saved her. She was hitting herself, all crazy, because she's a psycho, and I was doing all I could to help her. You've seen me, right? You know I help her all the time. She can't do anything without me, and now she's going to accuse me of things I've never done. I would never hurt her. You know that, right? She was hitting herself. I tried to fix her. I did. I tried. Some people just can't be helped.*

She texts my sister. She texts our mutual friends. She texts everyone we know before I have the chance to say anything.

What she doesn't know is that I didn't plan on saying a word.

I didn't plan on telling anyone what she did.

Instead, she ruined nearly all of my friendships before I left Boone. People stopped talking to me. No one would answer texts, even though they weren't about CK. If they did answer, they were curt and obviously uninterested in talking to someone who was *so cruel to someone who was soooo helpful* throughout my tragic cancer journey. When most derby people, who are notorious for drama and being in everyone's business, did talk to me, they pestered me for the reasons why we broke up.

I gave them an honest answer, and they would not believe me.

It's easier to believe a liar still on the team than an honest, useless person who can't walk.

Shouldn't I be more grateful for all the drunken nights I had to calm her down, despite being afraid for my own safety? Shouldn't I be more grateful for her accusations of me being mean and cruel to her, despite me giving her everything I had and tolerating her selfish behavior? Shouldn't I be more grateful that *she was so helpful?*

I am honestly tired of playing that game.

I'm sure if she's reading this, she will get pissed off all over again, but hey, that's art, baby.

That's truth.

boone, north carolina

One afternoon while casually watching Instagram stories, I see something posted by Derek, Jenna's husband. He uploaded a pic of a tiny, chubby kitten who sits amongst some leaves and sticks. Her bright blue eyes stare directly into my I NEED THIS KITTEN meter, which every cat lover has. I don't get too excited, though. I assume Derek is doing some construction for Habitat for Humanity, where he and Jenna both work, and this kitten likely belongs to someone they are assisting.

I message him anyway.

Who is that?!

He responds almost immediately. *It's a feral kitten at a worksite. There are about 30 cats living in a colony under this woman's house.*

I want her.

I need her.

I have to have her.

If we catch her, you can have her, Derek says.

Suddenly, I have hope in something. This kitten could never replace Pru, but she could give me something to do, something to care for; Duffles and Gatsby are basically self-sufficient, and I need a project. I need a baby. I need love.

I'll take her, I message him. My mom is going to hate me for this, but there is something about the kitten's toasted marshmallow body and raccoon tail that makes me think she was sent by Pru to help me get through the rest of this life.

I dreamt of Pru the other night. She had rich, luxurious fur that she never had in her actual life. She gazed at me with her doubly green eyes, and then looked down at three bear cubs who sat below her. One of the bear cubs had an injured paw. *I take care of them now*, Pru told me. *They need me here.*

Pru always loved kittens.

Although COVID-19 has begun to spread around the United States (but is not known as a pandemic or serious to Americans quite yet), my high school friend Jessica Blevins is getting married this weekend, and I will die before I miss it, even if I literally do die along the way. My friends Jodi and Vanessa will also be there; even though she lives farther away than my friends in North Carolina, Jodi has come to visit me more than people who live ten minutes from me. Vanessa lives in Florida, though, and I haven't seen her in years. She sent me everything from lotion to drones when I was in the hospital, and she always messages me to make sure I'm doing okay. Jessica, who was able to visit me once, has lived in the Nashville area for a long time and has taken mission trips all around the world. Whenever I look at her Facebook, she is either surrounded by wild animals or children from various orphanages. She had one of those children draw me an elephant, and then she sent me the sketch in the mail.

I still have it.

Maybe it's not entirely normal for high school friends to keep up with one another after college, jobs, and kids, but these are women I can count on. They didn't run away from me when the word *glioblastoma* came from my mouth. They message me, sent me mail, and cleaned my apartment.

Jessica, a devout Christian, was 37 and single before she met Joe. A talented musician, Jessica moved to Nashville and got heavily involved with the kind of churches who meet in warehouses. One of the American Ninja Warriors attends the wedding, and the only person in Jessica's bridal party the rest of us know is her sister-in-law.

Unlike the rest of us, Jessica had patiently waited for *adult things* like marriage and children. Not to say that Jodi and Vanessa and I made the wrong choices (well, I did at least), but Jessica never seemed to show any frustration when the rest of us had prom dates and engagements and babies and attention from potential lovers. When pulling out of her driveway one day, Jessica finally lost it and prayed to God that she *needed a miracle*. Everyone else was getting what they prayed for or wanted. Everyone else was getting those boyfriends and husbands. Everyone else was getting the babies and the families and the Christmases with children using wrapping paper rolls as samurai swords. Didn't Jessica deserve that? Didn't she, who never said a bad word about anyone and prayed for everyone daily, deserve a good man by her side? Didn't God, Jessica's God, answer the prayers of the faithful?

And then she met Joe.

Joe Miracle.

She posts about him on Facebook—something Jessica has never done in the past—and says, *Don't tell me that God doesn't have a sense of humor*. Although my beliefs have wavered throughout the years, I have to admit she has a point.

I believe the relationship, engagement, and wedding took roughly seven months, but #weblevinmiracles.

Jodi, Vanessa, and I show up at the ceremony, all wearing green. We did not plan this, but Vanessa and I perfectly match except that her dress has different sleeves. I cry immediately when I see Vanessa; we did so much together in high school. She was the only reason I got invited to the only high school party I'd ever been to, and while there, I took my first sip of alcohol. I thought I was such a badass, but in reality, I was super uptight and studied all the time, which is probably why I had to rely on Vanessa to get an invite anywhere. Vanessa didn't party, but she was friends with everyone. I had never met someone so good with people of all backgrounds. She could blend in anywhere but still stick out as the nicest, prettiest person in the room. She prayed for people but didn't judge them; people say things like that all the time, but with Vanessa, it's genuine. She has a wicked sense of humor, can't sit still, and wants everyone to be having a good time. I have learned a lot from her throughout the years. I noticed she never just said *hi* to people; she always followed up the *hi* with a *how are you? Tell me about what's going on with you today.* This was something that, as a high schooler, had never occurred to me. I shouldn't just give people a quick acknowledgment and move on; I needed to actually see what they were up to.

The ceremony is the ultimate Christian Contemporary Service, with praise and worship, two different pastoral messages, the raising of hands, communion, and the lighting of the unity candle. Jessica looks stunning in her beaded, rhinestone dress, and her brother and his wife sing during the unity candle business, which, as usual, seems to last longer than anything else in the ceremony.

Later, I ask Vanessa, who eloped like I did, how that went for her and her husband. *We drove up to this little house in Lexington, and this tiny old woman opened the door. She had avocado green couches and a bright orange loveseat. Straight out of the 70s. We didn't know that we needed to bring a witness, but then this other couple pulled up. It was an older guy and a younger woman who did not speak any English. I'm pretty sure she was a mail-order bride. I kept thinking, maybe this is a bad sign...*

We both laugh.

The way Joe looks at Jessica kind of restores my faith in marriage, she says and then rolls her big green eyes. We both laugh again. She's still married, but she tells me it's a grind. She's not unhappy, and she has a son, KJ, who sat beside me during the ceremony and uttered *pom pom* during praise and worship for some reason, but she tells me marriage is work and communication and effort.

I feel free as I listen to her.

Jodi has been married to Doug for fifteen years (fifteen years!), and they have two well-behaved, smart children and a farm of cats and dogs. My dad never fails to tell me Jodi's daughter *is one of the smartest kids* he taught when he was substituting after retirement. No one's life or marriage is perfect, but Jodi's seems pretty close.

She is trying to find someone to date her mother, who won't leave her alone.

After Jessica becomes Mrs. Miracle, we all step out into the foyer so the church people can quickly turnaround the makeshift chapel into a reception hall.

I open my phone to a shit show.

Dave is furious with me.

I have over 20 texts.

He's mad because I wrote he was a dishwasher in *Frontal Matter: Glue Gone Wild* when apparently, he actually made salads. He wants to sue me over this. He's mad because I'm at a wedding without him, and there will be people dancing and men *will be looking at me*. (Never mind I can barely walk, more or less dance. That seems like my worst nightmare, actually.) He's mad because even though he hates what I wrote about him, he thinks I should have used his real name, which makes absolutely zero sense to me. We aren't even together, and he's mad because I haven't responded to the 23 texts he's sent in the past hour while I'm at a wedding. He's mad because now he says he can't trust me, although I've done nothing to cause him to distrust me.[24]

He's also mad because CK sent him a nasty message.

She's also sending me nasty messages.

We try to eat barbecue at the wedding dinner, but I keep getting distracted.

Are you okay? Jodi asks me.

She wrote a book that really made everyone mad, Vanessa says, and we all laugh.

As I eat my barbecue, I think about the letters Dave wrote me. Emily and I analyzed those legal pad letters for each and every bit of mystery they contained. Once, long after I had turned 18, I typed up a letter to

---

[24] RED FLAGS RED FLAGS RED FLAGS.

him that expressed my anger and frustration about never knowing just *what the fuck was going on with us.* I typed and printed the letter on one of those sad printer pages where you rip off the perforated edges.

I had become perforated.

I was those rough edges.

This all happened during what Emily and I called The Summer of Worser, where we worked at tennis courts in Huntington and made minimum wage, which was just a little over five dollars at the time. Neither of us knew a damn thing about tennis, but we performed our duties the best we could. We leaf blew those courts like Ghostbusters, and we refilled the water jugs as if the park was preparing for a drought. Oh, and for sure, if we did not do these tasks properly, we heard about it from the tennis players before we heard from our boss, a lady named Mary Anne, who was being really nice to both of us because she just had a baby. We scheduled and rescheduled events, we listened to everyone talk about Patrick, *the kid who was gonna make it to Wimbledon,* and we dealt with Mike, who had an undying crush on Emily and would freeze his t-shirts in the ice machine so he would not sweat as much on the courts. On days when it rained, we did not have to go in, but we also did not get paid. We were living in a borrowed house with borrowed cable, and we would lounge around and watch Lifetime movies on those rainy days. We spent our paychecks on shoes and waited for the new Counting Crows' album that was sure to *be really fucking cool.*

And I wrote that letter to Dave.

I took a red pen and edited the letter.

I just find it funny how we spent all of this time writing to one another but not saying what we really mean. Am I losing it here, Dave? Have I lost my mind? You always signed your letters "love" and "stay safe." What is that supposed to mean? Am I like a little sister to you or something more? What in the fuck happened between us? What is going on? I feel like I deserve answers.

Then I wrote it again.

And again.

And again.

Dave was married by this time, and I knew it would be wrong to send the letter to him. This is where my brain has a bit of a gap: I know there was one version of the letter I ripped up, with the help of Emily, and then tossed the little confetti pieces of my heart in the trashcan. But what did I do with the other version? How many did I print? I think I actually sent one to him, but I never heard back. It was wrong of me, I know. He had a wife and a kid, and I was little more than a kid myself.

But I believed in this kind of love.

I believed *the boy next door* could be the one for me.

I believed this guy could actually be my soulmate.

His wife might have intercepted the letter and ripped it up.

I wouldn't have blamed her.

I never heard back.

Dave tells me now that he *tried to contact me* while I was in Auburn, but I never heard anything. Was my email broken? He said he heard I *had a boyfriend*. Well, I had a couple of boyfriends in Auburn, and none of them worked out. He was welcome to interject at any point, but he didn't.

But that's okay.

I tried things. I figured things out. I made mistakes.

I fell in love, fell out of love, took a weekend trip to Seattle because why not, joined roller derby, developed my first real crush on a girl, fell in love with Kevin, eloped, moved to North Carolina to be around my sister, developed an even more serious crush on a girl, got divorced, dated women, and swore I would never look at another guy again, and then got brain fucking cancer.

Everyone knows the story.

It's just that no one knows how it will end.

319

I don't know if I will have another surgery when more glue goes wild and a new tumor forms.

I've gone so many different directions with this, and I keep changing my mind.

That glue will keep going wild.

I don't know if I'm going to be mentally okay while living in West Virginia.

I know I have to move home for my own safety.

Then again, I don't know if I will leave my apartment again, especially since COVID-19 started killing the world, and I just don't want to take that kind of chance.

I do know that grocery and pharmacy delivery is a lifesaving option for me.

I don't know if anyone can save me.

I've lived this long, so maybe a cure is to come.

I doubt it.

I do know I love and respect Dave, for whatever reason, at least I do at this point, and I believe in soulmates again. I only stopped believing because I was stubborn. If two people can meet when they are 16 and 25 and then write letters for years and then finally admit that love still exists twenty years later, maybe anything can happen. He plans to visit at the end of March, despite the pandemic, despite being mad at me, and we will finally see this love story through.

I deserve it.

He deserves it.

We both deserve it, even if this is the worst decision I've ever made.

boone, north carolina

Derek and Jenna drop off my kitten, whom I have named Delilah, to my apartment after I get back from #weblevinmiracles. I can't believe I'm adopting a kitten while dealing with a terminal illness, but I can sense Delilah and I need each other.

During her first night alone with me, she jumps on the futon and purrs into my neck. She sleeps on my shoulder for a few minutes, and then she tries to nurse on my t-shirt.

I tell Jenna and Derek this story, and Derek says, *She has fully accepted you as her mama!*

Yes.

I needed her as much as she needed me.

boone, north carolina

My good friend Cho and I have been having a Netflix Party since the COVID-19 outbreak. We chose to watch *The Circle*, and the drama gets our minds off the madness happening in the world.

#Shubham4President

Cho has always been there for me.

I attended grad school with her husband, and at first, I thought he was a snob. He sat in the back of my Lit Theory class and gave everyone a hard time, especially during presentation Q & A. *I don't think you really understand what you're talking about*, he said to me. Yeah, no shit, I don't think any of us do, I thought with a sneer.

But then I got to know him better and realized he was actually pretty cool. He mentioned something about a wife, and I was shocked. *Yeah, my wife loves karaoke*. Wait. This guy who sat in the back of my Lit Theory class was married? What kind of wife could he have? She liked karaoke?

When I realized his wife was the perky and petite lady in cute high heels that always looked super organized at department meetings, I had to know more.

She was actually starting a roller derby team, and though I didn't consider myself athletic, I looked up the sport and read it fostered a *third-wave feminist aesthetic*, and I let my officemate drag me to the first practice.

My officemate left fifteen minutes after practice started, and I stuck with roller derby for a decade.

Cho, the league founder, quickly became known as the *roller derby Leslie Knope* to me. I overcame the intimidation I felt at first and got to know the kind-hearted leader who eventually became my boss at a writing center in Columbus, Georgia, and most importantly, a close friend. She and her husband now had two adorable daughters, both Pisces, who would take turns crying until Cho could do nothing else but let them console one another.

As a *Pisces Collector* myself, I can relate.

Whereas most of my friends either disappeared or purposefully cut me out of their lives, Cho remained. She and her family live close to Baltimore now, near her parents. Still, she does more than the people who live closest to me. Cho checks on me. She met me in Brooklyn for breakfast at a sweaty diner while my sister slept. She has Netflix Parties with me.

I need to focus on these types of friendships.

Cho. Nodya. Jodi. Rolli. Jessica. AMo. JC. Mel. Travis. Kate. Vanessa. People who do care for me.

On the morning of our last episode of *The Circle*, I check my Facebook Memories. It's often hard to look at any type of memories, because most of them either make me feel awful since I've changed so much, or terrible because it's like watching the diagnosis of brain cancer happen all over again.

March 29, 2018

I'm back in Boone! Thank you so much to everyone who sent mail. I couldn't believe how much I had once I got home. Thank you all so very much for thinking of me!

My main focus now is to keep myself comfortable. I am in a lot of pain and discomfort. With the donations from everyone, I was able to buy an adjustable bed, which will be very helpful to me.

Walking is going pretty well, but I have been using a cane for stability. I get pretty weak and tired, especially at night. I've had a few falls and need to be careful.

Please be patient with me as I continue to write thank you notes! I have a lot of pain in my dominant hand, so writing is difficult for me.

My short-term memory is also terrible now. If I don't respond to a text or message, I have simply forgotten. It is absolutely nothing personal. I probably saw the text or message and then got distracted by something else. As someone who once had an exceptional memory, this has been a difficult adjustment.

My computer would not connect to Wi-Fi at my parents' house, and I had very sketchy cell phone service in beautiful WV. I have a lot of messages to respond to, so I hope to do so within the next week. Thank you all for your patience!

Emotionally, this is been very overwhelming. The ability to plan is one of the areas affected by frontal lobe tumors, and I am really struggling with remembering plans and making them. I'm also having a difficult time just because the process of everything has been confusing, scary, and prevented me from being my best self. I'm so thankful for the support you all have shown me.

I ended up losing most of my hair. The doctor said it probably would take a year for it to grow back, if it does at all. I'm not into wigs, but I also hate the way my head looks. I feel small and tired a lot.

However, I got another fiction piece picked up a few days ago, so my creativity is still there! I'm so grateful for writing...

...and for all of you!

, Suzanne

As I read this, I think, how did I become so misunderstood? I was so honest about my feelings. I was so real. I was so forthright.

Why did people leave me when I was trying so hard to make everyone happy? Why did people abandon me when I was doing my best while simultaneously doing my worst? Why was this difficult?

Was it because I could still read and write? Would illiteracy be the thing to convince everyone I really wasn't doing so well and needed some support?

I guess not being strong enough to walk and having short-term memory issues was not enough for some people.

I lost more people than I did strands of hair.

I still have friends, I tell myself. I still have people. I still have my pets. I still have my sister and cousins.

I still have someone to watch Netflix with me from hundreds of miles away.

Sometimes normal is nice.

boone, north carolina

At the end of the day, though, I'm always alone, reflecting into my brain by myself as those cells grow and divide and grow and divide and grow and divide until they eventually take over my entire mind. I'm always amused people are thrilled to hear the cancer is *nowhere else in my body*. That's great, right? No. The cancer was in my brain and is still in my brain, and in case anyone has forgotten, the brain is the most important gift our body has to offer us.

Maybe it was a terrible idea to adopt a kitten before I move back to West Virginia with my parents, but Delilah is the most perfect little toasted marshmallow with the cutest raccoon tail. Gatsby loves her, and Duffles watches her climb curtains as if it is a television show. We are all happy and now completely quarantined and isolated since COVID-19 has begun its malignant spread throughout the United States. I fall into two of the five high-risk categories for getting the virus, so I go nowhere.

I see no one.

I do nothing.

I can't help but be a little smug. Oh, everyone is isolating and quarantining? Oh, everyone is bored at home? Oh, everyone is freaking out?

WELCOME TO THE LIFE OF A TERMINAL CANCER PATIENT, WORLD, minus the pain and agony.

Dave helps.

He calls.

When I'm too sad to answer, he calls back.

Sometimes he won't quit calling.

He doesn't give up on me, even though we still haven't seen each other yet.

A pandemic is a fine time to fall in love again.

Is this love or obsession?

I keep seeing a vehicle swing by my apartment window and suspect CK is driving by to see if I'm actually alone.

One day, I can't take the isolation anymore and make a quick drive-to-nowhere in my tiny Scion. I stand outside in my driveway and stare up at the sky. Since I'm not quite in a city or town, since I'm somewhere in between, I can see the stars perfectly from the gravel.

The Big Dipper.

Sirius.

Venus.

They have all been dead for centuries but still shine brightly enough for people light years away to see. I know one day this will be me, one day, but not quite yet.

These stars and I now have a pandemic to survive, but I am ready.

Diabetes? Not dead yet. Terminal brain cancer? Not dead yet. COVID-19? I'm following all the rules, but don't test me, bitch.

I am a constant nuclear reaction, and I, the one no one believed in, the one everyone thought would already be dead, will watch the world burn from my safe position below the night sky.

Acknowledgments

Thank you to Lisa, Barbara, and everyone at Running Wild Press; thank you to Brian and Steven from Finn Partners; thank you to my parents, Ted and Jenifer; thank you to my writing mentors and teachers, Tuckie, Sarah Perry, Prof. Van Kirk, and Dr. Moore; thank you to Sarah Goeke; thank you to my sister and my cousins; thank you to my Aunt Tammy; thank you to the friends who have stuck it out; thank you to Jeramy.

Thank you to anyone who doesn't get mad while reading this, right?

Running Wild Press publishes stories that cross genres with great stories and writing. Our team consists of:

Lisa Diane Kastner, Founder and Executive Editor
Andrea Johnson, Acquisitions Editor, RIZE
Rebecca Dimyan, Editor
Andrew DiPrinzio, Editor
Cecilia Kennedy, Editor
Barbara Lockwood, Editor
Chris Major, Editor
Cody Sisco, Editor
Chih Wang, Editor
Benjamin White, Editor
Peter A. Wright, Editor
Lisa Montagne, Director of Education
Pulp Art Studios, Cover Design
Standout Books, Interior Design
Polgarus Studios, Interior Design
Nicole Tiskus, Product Manager Intern
Alex Riklin, Product Manager Intern

Learn more about us and our stories at www.runningwildpress.com

Loved this story and want more? Follow us at www.runningwildpress.com, www.facebook/runningwildpress, on Twitter @lisadkastner @RunWildBooks

RUNNING

Wild

PRESS